Unto Another Generation

Saint Mary's Abbey/Delbarton, 1836 - 1990

A History

by

Giles Hayes, O.S.B.

Newark Abbey Press

2006

Newark Abbey Press
520 M L King Blvd
Newark, NJ

Copyright ©2006 by the Order of St. Benedict of New Jersey

ISBN 10: 0-9664459-6-1

ISBN 13: 978-0-9664459-6-1

Design and Layout
Sahlman Art Studio, Inc.
50 Christy Drive
Warren, NJ 07059

Printed in the United States of America

DEDICATION

This book is dedicated to
Benedictine monks and nuns,
living and deceased,
who have served the people of
the State of New Jersey
for more than 150 years.

FOREWORD

This book is part history, part chronicle, and part memoir. First, I did the initial historical research under the guidance of my mentor, Father Colman Barry, O.S.B., at St. John's University, Collegeville, Minnesota between 1959 and 1961, and I completed the research of St. Mary's Abbey through 1966 between 1972 and 1975. Excerpts of that history have appeared in a variety of magazines, and I have shared the entire corpus with historians who have asked for it. As a complete document, however, it never saw the light of day.

Some of the material which concerns the period before 1966 and especially the period from 1966 through 2000 are merely chronicle, a listing of significant facts and dates. The sources of this material have been the minutes of the Chapters and Archives of St. Mary's Abbey and Delbarton School and most especially the work of Father Peter Meaney, O.S.B., who died on the eve of my completing this book. Much of the material after 1966 and especially the facts and the interpretations from 1975 through the 1990s should be considered a memoir. I have been blessed to have lived the history of St. Mary's Abbey/Delbarton from the time I entered the freshman year at Delbarton in 1952 until the time I was elected the abbot of the St. Mary's Abbey community in 2006. After college and novitiate, I returned to Delbarton in 1959, began teaching here in 1962, and have enjoyed an uninterrupted career at St. Mary's Abbey and Delbarton since then. Having served as a School administrator since 1972 and as headmaster for nine years and having also served as master of novices in the 1990s, I have enjoyed many memories of the Morristown community. The archival collections, the *Courier* (the School newspaper), the *Archway* (the School yearbook), *Delbarton Today* (the alumni magazine), athletic department records and minutes of the parent groups have enlivened those memories.

I will note the many sources for this book in the bibliographical references at the end. Rather than include the hundreds of footnotes that could well be cited here, I have included the important documentation when appropriate within the text. The memoir sections in the last third of the text, however, are, by and large, memories supported by whatever documentation I could find. The historian of St. Mary's Abbey/Delbarton in the next generation will regard this memoir material as a primary source, and will be able to find support for it in the interviews of many of my peers as well as in issues of the *Courier* and the *Archway*.

Allow me a word about the last section of the book regarding Delbarton athletics. Initially, I never intended to devote so much space to each sport at Delbarton. After addressing the contributions of Father Stephen Findlay, O.S.B., and Mr. William O. Regan to the early history of Delbarton, however, I felt it important to research and write about the sports other than football. This was a daunting exercise because some of the sports did not begin at the School until the late 1970s and because the primary sources in the coaches' files and in the *Courier* or *Archway* either did not exist or were inadequate. For example, from the late 1960s through the mid 1970s, the *Archway* printed neither the text about the season nor the names of the athletes photographed. Nevertheless, I have tried to write as much as possible about sports other than football. To be sure, the final history of Delbarton athletics is yet to be written.

In addition, where does an author stop in mentioning names? One could mention none at all, or as many as possible. After going both ways, back and forth, in each draft of this book, my trusted advisors and I decided to take the middle course: list the appropriate names in the early years, the 1940s through the 1960s, but then limit the names mentioned in the 1970s through the 1990s to the representative few.

Finally, I take total responsibility for any mistakes in the above. I have made every effort possible to fact-check the details in the manuscript, including having as many confreres as possible read and re-read the manuscript. My hope is that the reader both enjoy and be inspired by the story of the 150 years of life of the St. Mary's Abbey monks of northern New Jersey.

The bulk of the material of the first two-thirds of this book was researched in the St. Vincent Archabbey and St. Mary's Abbey Archives, as well as in the minutes of the Chapter of St. Mary's Abbey. Formal interviews taken in the 1970s from monks who lived much of the St. Mary's Abbey/Delbarton history in the 1920s, 1930s, 1940s and 1950s, as well as interviews and conversations with monks of the 1970s through the present, helped to correct the details and improve this book. Within the year prior to publishing this material, more than 20 monks of St. Mary's Abbey as well as confreres at Newark Abbey, including Thomas McCabe, the author of the recent history of Newark Abbey and St. Benedict's Prep, have read and fact-checked all or part of this text.

I am particularly grateful to the monks of St. Mary's Abbey of the past who have collected the material of our history, assembled it, and made it available to the historians of the present. These men include Father Felix Fellner, O.S.B., Father Hilary Stephan, O.S.B., Father Martin Burne, O.S.B., and especially, as to my work, Father Peter Meaney. All of these men compiled brief histories or chronicles which make it easy for more modern historians to negotiate the Chapter minutes. I am particularly grateful to Father Augustine Curley, O.S.B., of Newark Abbey for his insights and encouragement as well as for his willingness to publish this book at the Newark Abbey Press. I am grateful also to Thomas McCabe, whose history of Newark Abbey and St. Benedict's Prep I was able to read in its first draft, making it possible for me to correct and guide my own thoughts regarding separation, the closing of St. Benedict's Prep in 1972, and its re-opening in 1973.

I am grateful as well to the many monks who have read this document and corrected it for grammar, style, and factual accuracy. I am also grateful to my confrere, Brother Eamon Drew, for allowing me to print his excellent graduate school research paper on the life of Abbot Martin J. Burne. This appears as Appendix 1. Most especially, I'm grateful to Mrs. Nancy Maguire, the wife of Tony Maguire '70, my collaborator, especially in researching recent Delbarton School history, and final editor of the book..

I am grateful to the monks of my community, St. Mary's Abbey, Morristown and my confreres and friends at our sister abbey, Newark Abbey, most especially to my classmate, and friend there, Abbot Melvin Valvano, O.S.B., and the principal twin architects of the new St. Benedict's Prep, Father Edwin Leahy, O.S.B., and Father Albert Holtz, O.S.B. All of these men, those mentioned and everyone else in our communities, have worked hard over the last two generations for Christ, for the church, for the poor, for the future leaders of our country, making our two communities significant instruments for the coming of the Kingdom of God in this land. This book is dedicated to these confreres in Morristown and Newark and to all Benedictine monks and nuns, living and deceased, who over the last 150 years and more have devoted their lives to the welfare of the people of the State of New Jersey.

Abbot Giles P. Hayes, O.S.B.
The Feast of St. Benedict
July 11, 2006

TABLE OF CONTENTS

INTRODUCTION

The past follows a religious community into the future. The past is present in the worship and work of a community; it affects its decisions, ministry, and style of life. If a community's history is known and understood, that history can minister to the community in the present. Knowledge and comprehension of the past frees man, and, in a community of religious men, leaves more room for the Spirit to breathe in the present. Consequently, studying the history of St. Mary's Abbey on the 150th anniversary of its establishment is not merely intended to praise dedicated men or illumine noble deeds. More than that, it is to liberate, to allow the Spirit of the Lord to work in the present and the future. As Benedictines in Morristown and throughout the United States progress through their second century, the issues and debates posed by their histories and by their fathers Wimmer and Zilliox continue to be timely and indeed perennial. The study of the histories of St. Mary's and Newark Abbey and the judgments monks have made on them, becomes a liberating force. Indeed, our history is both a reflection of God's design in the past and an invitation to be open to His will in the present and future.

PART ONE:

EARLY GENERATIONS

I

WIMMER TO NEWARK

In 1927, Benedictines from the urban center of Newark, New Jersey, established a foundation thirty miles west in Morristown. During the first eighty years of this foundation, Morristown monks have praised God daily in the celebration of the Eucharist and in prayer, and have served the Church throughout New Jersey in preaching, teaching, and in ministering the sacraments. The worship and work of the Benedictines of St. Mary's Abbey, however, must be understood in the context of its history. Monks offering the Eucharist, serving in a parish, or teaching in Delbarton School in 2007, live in a manner shaped by generations of monks before them. The roots of their ministry in the early twenty-first century are found in the Rule of St. Benedict of the sixth century. But the unique shape of their ministry has been determined by the history of European and North American Benedictines during the nineteenth century. On the one hand, this history reflects a conscious balancing of the active and contemplative elements of monastic life and also a related questioning of the compatibility of monastic observance in an increasingly industrial urban environment. On the other hand, it reveals a generous willingness of men to serve the Church as that service has been directed and guided by bishops and religious superiors.

New Jersey can boast of the first monastic foundation in North America. Prompted by the arrival of a wave of German immigrants in New York City in the 1830s, Bishop John DuBois of that see, whose jurisdiction encompassed northern New Jersey, appealed to priests in Germany to follow the immigrants and minister to their spiritual needs. Rev. Nicholas Balleis, O.S.B., a young Benedictine of St. Peter's Abbey in Salzburg, responded to DuBois' request. In 1836, he arrived in Newark to serve the Germans at St. John's Church on Mulberry Street and later at St. Mary's Church on High Street. By the early 1850s, Father Nicholas was ministering to more than five hundred German-speaking families at St. Mary's, before ill health, overwork, and frustration took their toll. Resulting in part from the destruction of St. Mary's Church during a riot of the "Know-Nothings" in Newark, Father Nicholas requested another assignment from his ordinary, Bishop James Roosevelt Bayley, of the newly created see of Newark. Bayley, not pleased to learn that he

Bishop James Roosevelt Bayley

might lose his one Benedictine, began a campaign to secure an abbey of Benedictines for his diocese. A convert from the Church of England during a period of virulent anti-Catholicism, this nephew of Saint Elizabeth Ann Seton and uncle of two American presidents, Bayley had the aggressiveness and perseverance to make his campaign succeed.

Bishop Bayley chose Abbot Boniface Wimmer, O.S.B., as the target of his persistence. Ordained a diocesan priest in Munich in 1831, Wimmer professed Benedictine vows at the Abbey of Metten in Bavaria in 1833. After pastoral work and teaching at Metten, he established a monastic community of fifteen members at St. Vincent in Latrobe, Pennsylvania, in 1846, ten years after Balleis had arrived in Newark. Like Balleis, Wimmer and his band of monks came to the United States to serve the needs of German immigrants. By the time Bayley first wrote to him in 1854, Wimmer had sent his monks to missions and parishes in four states, and in order to staff these and future mission stations, he had founded a priory and seminary at Latrobe. Before his death in 1887, he had laid the groundwork for hundreds of Benedictine abbeys, priories, seminaries, schools, colleges, and parishes throughout the United States.

In 1854, however, Father Boniface was not willing to accede to Bishop Bayley's request for monks. His opposition stemmed from two prejudices; his eventual yielding stemmed from a third prejudice. His first objection was an initial ambivalence towards, if not a fear of, urban life. At that time, when Newark's population numbered 32,000, he wrote to an associate about St. Mary's: "The parish has a fine location, the city can easily be reached, but I am afraid of cities." In response to Bishop Bayley's first request for help in 1854, Wimmer stated: "Why should we hurry into cities to draw upon us the wrath and hatred of others, well deserved, if we professed poverty and looked for riches." A month later, after Bayley ignored his first refusal and asked again, Wimmer expanded:

"In the country, far from the noise of the cities, we lead a happy life,
and if we are not doing first rate we are doing at least well....
How we would do in a city, I do not know; for a short while, maybe well enough,
after a while maybe bad enough, just in proportion to the exactitude with which
we observe our holy rule; but there is the fear, the fear we might lose the simplicity
of our manner, the poverty in our diet, the spirit of self denial and the pure
intention of our efforts.... The experience of nearly twenty five years of monastic
life and the guidance of past ages are raising great doubts as to whether it would
be good or evil for the order to settle in cities."

During the three years of correspondence with Bayley, Wimmer proposed another but related reason, his second prejudice, for refusing to send monks to Newark. He believed, incorrectly, that the majority of the German immigrants were settling in the rural areas of the Midwest and the Northwest. Consequently, he felt that the monks of his growing community should be sent to foundations in such states as Minnesota and Kansas. In 1855, when in Rome for the elevation of St.Vincent to abbatial status, he wrote to his prior: "We are now well established at St. Vincent.... Now we go West," which he characterized later in the year as: "the real home of German life and missions." In 1857, he responded similarly to still another Bayley request: "I do not know whether

Archabbot Boniface Wimmer (Abbot, 1855-1887)

it be not a temptation to me to turn at once East, when everything shows West." Bayley answered this by return mail in apparent anger and exasperation: "I cannot understand what East or West has to do with the matter when the question is the salvation of souls." Having suggested earlier that the Benedictines could open a school and seminary at St. Mary's, and serve at parishes and mission stations throughout the State, he added in this letter: "There are in this city some six thousand German Catholics, and the number is increasing.... I am certain that those who come to take charge of the mission will find plenty to do."

> *I*
>
> **In the country, far from the noise of the cities, we lead a happy life, and if we are not doing first rate we are doing at least well.... How we would do in a city, I do not know"**
> – Abbot Boniface

In April of the same year, a determined Bishop Bayley set aside argument for a new tactic, shorter and more demanding letters appealing from his authority. This procedural change in his campaign may have suggested itself to Bayley by Wimmer's own revelation of his third prejudice in some earlier letters to the bishop. Wimmer wrote to Bayley at different times: "I am very willing to do anything in my power to satisfy a good Bishop" (September, 1854); "The consent of a Bishop is a ... sure guide of a good success" (October, 1854); "I am convinced that the Church there (in the West) needs priests most and therefore I feel myself bound to give succor to those Bishops" (April, 1857). Consequently, when the temporary replacement for Balleis at St. Mary's asked to visit Europe, Bayley granted his request and wrote to Wimmer: "I now write to inform you that the Very Rev. Wm. Hasslinger is obliged to leave suddenly and unexpectedly for Europe. Could you not therefore send a priest or two to take charge of the mission and we can arrange matters afterwards." For an abbot determined to meet the needs of the Church, this demand from a bishop interpreting those needs was too strong to reject. Rather than take the time to compose a reply, Wimmer acted immediately by sending Father Valentine Felder, O.S.B. A week later Father Eberhard Gahr, O.S.B., arrived in Newark, and within the month, Father Rupert Seidenbusch, O.S.B. Wimmer had overcome his fears and ambiguities about Newark in this characteristic response to the will of a bishop. Some days later he credited Bayley's persistence in a letter to an abbot in Rome: "I sent missionaries to the West and I could not resist the appeals of the Bishop in the East."

In May, 1857, Abbot Boniface went to Newark to receive legal title to St. Mary's property from Bayley and to formally establish a priory there. In expressing his own feelings in a letter to Bayley, he stated a value which would motivate New Jersey Benedictines throughout their history:

> *"I avail myself of the occasion to express to your Lordship my kindest thanks for the undeserved benevolence and high opinion you showed to our Order, which I hope we will not only be anxious but also felicitous enough to answer to by our strongest efforts to serve you faithfully."*

Wimmer's promise of faithful service and Bayley's prediction that monks in Newark would have "plenty to do" were amply fulfilled in the next generation. In 1868, the priory established the

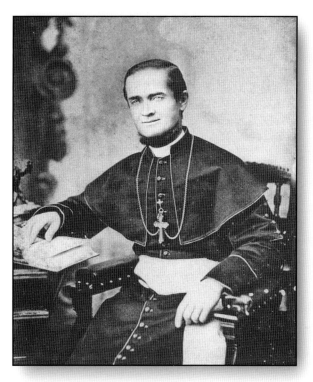

Bishop Winand Michael Wigger, D.D. –
Third Bishop of Newark

school Bayley wanted, St. Benedict's College, which graduated nearly three hundred students in college preparatory and business programs before St. Mary's became an abbey in 1884. Also during this time, more than twenty monks served in Newark and, at the Bishop's request, assumed responsibility for the care of souls at more than a dozen parishes and mission stations. These included: St. Mary's and St. Benedict's parishes in Newark, Sacred Heart in Elizabeth, St. Leo's in Irvington, St. Mark's in Rahway, St. Boniface's in Paterson, St. Francis' in Trenton, and missions in Plainfield, Basking Ridge, Bound Brook, Stony Hill, Westfield, Stirling, Summit, and Paterson. In the early 1880s, sensing that this apostolate would be best maintained if the Newark community were made an independent abbey, Wimmer set out to prepare the monks at St. Mary's for this transition. He was encouraged in his resolve by Bishop Michael Wigger, the third bishop of the Diocese of Newark, who shared Bayley's dream of an abbey in his see city.

In the spring of 1882, Abbot Boniface approved plans for building on High Street a monastery suitable for housing twenty monks. At the same time, he rearranged the horarium of the community in order to assure the regular observance of the Rule and the proper recitation of the divine office. Earlier, in 1881, he had considered purchasing a farm for the community "in the neighborhood of New York," but decided that he had "neither the money ($60,000) nor the men to manage it." In May, 1883, then, without the farm, but with the monastery completed and the monks ready to celebrate office in common, he wrote to Abbot Innocent Wolf, O.S.B., of St. Benedict's Abbey, Atchison, Kansas, that he was about to appeal for abbatial status for St. Mary's.

He stated that the financial stability of the Newark Priory and its parishes made this possible. Concerned for the continuing security of the foundation and for the expansion of its apostolate, but not apparently worried about either its urban setting or the compatibility of training young monks in a city rapidly approaching a population of 100,000, he concluded: "There is no doubt that an Abbot can be more saving than a Prior. He will likewise be in a better position to extend the activities of the house and apply its revenues, because he is empowered to receive novices. In this way an Abbot in Newark will be in a better condition than an Abbot in Atchison."

Wimmer fell seriously ill when he was about to submit the application for St. Mary's. His illness as well as the preparations he was making for the international celebration of the fifteen hundredth anniversary of Benedictine monasticism caused him to delay the request until the spring of 1884. In the meantime, Bishop Wigger offered to sell to the community a three-hundred-acre farm in Denville, New Jersey. With Wimmer's blessing, and after some discussion on the advisability of purchasing a farm twenty-five miles from Newark, the majority of the monks of St. Mary's approved the purchase. Neither Wimmer nor the monks, however, viewed the farm as a potential location of the proposed abbey. As Prior Gerard Pilz, O.S.B., wrote to Wimmer in April, 1884, they saw it rather as a location "especially suitable for raising vegetables, cattle, and cows."

In his 1883 decision regarding abbatial status for Newark, and as evidenced later in his letters to the first abbots of St. Mary's, Wimmer seemed to have resolved his earlier ambivalence towards urban life. Nowhere in his available correspondence of the 1880s does he appear "afraid of cities." In fact, in May, 1884, quite optimistic about the prospects of the future of monastic observance in Newark, he appealed to Rome on behalf of St. Mary's. Before the end of the year, Rome responded favorably, thus fulfilling the original hope of Bishop Bayley.

II

ZILLIOX LEAVES A LEGACY

James Roosevelt Bayley never experienced satisfaction from this event. He had died six years earlier while serving as archbishop of Baltimore. But Wimmer, continuing the debate with himself on monastic values, found another protagonist from Newark in Rev. James Zilliox, O.S.B., the first abbot of St. Mary's Abbey. Zilliox was born in 1849 in his family's home on William Street, Newark, in the shadow of St. Mary's Church, and was educated at St. Vincent. He professed vows as a Benedictine in 1866 and was favored by Abbot Boniface with a theological education in Ratisbon, Innsbruck, and Rome, where he was ordained to the priesthood in 1873 and awarded a doctorate in theology in 1875. "He was gifted particularly by nature and grace," wrote one of his classmates, "of amiable temperament, delicate sympathies, noble character; he had set before him the highest ideals of priestly and religious life, and strove arduously to attain them." As a measure of Wimmer's respect for the young monk, he appointed Father James master of novices at St. Vincent in 1877, when Zilliox was only twenty-seven years old, and in 1881 he appointed him prior of the abbey.

Father James returned this respect with perfect obedience to Abbot Boniface in spite of the fact that he disagreed with Wimmer on the activist direction American Benedictinism was taking. The near father-son relationship the two men enjoyed, as well as Wimmer's own heroic openness to debate and change within his community, provided fertile ground for nurturing American monasticism. The conflicts between Wimmer and Zilliox in the 1870s and 1880s exemplified the issues and tensions at the common roots of American Benedictinism. The history of the Morristown monks, indeed, of all Wimmer's sons, illustrates the manner in which these conflicts were lived out and resolved from generation to generation.

The conflicts between Boniface Wimmer and James Zilliox originated in the history of nineteenth century European monasticism. Civil authorities throughout Western Europe suppressed abbeys during the period of the French Revolution and the Napoleonic era. So thorough was this suppression that, by 1810, no monks remained in cloisters and few monastic properties were held by the orders in Germany and further west. In the 1820s and 1830s, however,

Catholic rulers in Germany and Bavaria, notably King Ludwig and his successors, began restoring monastic life and funding the mission work of German Catholics. Under their patronage, diocesan priests like Nicholas Balleis and Boniface Wimmer joined the restored communities, in part to live a life of prayer, and in part to establish bases for the parish and mission apostolates. Understandably, as the new monks followed the massive German emigration, the latter purpose predominated. The genius of Boniface Wimmer, his great contribution to American Catholicism, was his belief that long-range success in the care of souls in a mission land could only be accomplished through the efforts of missionaries teaching and preaching from permanent religious communities.

Abbot James Zilliox,
the first abbot of
St. Mary's Abbey

...he had set before him the highest ideals of priestly and religious life, and strove arduously to attain them.

Boniface Wimmer left Germany for the United States in 1846 before he could have been aware of or influenced by the second phase of the monastic revival in Europe which was taking place in Belgium and France. Here wealthy patrons of religion, scholarship, and the arts supported the work of Dom Prosper Gueranger, O.S.B., of the Abbey of Solesmes in the work of restoring Benedictine communities along more contemplative lines. In this later restoration of the monasteries, with parish needs adequately supplied by diocesan priests and with the responsibility of caring for extensive immigration almost nonexistent, Gueranger and the other founders, including Abbot Maurus Wolters, O.S.B., of the Abbey of Beuron in Germany, were able to place almost complete emphasis on prayer and scholarship. As the decades passed, their influence pervaded most of the European Benedictine communities.

James Zilliox came under this influence while in Europe in the 1870s. Reserved, always the scholar, not at all the aggressive missionary epitomized by his patron Wimmer, Father James found living the life of an American Benedictine difficult. "Here I have no rest," he wrote to a friend in 1876, "and have no chance for contemplation, which would be my only delight in this world." In fact, when this same friend wrote that Wimmer was the greatest Benedictine of the nineteenth century, Father James answered that Wimmer might be one of the greatest but that Gueranger was greater. Feeling that Benedictines should worship and teach only, he decried St. Vincent's extensive parish and mission apostolate. This work, he sensed, harmed monastic observance. In a letter to a friend he called Wimmer a *"perpetuum mobile,"* and continued, "the discipline in this house is not as it should be, much is wanting." While novice master at St. Vincent, he encouraged some of the novices to join monasteries in Europe, and when he himself asked to join the Abbey of Beuron, Wimmer made him prior of St. Vincent in charge of monastic discipline.

Abbot Boniface encouraged Zilliox' views, even his opposition, in a sincere attempt to secure for American Benedictines an appropriate balance of the active and contemplative values of monasticism. It is no wonder then, that in February, 1885, he promoted among his monks the election of his young protagonist for abbot of the newly created St. Mary's Abbey where, Wimmer felt, Zilliox would be able to enact some of his reforms.

In July, 1885, Abbot James was solemnly installed as the first abbot of St. Mary's. He resigned sixteen months later. During that time he spent six months at the Abbey, and the remainder, recuperating from tuberculosis, at St. Michael's Hospital, Newark, or at his parents' home. This illness took his life in 1890. Abbot James, nevertheless, left an important legacy to the Newark monks.

"Here I have no rest and have no chance for contemplation, which would be my only delight in this world."
– Rev. James Zilliox, O.S.B.

In August, 1885, with the approval of the capitulars, he proposed to sell the Denville farm, stating that education rather than agriculture should be the work of the New Jersey monks. In November, 1885, the fourteen capitulars affirmed this decision again, and voted unanimously to direct the Abbot to execute the sale when he received an appropriate bid for the land. The farm remained unused by the monks until 1895, when Franciscan sisters purchased it to build a rest home and hospital. With Wimmer, Zilliox and the first monks of St. Mary's Abbey harbored no fears of establishing monasticism in a growing city. Abbot James saw no inherent conflicts for monastic observance in either rural or urban environments so long as monks valued the rules of enclosure.

The first Abbot also opened a minor seminary or scholasticate at St. Benedict's College in order to promote vocations to the abbey. In addition, he returned the administration of the parishes in Rahway and Irvington to the bishop and curtailed the monks' weekend pastoral work in diocesan parishes and missions. At Wimmer's request, however, he assumed the responsibility for staffing the Benedictine parish of the Sacred Heart in Wilmington, Delaware.

Had he lived longer, Zilliox might have influenced the Newark and Morristown monks in more obvious ways. Surely his faith in Newark and his zeal for the monastic life and for the apostolate in education contributed to the remarkable growth at St. Mary's which began while he was abbot. These characteristics, an embodiment of what was already a half century of Benedictine tradition in Newark, represented his legacy to his successors in Newark and Morristown. Perhaps the best encomium on him and this legacy was penned by his mentor, Boniface Wimmer, when he wrote about St. Mary's during the month in which ill health forced Abbot James to resign:

With Wimmer, Zilliox and the first monks of St. Mary's Abbey harbored no fears of establishing monasticism in a growing city.

"There is beautiful order in this monastery, much better than in St. Vincent. The monks attend choir regularly, there is no idea of neglecting Mass, they do not miss chapter, waste time, or talk after recreation, etc. As far as I can see there is good understanding among them and they work diligently. In fact, it is a nice little monastery, and the food is good and sufficient."

"There is beautiful order
in this monastery…. In
fact, it is a nice little
monastery, and the food
is good and sufficient."
– Archabbot Boniface
Wimmer, O.S.B.

Writing these lines forty years after he began his missionary work in America, Wimmer must have felt proud of his own efforts and justified in the confidence he extended to his young friend and critic.

III

NEWARK'S LEGACY

The days of Wimmer and Zilliox preceded the founding of the Morristown community by two generations. During the intervening years, the manner in which the monks of St. Mary's Abbey responded to the ideals of Archabbot Boniface and Abbot James was dramatically affected by the needs of the Church in an increasingly industrial metropolitan area, and by the monks' willingness to fill generously those needs to the limits of their resources and endurance. Escalating immigration and urbanization in northern New Jersey advanced the activist spirit of Wimmer in Newark. The necessity for spiritual renewal and for educating young monks for the work of the Church enlivened the ideals of Zilliox. These needs and ideals resulted in establishing the Morristown community, which, in turn, benefited both from the continuing generosity of the Newark monks and, for a time, increased the ranks of the Newark community. Eventually, St. Mary's Abbey became two – Newark Abbey and St. Mary's Abbey/Delbarton. But the history of the two communities is rooted in the work and aspirations of hundreds of New Jersey Benedictines living during the administrations of the second and third abbots of St. Mary's Abbey, Newark: Abbot Hilary Pfraengle, O.S.B., and Abbot Ernest Helmstetter, O.S.B.

At the time of Abbot Hilary's election in 1886, Newark had a population of slightly more than 100,000. At Abbot Ernest's death in 1937, its population approached 400,000. During the same period, and as a result of massive immigration from Eastern and Southern Europe, the number of Catholics in northern New Jersey increased from approximately 100,000 to more than 1,000,000. This growth accelerated industrial and urban development in the area, giving the immigrants a significant role in the future of their new country. The monks, priests, and educators of St. Mary's Abbey, then, assumed responsibilities for the assimilation, education, and religious instruction of the immigrants, including responsibilities to both Church and country, the magnitude of which no other American Benedictine community at that time was called upon to assume.

Twenty-three young men joined the original fourteen monks of St. Mary's within the first five years of Abbot Hilary's administration. At his death, the community numbered nearly seventy

Abbot Hilary Pfraengle (Abbot, 1886 - 1909)

monks, a number which rose to nearly one hundred during Abbot Ernest's time. Although the Newark foundation, like other Benedictine communities, was originally founded to serve the German immigrants, fewer than half the men who entered the community during these years were of German descent. The work of assimilation had begun much earlier, however, since from its inception in 1868, St. Benedict's College held all classes in English. And as early as 1873, the school catalog listed a student body with a variety of immigrant names, only a minority of which were German. Before Abbot Hilary's death in 1909, the student body numbered more than two hundred; before Abbot Ernest's death in 1937 it numbered more than six hundred. The school sent thousands of its graduates into the professional, technological, and business ranks of the middle and upper-middle classes of the metropolitan areas of New York and New Jersey, thus contributing to the education and assimilation of Catholic immigrant families and to their quiet but profound influence on the life of the Nation. As the largest American monastic educational institution in the early years of the twentieth century, it was and continues to be unique among American Benedictine schools.

> As the largest American monastic educational institution in the early years of the twentieth century, it was and continues to be unique among American Benedictine schools.

The attention of the Newark monks to the pastoral care of immigrants equaled the attention they gave to the religious and academic education of three generations of immigrant youth. At the request of Bishop Wigger and also his successor, Bishop John O'Connor, as well as of the priests of the diocese, the monks applied to pastoral work whatever resources and time were available to them. Demographic change compelled them to set aside some of Abbot James' values. And again, the preservation of the faith of generations of immigrants among the increasing population of northern New Jersey placed them in a role unique among American Benedictines.

In 1886, the community conducted the parishes of St. Mary's and St. Benedict's in Newark, Sacred Heart in Elizabeth, and Sacred Heart in Wilmington, Delaware. To these Abbot Hilary added St. Raphael's in Manchester, New Hampshire, St. Elizabeth's in Linden, and Blessed Sacrament in Elizabeth. Abbot Ernest added St. Joseph's in Maplewood, Notre Dame in Cedar Knolls, and St. Christopher's in Parsippany. In 1906, twenty percent of the priests of the Abbey served full time in parishes. Before then and later, nearly half of the priests teaching at St. Benedict's also celebrated the

Abbot Ernest Helmstetter
(Abbot, 1910-1937)

Eucharist and administered the sacraments daily at nearby convents, hospitals, and diocesan parishes, while nearly all did weekend pastoral work at diocesan churches in northern and central New Jersey. In this way the monks ministered to Catholics during these years at nearly one

St. Mary's (German) Roman Catholic Church, 532 High Street

Bishop John J. O'Connor – Fourth Bishop of Newark

hundred parish and convent communities. By accomplishing work perhaps unparalleled by any other religious community of men in the area, the Newark Benedictines have had a significant impact on the Catholic life of New Jersey and left a remarkable legacy of apostolic service to the Morristown monks who followed them.

Not all requests for aid, however, could be answered. In 1890, Abbot Hilary received the deed for another parish in Wilmington, Delaware, but returned it to the bishop of the diocese because the community could not staff the parish. At the same time, he sought two parishes in New Brunswick from Bishop Wigger but quickly withdrew the requests, and the community voted not to staff a school in Wilmington or begin pastoral work on property which the community owned in Westchester County, New York. He also abandoned a plan to purchase property and establish a foundation in Norwalk, Connecticut. Limited resources taxed the monks under Abbots Hilary and Ernest, so these and other requests had to go unanswered. But, as Boniface Wimmer "could not resist the appeals of the Bishop in the East," Hilary Pfraengle could not resist the requests of a bishop in the north.

Even before his blessing as the second abbot of St. Mary's, Abbot Hilary received a letter from Bishop Denis M. Bradley of Manchester, New Hampshire, asking him to establish a Benedictine foundation in his diocese. Bradley dreamed of a Benedictine college and seminary for poor first- and

> By accomplishing work perhaps unparalleled by any other religious community of men in the area, the Newark Benedictines have had a significant impact on the Catholic life of New Jersey and left a remarkable legacy of apostolic service to the Morristown monks who followed them.

second-generation immigrant youth of New England. Abbot Hilary, however, denied Bradley's first request, since he was unable to determine the mind of the community on the project. But as Bradley may have known, Pfraengle, the former rector of the seminary at St. Vincent and a doctor of theology like Zilliox, was personally disposed to starting the foundation and the college. Bradley, then, continued to press the matter. Nevertheless, because of urgent business in Newark, the abbot was able to resist his pleas for more than a year. Finally, in 1887, Abbot Hilary journeyed to Manchester as a guest of the bishop. He returned fully convinced of the merits of a foundation in New Hampshire. In the same year, the St. Mary's community opened St. Raphael's parish in Bradley's see city.

The bishop regarded this as a good beginning, but he continued to request the abbot and his capitulars to establish a college in Manchester. Pressured on the one hand by the persistence of the bishop, and on the other by pastoral and educational needs in northern New Jersey, Pfraengle queried Wimmer on the opportunity in New Hampshire. In May, 1887, the aging Archabbot responded with a caution which clearly reflected the will of the founder for the Newark community:

"The place in Manchester seems really (to) be acceptable, if only care of souls is the ambition, and a day school left to your good will; only I beg leave to remark, it might be a little premature, since you have so few priests. Newark—your day school there must be your main care, since your Abbey depends chiefly on its good standing."

A number of monks in Newark, albeit a minority, shared Wimmer's caution. Led by the prior of the abbey, Father Ernest Helmstetter, who would succeed Abbot Hilary in 1910, they delayed the opening of the college in Manchester for a few years. Circumstances, however, minimized the impact of this opposition. First, the large number of candidates entering the community in the late 1880s and early 1890s provided manpower for an expanded apostolate. In addition, St. Mary's had a sufficient number of priests with earned doctoral degrees to conduct a college and seminary. Finally, Bishop Bradley assured Abbot Hilary of the financial support of the clergy and laity of the Manchester diocese. Consequently, in 1889 and 1891, while already carrying a significant debt, the Newark monks voted nearly $70,000 over the minority's opposition to purchase land and begin building for the college. With one building completed, the college opened in September, 1893, in the midst of a national economic depression. Because of both Abbot Hilary's and Bishop Bradley's desire to provide an education for the sons of poor Catholics, the annual fees for tuition, room and board were set at $180. In addition, to focus on assimilation and to appeal to a wide variety of immigrant groups, Bradley and Pfraengle chose to place the college under the patronage of an English Benedictine, St. Anselm.

> "Newark—your day school there must be your main care, since your Abbey depends chiefly on its good standing."
> – Archabbot Boniface Wimmer, O.S.B.

Students in St. Benedict's, 1922.

During the next 25 years, the St. Mary's Abbey community voted nearly $400,000 for the expansion of St. Anselm's, while they spent less than half that sum on St. Benedict's Preparatory School and the monastery in Newark. The monks even gave their abbot to Manchester for a time. In the late 1890s, in an effort to solve financial and administrative problems at St. Anselm's, Abbot Hilary sought and received permission from the Sacred Congregation of Religious to live in New Hampshire, where he stayed for five years.

The Manchester community provided St. Mary's with a college and a school of theology for the training of young monks. As St. Anselm's grew, however, its community attracted many men whose vocation had little relationship to the abbey in Newark. This became increasingly the case in the early 1920s, corresponding with the completion of a building program for the monastery and college in Manchester. Abbot Ernest, therefore, began discussions among the New Jersey and New Hampshire Benedictines regarding the creation of an independent abbey at St. Anselm's. In the spring of 1927, the community voted overwhelmingly in favor of independence. In the following summer the authorities in Rome raised St. Anselm's to the status of an abbey, and thirty monks of St. Mary's transferred their stability to Manchester. As by a providential response to Newark's continuing generosity, this number was replenished by candidates to the Newark community within the next seven years.

IV

FORMATION OF MORRISTOWN

In early 1925, anticipating independence for St. Anselm's and the resultant need for a house of studies for the young monks of St. Mary's Abbey, Abbot Ernest began looking for a suitable location. He considered two sites: the Darlington estate in Mahwah and the Delbarton estate in Morris Township. Few records survive that suggest the reasons for the eventual choice of the Delbarton site, and no discussion regarding the selection can be found in the written minutes of the Chapter. But the Abbey's oral tradition recounts a quaint legend regarding it, and legends have a way of carrying a kernel of truth. According to tradition, elderly Father Ambrose Huebner, O.S.B., the first prior of St. Mary's under Abbot James and one of the first monk residents of Delbarton, preferred the Morris Township site over Darlington, while the majority of the community favored the Mahwah estate. In his simple faith, he journeyed to Delbarton and planted Benedictine medals along Mendham Road, convinced that the founder of the order, thus rooted at Delbarton, would guide the deliberations of the community. However, tradition also recounts that Bishop Thomas J. Walsh, the fifth bishop of Newark, asked Abbot Ernest that the Benedictines choose Delbarton because he wanted to purchase Darlington for the diocese. For whatever reason, on August 18, 1925, Father Ambrose's preference became the community's choice. On that day, the Chapter of St. Mary's Abbey voted by a significant majority to purchase Delbarton and thus assume a large debt. The estate, formerly owned by Luther Kountze, a wealthy New York and Colorado banker, cost $155,000. Ten percent of the total was paid immediately, the remainder on December 1, 1925.

The Newark monks generously extended themselves again for their apostolic work. And the foundation they were about to establish in Morris Township would, over the years, make further demands on their resources. In time, Delbarton, their monastic child, would provide a return on their investment in the training of monks. But, by the often peculiar workings of history, the child would one day become the father of Newark. Historical forces beyond independence for St. Anselm's also contributed to establishing monasticism in Morristown. These forces were related to the legacy which the first abbot of St. Mary's left his community.

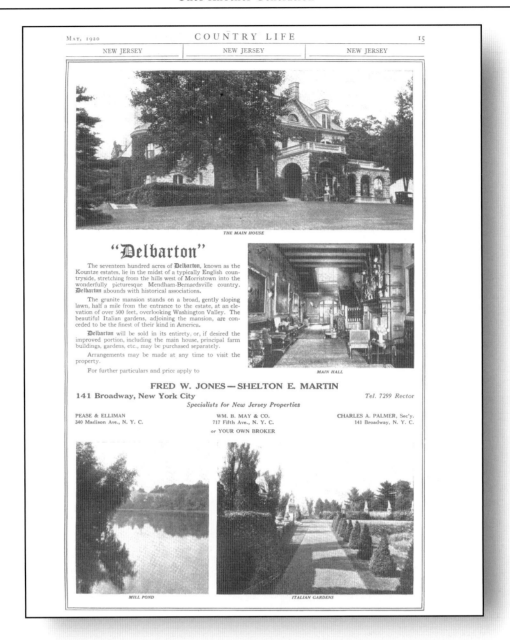

Marketing piece for the sale of the
Delbarton estate, 1920

The monastic ideals of James Zilliox were shared by his two successors. A contemporary of Abbot James, Abbot Hilary was his schoolmate in Innsbruck and Rome during the 1870s. In addition, Abbot Ernest was a junior monk under Abbot James and a student in St. Vincent Seminary when Zilliox served as its rector. Both of the later abbots observed poverty carefully and demonstrated that faithfulness to monastic observance and discipline which Abbot James preached and lived. Abbot Hilary was well known not to tolerate abuses and carelessness in the recitation of the divine office. And Abbot Ernest, throughout his life, faithfully attended choir, even during the long, protracted illness before his death in 1937. Both, like Zilliox, taught by their example; but neither, unlike Zilliox and other abbots in America, enjoyed the luxury of a small community isolated from the incessant demands of a growing Church. These demands shaped the monastic regulations in Newark and Manchester in ways that James Zilliox might not have approved, but which Boniface Wimmer would have understood.

In 1888, Abbot Hilary arranged the monks' horarium around the work of the day. Earlier, Abbot James had sought to subordinate the work to the horarium. Abbot Hilary required the monks to rise at 4:30a.m. and begin the morning hours of the divine office at 4:50a.m.. After the community prayed Lauds, Prime, Terce, Sext, and None, some of the priests went to nearby parishes and convents to celebrate Mass, while others offered Mass privately and participated later in the conventual Mass. Classes at St. Benedict's followed breakfast at 7:15a.m., and the venerable German tradition of haustus from 3:00p.m. to 3:45p.m. followed classes. Because many could not attend the community meal at noon, no canonical hours were held at that time. Vespers and Compline were recited at 8:30p.m., followed by anticipated Matins. Such a schedule allowed the monks to be fully engaged in schoolwork and some pastoral responsibilities and enabled them during the same day to attend most, if not all, of the monastic prayer.

An illustration of the degree of their commitment to the school and pastoral responsibilities is suggested by their attendance at Chapter meetings. While in 1885 and 1886, according to the testimony of Boniface Wimmer, one hundred percent of the community or fourteen capitulars attended chapter regularly; ten years later, in 1895 and 1896, the Chapter minutes indicate that fewer than fifty percent of those resident in Newark, or eight or nine capitulars, were able to attend.

In March, 1898, Abbot Hilary presented to the monks for possible adoption by the community the ceremonial and monastic regulations of the Beuronese Congregation. After discussion, they accepted the ceremonial, but not the choir regulations or horarium. In 1907, he moved the time for the recitation of Vespers to immediately after dinner and before evening recreation; Compline and Matins remained at 8:30p.m. Shortly after his election in 1910, Abbot Ernest changed the hour of None from before morning Mass to before lunch. In addition, he completed the construction and remodeling of the choir chapel begun by Abbot Hilary.

Both men frequently exhorted the monks about monastic observance and taught by their example. The positive memory of them in the community, as well as the fact that they were both valued for their advice and leadership in other religious communities, is a testament to their holiness. But perhaps they were best exemplified in the lives of their monks. During their fifty years of guiding the monks of St. Mary's, more than one hundred students of the men at St. Benedict's Prep (between 1870 and 1927) were impressed enough by the life of the community that they too chose to seek God at St. Mary's Abbey.

Evidence suggests, however, that both abbots felt a need for a less active life. Both, with many of their capitulars, may have believed that the city pressing in around them not only limited expansion in Newark but also detracted from the proper monastic observance, especially for young monks and the elderly. These concerns occurred frequently in the later history of the Abbey, but as early as 1909, a few months before his death, Abbot Hilary touched upon the expansion question in a long speech to the capitulars. He did not, however, suggest moving the Abbey from Newark. The secretary of the Chapter summarized the speech:

> *"(He said) here in the city we would always be pressed for space and could not*
> *develop as we ought. He spoke of looking about for some farm of about 100 or*
> *more acres, with running water, not too far from the city, etc. It was remarked*
> *that our Denville farm...would have been just the right kind of place."*

Despite the fact that Abbot Ernest, a native of Newark, appeared committed to the development of the school and monastery there, he and the community periodically reviewed the need to expand out of Newark. In 1918 came such a time. It is not clear whether in 1918 he already anticipated independence for Manchester and, consequently, sought a site outside the city to be used as a house of studies, or whether he and the community actually proposed to move St. Benedict's. But, in the summer of that year, with a strong majority vote, the Chapter authorized Abbot Ernest to buy the four-hundred-acre Sully Farm in Hackettstown for $25,000. The monks discontinued the project in September when they discovered that the full title to the property was not free to purchase. A few months later, in 1919, affirming his intentions to expand in Newark, Abbot Ernest approved an expenditure of $130,000 for a new classroom building and gymnasium at St. Benedict's.

M .... more than one hundred students of the men at St. Benedict's Prep (between 1870 and 1927) were impressed enough by the life of the community that they too chose to seek God at St. Mary's Abbey.

The search for land outside the city intensified as independence for Manchester approached. In June, 1923, Abbot Ernest and the Newark monks considered another purchase, a six-hundred-acre farm in Gladstone. But they judged this as unacceptable due to its distance from Newark and its

Newark, view of Broad and Market Streets, 1920

1928 Scenes of Morristown: The Railroad Station (above) and the
Morristown Public Library (below).

(Photos courtesy of Floyd W. Parsons, EM, editor-in-chief of *New Jersey: Life, Industries & Resources of*
a Great State. Published by New Jersey State Chamber of Commerce, Newark, NJ, 1928.)

price, which they anticipated being close to $300,000. Two years later, with the Diocese of Newark and St. Mary's Abbey searching for land, the monks chose Delbarton.

The foundation of the Morristown community, prompted in part by the need to replace St. Anselm's as a house of studies, was also rooted in an apparent anxiety to assure the regular observance of monastic life in a setting other than that which imposed the increasing demands of the active life and increasing limitations on the facilities to sustain that life. Abbots Hilary and

Ernest and the Newark monks of the first third of the century identified more with the ambivalence of Wimmer's early days than with both his resolution of that ambivalence during the 1880s and Zilliox's confidence in the growing city. It remained for the St. Mary's monks of the second third of the century to resolve that ambivalence, and, for those in Morristown, to fulfill their founders' aspirations as well as return the generosity which gave them sustenance.

1928 Scene of Morristown: Route 24 from Morristown to Convent.

(Photo courtesy of Floyd W. Parsons, EM, editor-in-chief of *New Jersey: Life, Industries & Resources of a Great State.* Published by New Jersey State Chamber of Commerce, Newark, NJ, 1928.)

Formal Garden view with the backs of statues of Alexander and Darius on the right and left and two of the four virtues in the center.

V

PIONEERS

In early 1925, when Father Ambrose Huebner planted the Benedictine medals on the Delbarton property, the Kountze estate was not fit for occupancy by a community of monks. During the five years between Luther Kountze's death in 1920 and St. Mary's purchase in 1925, the estate came under new ownership twice, once by two sisters who sought to make a year-round home there, and a second time by the officers of a health spa intent on creating at Delbarton a spring and summer resort. Both occupants left the property after failing to meet payments to DeLancey Kountze, Luther's eldest son and chief officer of his late father's estate. When the last of the two occupants left in 1923, the realtor retained a resident caretaker, Mr. Joshua Skidmore and his family, to maintain the property.

Luther Kountze had developed the estate in the early 1880s from property purchased from four farmers. After moving the 18th century home of one of the farmers from its former site to a new position in the valley one hundred yards east, he built an imposing gray stone mansion in its place. Completing it before 1890, he then created the formal Italian garden adjoining on the west side of the mansion. Shortly after the turn of the century, he began but never completed a Greek garden east of the mansion. To provide the mansion with running spring water, he built a water tower at the highest point on the property two hundred yards south of the mansion. Among the woodland streams in the valley to the west, he installed the mechanical equipment to pump the water to the tower. In addition, he built a creamery and workmen's cottages near the southeast corner of the estate, a barn further in the valley east of the former farm house, a gardener's cottage three hundred yards southwest of the mansion, and a carriage house between the gardener's cottage and the mansion. Although he and his family used the estate as a summer home only, in the 1890s he began a year-round farm there. At the same time, he hired a professional horticulturist to design patterns for roadside greenery and plant rare and valuable trees and shrubs. Except for a few minor repairs carried out by the occupants of the early 1920s, such as the installation of porcelain door knobs and bath tubs in the mansion, little had been done to modernize the property or its buildings since the turn of the century. In addition, after 1923 visitors had vandalized many

Luther Kountze: c. 1890

of the buildings, and lawns and fields were allowed to grow wild. The caretaker after Kountze's death had more than he could do to maintain the estate in its former glory.

Prior to the arrival of the monks at Delbarton, in 1926, the community voted to install a boiler and a steam heating system in the mansion. During the summer of 1926, with heat guaranteed for the following fall and winter, four monks established a monastic community at Delbarton. Abbot Ernest sent Father Edward Bill, O.S.B., to serve as the first superior. Along with Father Edward went the aging pioneer, Father Ambrose Huebner, whose request to contribute what he could to maintain the property was fulfilled by Abbot Ernest. Shortly after

arriving, however, Father Ambrose broke his hip in a fall. To care for him, then, the abbot sent Brother Aloysius Hutten, O.S.B., a professional registered nurse. In addition to his medical duties as nurse for Father Ambrose and infirmarian for the small community, Brother Aloysius also contributed his considerable talents as master cabinetmaker and carpenter to refurbishing the buildings and grounds. Father Norbert Hink, O.S.B., the fourth of the pioneers, took up residence at Delbarton while serving as pastor at Notre Dame in Cedar Knolls, a parish the community took over in the same year. Father Norbert, a professional artist, redesigned and redecorated the first floor of the mansion.

These monks had much to accomplish before the arrival of the larger community of young monks in the school of theology. With

Father Ambrose Huebner on the second floor porch of the former Kountze mansion, 1930s

the help of Kountze's caretaker and Mr. Alphonse Helmer, who became a full-time resident of the property and maintenance engineer for the community in 1929, preparations for housing the larger community took three or more years. They cut the lawns and fields, remodeled Kountze's armor room into a chapel and his music studio into a monastic refectory. They repaired the damage caused by vandalism and the plumbing and lighting and performed minor repairs on the roads, cottages, and barn. Brother Aloysius and Alphonse Helmer did extensive carpentry and masonry work which continues to stand to this day. A postulant to the community, John Mullin, arrived to help in the winter of 1928, and during the summers, scholastics (college candidates for the community) and clerics (recently professed monks studying philosophy and theology at St. Anselm's), assumed summer residence at Delbarton to advance the preparations and work on the farm.

The monks rejuvenated the Kountze farm in the late 1920s, not long after the four pioneers established the foundation. Brother Isidore Stumpf, O.S.B., the farm manager, planted and

Pillars in Formal Garden; the design has been
attributed to Stanford White

Brother Isidore Stumpf

Brother Aloysius Hutton, 1964

maintained vegetable gardens, fruit orchards, and fields of grain, and directed the harvests of corn, alfalfa, and hay. His principal assistant in the early days, Brother Peter Ohlheiser, O.S.B., cared for the animals on the farm, chiefly cows, chickens, and horses. In the early 1930s, Brother Albert Becker, O.S.B., joined the staff and continued to serve with Brothers Isidore and Peter through the 1930s and 1940s. They received assistance from time to time from many of the brothers and clerics, including Brother Joseph Heeney, O.S.B., who served the community in the mansion for more than five years during the early period.

Old Main in 1920s

VI
EARLIEST YEARS IN MORRISTOWN

It is not known when the monastery in Morristown was canonically established as a dependent priory of St. Mary's Abbey. Since no written records of this exist in the Abbey or diocesan files, authorities later inferred that Bishop O'Connor and Abbot Ernest made a verbal agreement in 1926. In 1938, when Rome created the Diocese of Paterson to include Morris County and, therefore, St. Mary's Monastery, Bishop Thomas McLaughlin of Paterson and Abbot Patrick O'Brien, O.S.B., Abbot Ernest's successor, rectified the oversight by formally establishing the priory. Earlier, however, in 1930 and 1931, the Newark monks opened the house of studies at Delbarton, transferring the theological students from Manchester to Morristown. This influx of young monks to year-round residence at Delbarton confirmed the foundation in the purpose of its existence and assured the regular observance of monastic life there. The event occasioned Abbot Ernest's appointment of the first prior of St. Mary's Monastery, Father Vincent Amberg, O.S.B.

Perhaps no other monk in the early days shaped the monastic life and determined the future of the Morristown community more than Father Vincent. He came to Morristown rooted in the ideals and traditions of the abbey and rich in the experience of administration and spiritual leadership. Born in Newark just as Boniface Wimmer prepared to elevate St. Mary's Priory to an abbey, a graduate of St. Benedict's Prep and a young friend and altar boy of Abbot James Zilliox, Father Vincent joined the community in the 1890s and was ordained to the priesthood near the turn of the century. During Abbot Hilary's last days, he served as headmaster of St. Benedict's. At that time, he supervised the planning for the addition to the school which was completed after Abbot Ernest's election. In 1910, Abbot Ernest appointed Father Vincent prior and procurator of St. Anselm's. In Manchester for seventeen years, he planned and supervised an extensive

> Perhaps no other monk in the early days shaped the monastic life and determined the future of the Morristown community more than Father Vincent.

Prior Vincent Amberg

building program for the priory and college, taught in the college and the school of theology, and directed the monastic observance of the monks. In 1927, he returned to Newark after leading preparations for independence in Manchester and arranging for the election of its first abbot. He served as prior in Morristown until 1945 and as procurator of the monastery there until his death in 1965.

Father Vincent possessed a gentle heart under a gruff exterior. The former did not often reveal itself in his early days at Morristown, since he might well have felt that the superior of a struggling community should be the example of Spartan discipline. It revealed itself, however, amidst the characteristic directness of his private conferences with monks and was evident as well to the large number of penitents who came to him during his more than thirty years at Delbarton, including many monks, diocesan priests, and two bishops.

Father Vincent himself adhered closely to the rules of monastic observance and expected the young monks to do the same. And as he himself lived in poverty, not spending unnecessarily, and keeping account of every penny spent, he also demanded this of those around him. A whole generation of St. Mary's monks rarely enjoyed as much as an ice cream cone during those frequent commutes between Morristown and Newark; and they knew well that PV, as Father Vincent was called, fully expected the change returned, even if it were only a nickel, from those infrequent shopping trips. But Father Vincent's support for his confreres, his strict observance, and his administrative discipline securely anchored the pioneer community during the difficult days of the 1930s and early 1940s.

Father Vincent also held the title of rector of the seminary during the early years. Drawing his lessons from a broad experience, enthusiastic or reserved as the topic demanded, always knowledgeable, he taught moral theology to the clerics until the late 1950s and canon law until the 1940s. Father Bede Babo, O.S.B., the socius and immediate superior of the young monks, taught dogmatic theology. Although classes were held in English, Fathers Vincent and Bede assigned the staple Latin texts, Sabetti-Barrett and Tanqueray. The clerics attended moral theology, canon law, and dogmatic theology twelve times a week. Classes in liturgy, homiletics, and later, Scripture, met less frequently in those years, and were taught by a number of confreres including: Fathers Ninian MacDonald, O.S.B., William Koelhoffer, O.S.B., Ambrose Gallagher, O.S.B., Michael Ducey, O.S.B., and Hugh Duffy, O.S.B.

During these years the community numbered fifteen to twenty monks. The number swelled during the summers when the recently professed novices and the young clerics returned home from St. Vincent or St. Anselm's. It increased also during the occasional years in the early 1930s and early 1940s when the scholastics took their first two years of college at Delbarton. All prayed, lived, and studied in one building, the old mansion – one community of men spanning three generations, united in their relationships with one another by common observance, some hardships, a single purpose, and a pioneering spirit.

The clericate at St. Mary's Abbey/Delbarton in 1939: Kneeling, left to right:
Fraters Ignatius Kohl, Adrian McLaughlin, Mark Confroy, Alfred Meister,
Frederick Muench. Standing, left to right: Edmund Nugent, Jerome Fitzpatrick,
Leo Beger, Gilbert Crawford, Leonard Cassell, William Fagen, Kenneth Mayer.

Brother Ambrose Kelly (L) and
Brother Albert Becker (R), 1950s

The life of prayer and study in the mansion developed community and spirit, but the monks also found community in ways that may have been more subtle, yet just as profound. If it can be said that Father Vincent was the guiding force of the monastery, the experienced monks around him, especially the professed brothers, embodied the monastic ideals of St. Mary's in their work and prayer. In their frequent and often informal daily contact with the clerics, the brothers conveyed these ideals to them. The example of these older and more mature men, skilled in their work and confirmed in their vocations after many years of seeking God, was ever present to the clerics. The stalwarts of the first twenty years in Morristown were Brothers Aloysius, Peter, Albert, and Isidore. A young monk would go to one for medical care and transportation, to another with a maintenance problem, to the others for a work detail in the fields or with livestock in the barn. Although work with the brothers was never easy, it was nearly always exhilarating, especially when working with confreres or when it would help supply the common table. And it provided a regular cycle for the year, giving additional order as well as variety to the monastic routine. Few monks of this time forgot the annual corn harvest with Brother Isidore, the last major effort of the summer and an occasion for the final community celebration before the start of school.

The brothers wasted few words and tolerated no nonsense. Yet they communicated to the clerics an understanding of the ways of youth and an appreciation for help generously given. Faithful, supportive, they worked quietly yet tirelessly for St. Mary's and the Church. Their contribution to the Abbey was obvious in the food they put on the table or in the conveniences they provided. Their contribution to the Church, though less tangible, lived on in the young monks who learned from them.

Recreation also formed community. Clerics gathered daily after lunch and dinner for playing cards, for listening to the radio, or for taking long walks on the property or in Jockey Hollow, the National Historical Park opened to the south of Delbarton in the mid-1930s. In the late afternoon, they enjoyed the traditional German haustus of soda, beer, and snacks, the latter usually favorite delights left by visiting parents on previous weekends. The rolling terrain on the property and in the park, as well as a measure of snow, provided for winter sports. The 1930s through the 1940s were good years. The vast lawns supplied the playing fields for summer sports. Almost nightly, teams of monks contended with each other in baseball or softball, with the length of games determined only by the ringing of the bell for divine office. Everyone had the opportunity to play, whether talented or not, but periodically the Benedictine "all-stars" assembled to meet challenges from club or semi-professional teams in the area or to offer the challenges themselves. The Benedictines rarely lost. Furthermore, the monks combined work with the anticipation of recreation when in the 1930s they excavated the lake near the pond on the northeast corner of the property. Now called Lake Vincent, the new facility provided recreational fishing, swimming, and boating.

Old Main, circa 1930

VII

NEWARK'S GENEROSITY TO MORRISTOWN

St. Mary's Abbey established the Morristown foundation on the eve of the stock market crash and the Great Depression. Sustaining this foundation during the depths of the economic collapse of the 1930s drained the resources of the Newark monks. Again, a faith in the future of their community and a willingness to respond to the needs of the Church prompted Newark's characteristic generosity during these days. Once more, and not for the last time, they put aside their own needs for the needs of others.

Vegetables for the common table were their only daily, tangible returns from Morristown. Nevertheless, within the next generation dozens of monks trained in Morristown staffed the Newark parishes and St. Benedict's Prep. And in later decades, many of these monks went to Newark after a year or more of teaching experience gained at Delbarton School. But, even in the light of this eventual return in manpower, the accumulated revenues the Newark monks forwarded to Morristown demanded from them considerable sacrifice in terms of the immediate needs of the Newark school and monastery. For twenty or more years, from the late 1920s to beyond 1945, the Abbey sent a check of $1000 each month to Father Vincent Amberg. With extraordinary expenditures in taxes and in the repair of plumbing, lighting, and heating, the average minimal cost of maintaining St. Mary's Monastery, Morristown, annually came to between $15,000 and $20,000. In addition to this expense, the Newark monks accepted other financial responsibilities. During the decade of the Depression, they voted to send nearly $50,000 to Benedictine abbeys and parishes facing financial disaster. They also extended themselves in practical daily charity. As a religious community located in the midst of an urban environment, the Newark monks received frequent requests for food, clothing, and money. For years, in fact, the community ran a

> Again, a faith in the future of their community and a willingness to respond to the needs of the Church prompted Newark's characteristic generosity during these days. Once more, and not for the last time, they put aside their own needs for the needs of others.

Newark "Four Corners" – Market and Broad Streets, 1928

(Photo courtesy of Floyd W. Parsons, EM, editor-in-chief of *New Jersey:
Life, Industries & Resources of a Great State.* Published by New Jersey
State Chamber of Commerce, Newark, NJ, 1928.)

soup kitchen on High Street, feeding a substantial hot meal daily to the poor and unemployed who came to them.

In this period, therefore, in order to help cover these costs and minimize the sacrifices they were making for St. Benedict's and the monastery in Newark, some monks recommended that the community look for additional sources of income consistent with their apostolate. Consequently, in the spring of 1932, Abbot Ernest appointed a committee chaired by Father Vincent to investigate the desirability and feasibility of opening a day school at Delbarton. Abbot Ernest was then serving as President of the American Cassinese Congregation of Benedictines. In this capacity he left Newark in April for a series of visits to other abbeys, expecting that the committee would complete their work by his return. The committee worked quickly, reporting back to the community on May 7, before Abbot Ernest's return, that the Abbey should start a school at Delbarton as soon as possible. With the prior presiding in Chapter, the capitulars voted by a strong majority to endorse the committee's report to Abbot Ernest.

Misfortune, however, and considerable embarrassment for Abbot Ernest and the Newark Benedictines terminated the decision to open Delbarton School at this time. Somehow, members of the press learned of the Chapter vote and misinterpreted it to mean that the monks of St. Mary's were about to open the school. In point of fact, the vote merely represented support for the findings of Father Vincent's committee. Final decision on the school would have to await Abbot Ernest's counsel and approval, more Chapter discussion and voting, and permission from the ecclesiastical authority of the diocese, Bishop Thomas J. Walsh. Nevertheless, a reporter printed the story as he understood it. Unfortunately, the newspaper article then came to the attention of the bishop.

Walsh, disturbed by this apparent breach of Church protocol, looked forward to the return of the abbot for an explanation. Some weeks passed before the bishop, abbot, and prior unraveled the misunderstanding, but, as a result, the community dropped the plan to establish a school at Delbarton. Through these months of May and June, the secretary of Bishop Walsh, Father Thomas McLaughlin, observed with empathy the intentions and embarrassment of the Newark community. In a few years, as the first bishop of the Diocese of Paterson, he would remember their good will.

Newark continued to struggle through the Depression without that additional source of revenue. Some men, therefore, in counting the cost of sustaining Morristown, spoke of selling Delbarton. Abbot Ernest apparently disagreed with this position, even to the point of wanting to expand in Morristown by building a large monastery there. But after 1935, with old age and ill health sapping his strength, he was unable to exercise the aggressive leadership of his earlier days. Abbot Ernest died in the summer of 1937. He served the Church for twenty-seven years as abbot, almost sixty years as a monk, and more than fifty years as a priest. Before his death he expressed regret that he was unable to resolve the questions regarding Morristown and more effectively provide for its future. Reluctantly, he left this work to his successor.

VIII

MORRISTOWN'S CHARTER

Ill health prevented the fourth abbot of St. Mary's from attending the Chapter meeting that elected him in August, 1937. He then served the community as abbot for thirty years. Patrick O'Brien quickly assumed the responsibilities Abbot Ernest left for him. During the next third of the century, he directed the Newark and Morristown monks through a period of their greatest expansion as well as their greatest trial.

Abbot Patrick's vocation matured in Manchester, New Hampshire, the town of his birth. He attended St. Anselm's College and, for four years, taught high school in New England before joining St. Mary's Abbey. After completing theology in Manchester, he taught there and at St. Benedict's for a time. He then began pastoral work at St. Joseph's parish, Maplewood, where he served until his election.

Abbot Patrick enjoyed many of the characteristics of his predecessors. Like Wimmer, he was a builder who lived to see the remarkable growth of his community and the expansion of its facilities. Like Zilliox, he was a man of piety, quick to exhort his monks to holiness and faithful observance of the Rule by his words and example. Like Abbots Hilary and Ernest and three generations of St. Mary's monks before him, he was generous, open to the needs of all, willing to spend himself to the limits of his strength.

Abbot Patrick met his responsibilities through a period of unparalleled change and challenge in the American Church and culture. He saw the beginnings of the Liturgical Movement, the conclusion of the Second Vatican Council, the progress of the great migration of peoples to the urban North, and the gradual alienation of Americans from their political and social institutions. Inevitably, any religious community would be affected by such developments. But mid-twentieth century America had an enormous effect on St. Mary's, an abbey supporting one community located in an urban setting undergoing radical economic and demographic change and another community located in an expanding middle-class, suburban environment projecting different needs. But Abbot Patrick possessed both the single-mindedness and decisiveness to face these challenges and the holiness and generosity to sustain his community through them. Like most Americans, he may not have satisfac-

Abbot Patrick O'Brien (Abbot, 1937-1967)

torily resolved the period's tensions, but more complete judgments on decisions made then must wait for a later history. Viewed as a whole, however, and in the perspective of only a few years, even the bare outline of the period illumines the strength of Abbot Patrick and his community.

During late 1937 and early 1938, the abbot directed his attention to the physical details of the monasteries and the observance of the monks, apparently taking stock of the opinions of the men around him. In the spring of 1938, however, he forcefully addressed himself to the unanswered questions about Morristown. In a chapter meeting of May 12, he read a lengthy statement on what he called "the Delbarton situation." He put the statement in writing, he said, "because I wish my position to be emphasized and perpetuated." Abbot Patrick, evidently, had developed strong feelings on the matter, feelings which he held consistently throughout his administration. Because of the significance of this memorandum concerning the history of St. Mary's Abbey for the next thirty years, the memorandum should be studied in full.

After briefly discussing the history of the purchase of Delbarton, he described its convenient location and material advantages. He pointed to the importance of Delbarton as a place for the infirm and noted that the community in Newark did not have the accommodations for the priests, brothers, and clerics resident in Morristown. Interpreting the purpose for the expansion to Delbarton and implying his view for the future, he said:

> *"Delbarton as it stands today is of great value to us. It has everything that could*
> *be desired for a present home and a future monastery. It was bought and*
> *developed with the idea of a future expansion of the community."*

Then, identifying with the early Wimmer, but not the Wimmer or Zilliox of the 1880s who accepted the possibilities of monastic life in cities, he continued:

"We must have a suitable place for training our clerics. We shall surely agree that the city is no place for such training, for developing sincere members of the Benedictine Order. This has been proved by experience. The distractions in the city hinder not only the progress in study, but also the spirit of recollection, of true asceticism...Delbarton is furthermore necessary for religious purposes. We are all members of a semi-contemplative Order and we must at times find a place for spiritual refreshment and for the rejuvenation of our inner life. It cannot be gainsaid that life in a city is a deterrent to religious progress. Some cannot be persuaded of this, but the fact is attested by the very nature of religious life."

This said, he explicitly cited the problem which made him take the extraordinary step of reading a prepared memorandum in Chapter. With his characteristic directness belying his small stature and gentle demeanor, he advanced in detail, seeking to discern the future:

"The question has at times been asked by a few of our capitulars, "Why not sell Delbarton?" It is obvious that such a proposal is not only impractical, but also poor business....The price paid was considered low and the transaction a bargain....When we consider the saving of hospital bills for months and for years...the saving of maintenance bills for priests, clerics, brothers, and students (who would have to be provided for, if not at Delbarton, then somewhere else); the recreation and rest place for the tired and fatigued; the prospects of a home in our

A view of Newark around 1912 looking west. The Abbey is in the upper left quadrant.

olden days; the prospects of a school when St. Benedict's Prep, on account of
parochial high schools, or a Catholic community school, would no longer have any
purpose; when our parishes would be supplied from the secular clergy; these and
many more reasons refute the cry: "Sell Delbarton."

He then appealed to history with some overstatement:

"Let us not make the same mistake made by our monastery and by other
monasteries in the past. We had in our possession properties in the city and in the
country, i.e. Denville, and after difficult pioneering work and expense just when
we were about to reap the benefits, these were sold much to our later regret."

For the benefit of some monks, he added reassuringly: "Some fathers desire the sale for fear they will be reassigned there. Still, there never will be a time when we shall be forced to live at Delbarton, unless necessity require it."

Abbot Patrick concluded forcefully, giving a hint of the direction of his leadership in the next few years.

"Therefore, considering our investment; a necessary home for novices, clerics,
priests; for the sick, aged, convalescent; a home for retreats; a prospective
school which we hope to have when our forces are adequate; considering
all these things, we must naturally deem it imprudent to dispose of
Delbarton at present; and I personally wish to go on record tonight as being
heartily in favor of its retention and development."

This wide-ranging memorandum and the manner of its delivery clearly revealed the mind of the abbot on the Morristown foundation. It most likely ended all serious discussion of selling the Delbarton property. In fact, the decisive leadership of Abbot Patrick revealed here prompted the positive response from the community for his many proposals the next year regarding the development of Delbarton.

> *"The distractions in the city hinder not only the progress in study, but also the spirit of recollection, of true asceticism..."*
> - Abbot Patrick O'Brien, O.S.B.

Within only a few weeks of this memorandum, the community voted $15,000 to build in Morristown a more than thirty-room brick monastery on the top of the hill, just east of the water tower. The monks also voted to open immediately a novitiate on the third floor of the mansion, rather than continue to send novices to St. Vincent Archabbey. In addition, they accepted a proposal to have the newly professed clerics attend philosophy classes closer to home in Darlington. The last two of these three decisions were reversed in 1939 and 1940, when both novices and philosophers returned to Latrobe, but the first decision was vigorously carried out by Father Vincent Amberg.

Striving to have the new monastery building completed by the spring or summer of 1939, Father Vincent is said to have occasionally led a crew of brothers to the site to continue the work of the carpenters and masons after the workmen went home for the day. This help assured the scheduled completion of the building, but the original $15,000 allocated for the project proved to be inadequate. Consequently, in April, 1939, Abbot Patrick asked for and received permission from the Chapter to sell three buildings on Niagara Street, Newark, formerly properties of Abbot Ernest's family, for $5900, with the money realized from the sale assigned to complete payment on the Morristown monastery.

The events of the next month, May, 1939, were equally significant for the future of the Morristown monks. Bishop Walsh's former secretary, Thomas McLaughlin, had come to the newly created Paterson diocese as its first bishop in mid-1938. In the following months, perhaps during some of his frequent visits to St. Mary's Monastery, he expressed concern to Abbot Patrick that his diocese was inadequately supplied with Catholic schools. Bishop Griffin of the Diocese of Trenton, also a frequent visitor to the Morristown community, voiced the same concerns for his own diocese.

> "...the prospects of a school when St. Benedict's Prep, on account of parochial high schools, or a Catholic community school, would no longer have any purpose;.... and many more reasons refute the cry: "Sell Delbarton."
> – Abbot Patrick O'Brien, O.S.B.

Both men stated that they would like to see a Catholic boarding school established for boys to compete with The Lawrenceville School, The Peddie School, Blair Academy, and the traditional boarding preparatory schools in New England. In May, 1939, Bishop McLaughlin held a lengthy and direct conversation with Abbot Patrick on this topic. During this conversation he stated that St. Mary's Abbey would meet important needs of the diocese by opening a "residential high school"

St. Benedict

at Delbarton. Abbot Patrick answered that the community had considered this earlier and that the community might be well disposed to the idea again. When the abbot finally asked the bishop if such a school could open in September of the same year, McLaughlin responded, "Yes." Therefore, on May 8, the abbot brought the proposal for a "residential high school" to the capitulars, who accepted the project by a strong majority.

PART TWO:

MAINTAINING UNION

IX

TOWARDS SELF-SUBSISTENCE

Very few religious communities ever began a school with but four months' preparation. The clouds of a World War and a lingering economic depression further complicated the opening of Delbarton School. However, the first headmaster, Father Augustine Wirth, O.S.B., and his staff quickly prepared the classrooms and the living quarters in the Kountze mansion. Most of the monks living there had recently vacated the mansion for the new monastery. But Delbarton was blessed with facilities at the beginning; the want of a student body presented the major problem now. To create one and to promote the school, Father Augustine and his principal associate, Father Claude Micik, O.S.B., canvassed selected neighborhoods in New Jersey through the late spring and summer months. Their work resulted in a fall term enrollment of twelve boarding students in grades seven and eight.

In 1939, Delbarton School offered a seventh and eighth grade curriculum of religion, arithmetic, English, civics, and geography. A similar program was available to the few sixth grade students enrolled in 1940, and Latin and algebra replaced arithmetic and geography for the ninth graders in 1940 and 1941. With a housemother in residence and some of the scholastics involved in extracurricular activities, along with five full-time staff members, including Brother Aloysius Hutten as infirmarian, the students received an appropriate measure of both attention and discipline. In return, they contributed to the mansion a new life and rhythm not heard there since Kountze's children were young, fifty years earlier. From the following code of conduct, which included the original rules of discipline of Delbarton School, the spirit of Delbarton's first twelve-year-olds as well as the travail of its first teachers might be inferred. Capitalization and underlining from the original have been maintained here.

> *"Your room is a place for study. <u>Silence</u> is essential for <u>Concentration</u> on your*
> *Studies. Therefore, any form of <u>disturbance</u> is out of place during Study Time.*
> *<u>Visiting</u> in rooms is strictly forbidden at <u>all</u> <u>times</u>. <u>All</u> <u>boys</u> should always be*
> *together for all extracurricular activities. Don't be a Lone Wolf.*
> *ACT AS GENTLEMEN AT ALL TIMES AND IN ALL PLACES."*

Father Augustine Wirth, Headmaster (1939-1942),
and Prior Vincent Amberg

The efforts of Father Augustine Wirth and Father Claude Micik bore fruit as the enrollment increased to more than twenty students by 1941. During this time, however, Father Augustine's health began to fail, and Abbot Patrick developed some concern that the School was not becoming a high school soon enough. The Abbot interpreted Bishop McLaughlin's request and the community's will, expressed in chapter in May, 1939, as his responsibility to fulfill.

Father Stephen
Findlay, Headmaster,
1942-1967

Consequently, in late August, 1942, after considerable thought and some consultation with his counselors, he called young Father Stephen Findlay, O.S.B., into his office and said: "I've decided I'm going to send you to Delbarton." In the same statement, before allowing Father Stephen to respond one way or the other, he added, "You will do it under obedience."

Father Stephen was ordained to the priesthood in 1937 and trained to serve the Church as a theologian and canon lawyer. When he received his doctorate in canon law from The Catholic University of America in 1940, he could not have known that in two years he would become chief administrator of Delbarton's spirited twelve-year-olds. He prepared for this responsibility in fewer than three weeks during the late summer but went on to have the benefit of more than twenty-five years to learn the position. He learned well, because under his administration, Delbarton School earned its place as one of the distinguished Catholic preparatory schools in America.

Abbot Patrick directed Father Stephen to make Delbarton School both a four-year high school and a self-sustaining institution within the St. Mary's Abbey community as soon as possible. The new headmaster accomplished these goals before the end of the decade. When Father Stephen began his work, twenty students were enrolled at Delbarton; in February of his first year, the number reached thirty-one. During the next school year he increased the faculty to thirteen monks and the student body to more than fifty. He opened the tenth grade in 1944, but because the World War seriously limited the availability of science equipment, he was unable to provide the science courses important to the eleventh and twelfth grades until after the war. Consequently, he delayed the opening of the eleventh grade until 1946 and the twelfth grade until 1947. In June, 1948, the first twelve college preparatory graduates of Delbarton School received diplomas from a proud Abbot Patrick. The young graduates, however, could not have fully appreciated the extraordinary efforts and sacrifices the Newark and Morristown monks had expended to make that day in June possible.

From his earliest days in office, Father Stephen recognized the importance of a faculty dedicated to the School. He was fortunate to have had with him from the beginning such confreres as Fathers Adrian McLaughlin, O.S.B., Frederick Muench, O.S.B., Kenneth Mayer,

Graduating Delbarton School middle school students and faculty, 1945; faculty Left to Right, Father Augustine Verhaegen, Father Kenneth Mayer, Father Frederick Muench, Father Adrian McLaughlin, Father Stephen Findlay, Father Mark Confroy, Brother Aloysius Hutten, Father Ninian McDonald.

Father Stephen's early stalwarts at an assembly in the Main Building, front hall, 1948.
Left to Right: Father Adrian McLaughlin, Abbot Patrick O'Brien,
Father Stephen Findlay, Father Felix Pepin, Father Kenneth Mayer,
Father Peter Meaney, Father Frederick Muench.

O.S.B., and Arthur Mayer, O.S.B., who provided continuity on the faculty through the length of his administration and who still served on Delbarton's faculty or board of trustees into the late 1980s. The dedication and loyalty of these men to the community's new venture were shared in the early and mid-1940s by Fathers Alfred Meister, O.S.B., Leo Beger, O.S.B., Leonard Cassell, O.S.B., Lucien Donnelly, O.S.B., Felix Pepin, O.S.B., and Brother Denis Robertson, O.S.B.; two monks from St. Paul's Abbey, Newton, Thomas Tyson, O.S.B., and Andrew O'Sullivan, O.S.B.; and monks of the earliest years, Fathers Augustine Wirth, Claude Micik, Mark Confroy, O.S.B., Ninian MacDonald, Augustine Verhaegen, O.S.B., and Aloysius Hutten. In 1946, Father Stephen added to the faculty the first full-time layman, Mr. William O. Regan, who began then and served in an uninterrupted and distinguished career as athletic director and head football coach until 1987. The amount of time these men devoted to the Delbarton students is incalculable. The New Deal eight-hour-day reform, enjoyed then for the first time by so many of their contemporaries, they never knew. In addition, nearly all of the young monks resident in the monastery also contributed to the School, and many of them later joined the faculty full-time to serve under Father Stephen for ten or more years. Gradually, the community established a stable faculty at the School, a necessary component of the institution's growing self-subsistence.

X

TENSIONS OF TWO COMMUNITIES

The Newark monks continued to support the Morristown community and school during the 1940s, even as they had assisted St. Anselm's a generation earlier. However, some of the questions asked in the 1930s remained. In early 1941, before Father Stephen Findlay became headmaster of Delbarton, Father Vincent Amberg made a request of the community in Chapter which occasioned a discussion that continued intermittently over the next quarter century. He proposed an expenditure for the construction of garages to serve both the monastery and school in Morristown. The community eventually rejected the motion, but regarding the discussion preceding the vote, the secretary of the Chapter noted the earliest recorded consciousness of a separate identity for the two schools of the community. He wrote that one monk said "something should be done for Delbarton," and another, "a building fund should be set aside for St. Benedict's Prep." The second comment might have been occasioned by the speaker's realization that since 1925 much had been done for Delbarton while expansion continued to be limited in Newark. In fact, the hope of the second monk was not fulfilled for nearly twenty years.

In the following year, however, as though oblivious of their own limited financial resources, but characteristically generous and self-sacrificing, the monks of St. Mary's Abbey voted to give, unencumbered and at no cost, 48 building lots which they owned in Wilmington to the bishop of that diocese, Edmund Fitzmaurice.

> .... since 1925 much had been done for Delbarton, while expansion continued to be limited in Newark.

In 1943, after Father Stephen's first year as headmaster, another event prompted the periodic discussion of priorities between Newark and Morristown. In May and June, Fathers Vincent and Stephen agreed that, if fully utilized, the existing facilities of the School could accommodate as many as fifty boarding students. To achieve this immediate goal, Father Vincent proposed what he regarded as minor alterations for Kountze's carriage house, then used as the gym but later called Chapter Hall. He began the alterations in the early summer with monies on hand. Father Stephen, in turn, admitted the additional students to the School.

In late August, however, Fathers Vincent and Stephen realized that the existing funds were not, in fact, adequate for the alterations, so Father Vincent made a request of the Chapter on September 3 for an additional $5000 to complete the work. At that time Father Stephen presented Delbarton School's financial report for 1942-1943, his first year in office.

Income

    Board and tuition $12,250.00

Expenses

    Teacher salaries 50.00

    Board for students 4,780.00

    Supplies, maintenance, staff 4,000.35

                                            8,830.35

In spite of the more than $3000 profit for the year and the sum spent since June on the remodeling of Chapter Hall, the capitulars rejected Father Vincent's request. In the discussion, some counseled again that the Morristown community should try to live within its budget and be careful about expanding too quickly at the School.

During the following week, however, Abbot Patrick scaled down Father Vincent's request to $3000, an expenditure which, by Benedictine statute, he could authorize with the approval of the seniors, five members of the Abbey serving as his special advisors and as officers of the monastic corporation. He then saw some of the seniors privately, received their approval for the expenditure, and authorized Father Vincent to continue the repairs. The abbot, however, did not see two of the seniors because they were away from the Abbey at the time and did not get the approval of the other members at an official meeting, but privately. Abbot Patrick later regretted these errors in judgment and in a few months, apologized to the chapter for them.

As the remodeling advanced, opposition to Abbot Patrick's actions grew. They culminated at a Chapter meeting held on November 10, 1943. This meeting was occasioned in part by the signing of a petition by nearly every member of the community calling for the establishment of a long-range plan regarding the future of St. Mary's Abbey and St. Benedict's Prep School. In a free and frank discussion of nearly two hours in which more than twenty members spoke, Abbot Patrick asserted that he agreed with the content of the petition but not with the act of petitioning. Some monks defended both the content and the process. Like the lone monk's statement in 1941, however, apparently nothing came of the petition, since the discussion quickly moved to the matter of the remodeling and expansion at Delbarton School. Again, monks warned about uncontrolled growth and counseled living within a budget. Finally, the Abbot presented a motion asking the capitulars for authorization to spend $3000 to complete repairs on Chapter Hall, the same authorization he received from the seniors in September. The motion was defeated by a vote of eighteen to seventeen. Abbot Patrick directed Father Vincent, then, to re-modify or cease the

Chapter Hall, Kountze Family carriage house which served as the Delbarton gymnasium until it was destroyed by fire in 1947.

alterations and pay the contractors with whatever budgeted funds he already had available. As the future would suggest, this forced economizing may have been providentially designed.

In April, 1947, three and one half years after the events of November, 1943, Chapter Hall burned to the ground. Since it served as the gym and an activities center as well as a residence hall for some students, Chapter Hall was the center of life at Delbarton School. However, it was underinsured. But the fire occurred while the monks and students attended breakfast, thus preventing loss of life. On balance, then, circumstances mitigated the tragedy for the young school. In the end, discussions and decisions made by the community during the months after the tragedy resulted in unanimity at St. Mary's regarding expansion in Morristown, and finally, in financial independence and self-subsistence for Delbarton School.

External forces also contributed to these results. At that time, according to the constitution of the American Cassinese Congregation of Benedictines, of which St. Mary's was a member, each abbey was visited every three years by a committee of two or three abbots elected for this purpose from the Congregation. Visitators functioned as observers and listeners, interpreting to the community at the end of their three-day visit what they thought were the needs of the community in light of what they were told and what they observed compared to the Rule and the statutes of the Congregation. On these ordinary visitations, they served as advisors, not decision makers. The closing statements of visitators, however, usually affected directions a community would take following the triennial visit. At St Mary's Abbey during the 1940s and 1950s, the visitators had a profound effect.

In 1946, the abbot visitators recommended that the community study its current situation and plan for community development, both in Newark and Morristown, in an ordered way. This visitation and the destruction of Chapter Hall prompted a series of important community discussions from May to December, 1947, regarding the future of the Abbey and its schools.

At a Chapter meeting held on May 26, 1947, the community conducted a wide-ranging discussion on topics of concern. Four themes surfaced in their deliberations: that the community concentrate its apostolic work in either Newark or Morristown; that in recent years the community had over-extended itself; that Delbarton should become a day school only; that the future of Delbarton should be determined only after the future of Newark and St. Benedict's Prep had been determined. Many men contributed to this open forum, offering their opinions on the merits of these and related questions. In a statement reflecting his views of the previous decade, views which guided him through the remaining decades of his administration, Abbot Patrick said that St. Mary's Abbey needed both the Newark and Morristown communities and schools. The secretary of the Chapter summarized his reason as: "The uncertainty of the future dictates the wisdom of maintaining (our) present set-up." The abbot then appointed two committees to study the future

Pergola and statues on southside of Delbarton Formal Garden.

of the Abbey, one to study the future of Newark; the other, to study the future of Morristown. With a view to promoting unity, he integrated each committee with priests resident at both locations. He charged the members to "determine the future for twenty years" and asked for their recommendations within the next few months.

Both committees reported back before the end of June, with the Newark group recommending that general community discussions be held on their topic during the fall of the year, and with the Morristown group making specific recommendations for immediate approval by the Chapter. This committee proposed that the size of Delbarton School be set at one hundred boarding and fifty day students. They further recommended that, to prepare for this increased enrollment, the community approve an appropriation of $110,000 to build a new gymnasium building and remodel the Brothers'

> Assisted by the Delbarton Mothers' Guild and Fathers and Friends, founded by Father Stephen in 1946 and 1947, the School became self-subsistent.

House. They proposed that the $50,000 fire insurance claim for Chapter Hall be assigned to the $110,000 appropriation and that the monks at Delbarton School be required to raise the remaining $60,000. In a demonstration of unanimity, the capitulars voted in favor of these proposals by a significant majority. In later months the community increased the appropriation because the new Delbarton gymnasium, originally projected at a price near $100,000, eventually cost $125,000. With the completion of the gym for the 1948-1949 school year and with the addition of rooms for fifteen to twenty boarding students in the Brothers' House, the School's facilities remained adequate through the mid-1950s. As specified by the Chapter vote in June, 1947, Father Stephen and members of the Delbarton faculty, independent of the rest of the community, raised the money for these improvements. Assisted by the Delbarton Mothers' Guild and Fathers and Friends, founded by Father Stephen in 1946 and 1947, the School became self-subsistent.

The meetings recommended by the Newark committee occurred during the fall and early winter of 1947. Discussions were characterized by a sense of unity and an acceptance of diversity within the one Abbey. In the meeting of October 30, monks, for the first time in the recorded minutes of the Chapter, used the term "separation," but the majority of the members valued more the benefits of one community. Some members explicitly branded separation premature. In a sensitivity for Newark's unique apostolate and in an awareness of the growing difference between the Newark and Morristown environments, one monk suggested that St. Benedict's should be increasingly valued as a location "more appropriate for work with the poor."

Some monks recommended that the community build an auditorium and gymnasium complex at St. Benedict's Prep. When the series of meetings ended in December, however, the community appeared to agree on the desirability of this proposal, but made no financial appropriation for it. Again, as in 1941 and 1943, nothing would result from this recommendation for another eleven years.

XI

SEEKING GOD

Benedictine monks dedicate their lives to seeking God. In his Rule for monks composed in the sixth century, St. Benedict taught that an obedient monk is one who truly seeks God and performs his work in a context of a life of prayer and Scripture reading lived in community under the authority of an abbot. Teaching at Delbarton and developing the facilities of the School, therefore, played a role in the lives of the Morristown monks subordinate to the larger role of seeking God. As much as they may have been consumed daily by teaching, prefecting, studying, coaching, and raising money, their worship and prayer transformed their work and continued to remind them of what they professed when they took vows. This spiritual anchor of their lives, even as it enriched them, imay have helped free them to expand their work and resources to the limits. It surely represented the bond, under one abbot, that preserved their unity and fellowship with the Newark monks as circumstances propelled the communities in different directions. Single-mindedly again, Abbot Patrick insisted that the monks he served not forget their calling to seek God.

Within a few weeks of his election in 1937, Abbot Patrick changed the daily horarium in a way more in keeping with the arrangement of the day by St. Benedict. He moved the hour of Vespers, prayed after dinner under Abbots Hilary and Ernest, to the time of sundown in the late afternoon, and required that on feasts and holy days it be sung rather than recited. Later he moved Vespers to the early afternoon. Although he continued the practice of anticipating Matins and Lauds at 8:00p.m. and later at 5:00p.m., he moved Compline from its original place after Vespers to the more appropriate last hour of the day at 7:30p.m.. In addition, he encouraged the singing of Compline. With these changes, he moved the rising time from 4:30a.m. to 5:00a.m..

The Chapter notes demonstrate that Abbot Patrick regularly exhorted his monks to faithful observance. During these early years, the secretary of the Chapter records that he asked the monks to make culpa to him should they miss office, that evening work activities should not excuse them from morning prayer, that no purchases should be made without the permission of the procurator or headmaster, that the greatest charity should be extended to guests, and other exhortations pertaining to the teachings of St. Benedict's Rule.

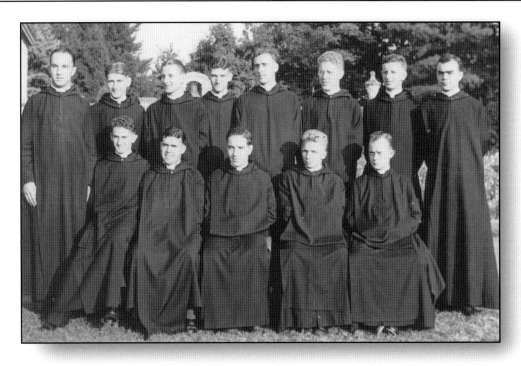

The clericate in 1938

In 1943, Abbot Patrick collected his exhortations in a small booklet. A remarkable mirror of his piety, the booklet also reflected the spirit of his distant predecessor, Abbot James Zilliox. Since it also represents the values learned by a generation of Newark and Morristown monks, portions of it deserve recounting:

"When we pronounced our vows, we took upon ourselves the Benedictine life as our profession. It follows from this that our most important duty is to be good Benedictines. Other activities, such as teaching, preaching, parish work, etc., are secondary and must not be preferred to our monastic duties. We may engage in these works only if they do not prevent us from being good monks...
In our professional life as Benedictines, the most important duty is the Divine Office...Our other work must be so arranged that it does not ordinarily interfere with the Divine Office...Walks may be taken after classes.

"....In our professional life as Benedictines, the most important duty is the Divine Office..."
– Abbot Patrick O'Brien, O.S.B.

This does not include visits to homes or places of amusement, such as movies, plays, etc. Special permission is required for these...

All should carefully avoid unkind remarks and criticism and refrain from saying anything that might disturb the peace and harmony of the community...

Permission to go out at night should be infrequently given. There are times when absence from the monastery is legitimate, but to be looking for and to take advantage of every opportunity to go abroad is dangerous and entirely out of harmony with religious life. It destroys the spirit of prayer and recollection, and in time, it engenders a love of the world and worldly things and a disgust for everything that is spiritual....

No monk may possess money or use it without permission. To meet an emergency which may occur when walking in the city, one may receive 75 cents from the procurator once a month. This money, however, may not be spent at will....

A conscientious priest will at frequent intervals read over the ceremonies of the Mass so that he may not become careless or remiss. He should carefully observe the "vox alta", the "vox media", and the "vox secreta", whenever they are prescribed, unless the nearness of the altars will disturb another priest....."

Abbot James' spirituality remained timely for Abbot Patrick. Although Abbot Patrick may have changed the tone of his admonitions as values of self-renewal and self-actualization became current in the 1950s and 1960s, and, during periods of inflation and higher prices, may have allowed a monk more than seventy-five cents per month for emergencies, the basic values in his teaching remained the same throughout his life.

Prior Hugh Duffy

During the late 1940s and early 1950s, as the size of the monastic community in Morristown grew to as many as thirty monks during the school year and to fifty or more during the summer, Abbot Patrick redistributed administrative responsibilities. In 1945 he assigned Father Hugh Duffy, O.S.B., to the office of prior to succeed the aging Father Vincent, who continued as procurator of the Morristown community until his death twenty years later. Father Hugh, formerly the pastor of the Abbey's parish in Cedar Knolls and occasionally the Scripture professor at the school of theology, was New-England-born like Abbot Patrick and educated in Europe after ordination to the priesthood. Before returning to St. Mary's, he spent two years at the German Abbey of Maria Laach of the Beuronese Congregation, the same congregation James Zilliox sought to join in the 1870s.

An urbane, articulate gentleman, the new prior brought a style to the community which endeared him to the young monks. By imparting this style, he introduced into the community's routine many of the monastic practices he learned in Europe. In addition, he possessed for his day an unusual knowledge of the Church's liturgy which enriched the worship of the community.

Prior Bede Babo

Also at St. Mary's Monastery in those years was Father Augustine Verhaegen, a monk of the ancient Abbey of Afflighem in Belgium and an accomplished musician and student of plain chant. Together, Fathers Hugh and Augustine developed in the monks an appreciation of and the skills for the appropriate celebration of the Eucharist and the divine office. This enhanced the spirit of the group, sensitized the monks to the values of the Liturgical Movement in the Church, and educated them for this important part of their apostolate at mid-century. More than this, it placed a high value on worship, confirming the teachings of Abbot Patrick and improving monastic observance.

Father Hugh esteemed the vocation of the professed lay brother in the monastic community. He promoted non-clerical vocations and, with Abbot Patrick, encouraged the brothers to attend all of the hours of the divine office. Prior to this period, under Abbots Hilary Pfraengle and Ernest Helmstetter and throughout the congregation, the prayer life of the brothers was limited to recitation of the rosary or the Little Office of the Blessed Virgin. Father Hugh, however, expanded this significantly at St. Mary's, and in doing so, anticipated monastic reforms that would not come in some abbeys until the 1960s.

Father Hugh also introduced important changes into Morristown's horarium. In the late 1940s, he moved Lauds, a morning hour, from the evening of the previous day to the dawn hour. He placed Prime after Lauds, then private Mass for priests or meditation for the clerics and brothers, Terce, breakfast, and

Prior Michael Collins

then sung conventual Mass, followed immediately by classes. Sext and None were assigned for the period before lunch, and Vespers after lunch. Matins continued as anticipated at 5:00p.m., followed by spiritual reading. Compline he ordered sung at 7:30p.m.. In addition, on Sundays and holy days Father Hugh had conventual Mass celebrated solemnly later in the morning and Vespers sung at 3:00p.m.. Except for minor changes, such as reversing the order of breakfast and conventual Mass during the week, Father Hugh's order of the day remained in force in Morristown until the changes in the Eucharistic celebration and the divine office throughout the universal Church during the late 1960s. Heart disease caused Father Hugh to resign the office of prior in 1952. Father Bede Babo succeeded him until 1956, when Father Michael Collins, O.S.B., began a twelve-year term. Father Michael was followed by Father James O'Donnell, O.S.B. in 1968.

Before assuming the responsibility of prior, Father Bede served as socius of clerics from 1931 to 1950, when he was succeeded by Father Leonard Cassell, who, in turn, served as Scripture professor at the school of theology until the late 1960s. Father Denys Hennessey, O.S.B., also a professor in the school of theology, followed Father Leonard as socius in 1952, and Father Adrian McLaughlin succeeded him in 1956. When Father Adrian became dean of studies at Delbarton School in 1960, Father James succeeded him as socius and taught theology until 1967. Father Christopher Lind, O.S.B., professor of moral theology since 1956, followed Father James as socius, and after him Father Adrian accepted another term in the position. In the school of theology Father Stephen taught canon law from 1942 until the late 1950s. Fathers Michael Collins and Gregory Schramm, O.S.B., taught homiletics and catechetics; Father Gerard Carluccio, O.S.B., taught dogmatic theology, and Father Austin Queenan, O.S.B., Church history.

In 1941, St. Mary's Abbey began sending its novices to St. Benedict's Abbey for their first year of monastic life. This arrangement continued until the completion of the new monastery in Morristown in the mid 1960s when Father Martin Burne, O.S.B., became the master of novices at the Abbey. After a short period in the early 1940s when the scholastics and newly professed attended college in Kansas, both groups went to St. Vincent. From the late 1950s through the early 1960s, the newly professed received philosophy training at St. John's Abbey, Collegeville, Minnesota, while the scholastics attended a variety of schools including St. John's, St. Benedict's, and St. Bernard's in Alabama.

As his piety and spirituality resembled that of James Zilliox, Patrick O'Brien's view of the pastoral ministry resembled that of Hilary Pfraengle and Ernest Helmstetter. In addition, the demands of the Church imposed on the Morristown monks during the early days of the Diocese of Paterson were not unlike those imposed on the Newark monks fifty years earlier. Nor was the response less generous. From the days of the Great Depression, when Father Vincent Amberg regularly journeyed on weekends to St. James Church in Springfield and Father Bede Babo to St. Cecilia's in Rockaway, the Morristown monks counted service to Catholics in northern and western New Jersey, and more recently central and southern New Jersey, among their highest priorities. Since 1926, without interruption, they have ministered to the faithful of Cedar Knolls, and from that time until the late 1950s, to its mission church and later parish, St. Christopher's in Parsippany. Through the years, nearly all the priests of the community administered the sacraments every weekend at parishes in the Dioceses of Paterson and Trenton. The churches where the monks worked ten or more years included: St. Vincent's, Madison; St. Patrick's, Chatham; Sacred Heart, Dover; Assumption and St. Margaret's, Morristown; Sacred Heart and St. Cecilia's, Rockaway; St. Mary's, Wharton; Holy Family, Florham Park; Our Lady of Perpetual Help, Bernardsville; Christ the King, New Vernon; St. Joseph's, Mendham; St. Lawrence, Chester, when it was a mission of St. Joseph's; St. Elizabeth, Far Hills; St. Bridget, Peapack, and Our Lady of the Mount, Warren.

In addition to this pastoral work for the laity, the monks served daily many of the convents for sisters in the area. These include: the Sisters of Christian Charity, Mendham; the Sisters of Charity, Convent Station; the Sisters of St. John the Baptist, Peapack; the Carmelites, Morristown; and the Filipinni Sisters, Morris Township.

XII

MAINTAINING UNION, BUILDING A CHURCH

The Chapter decisions of 1947 resolved only for a time the questions related to the two communities and schools of St. Mary's Abbey. Abbot Patrick sought to maintain the unity as evident from June to December of that year by spending as much time as possible in Morristown and Newark, by holding common Abbey celebrations and retreats, and by having clerics spend weekends and school vacations in Newark. In addition, under his leadership at mid-century, the community occasionally compromised on Abbey expenditures, albeit often without any apparent design, by accompanying within a short period of time a financial appropriation for one of the schools or monasteries with a similar appropriation for the other school or monastery.

However, the natural growth of the Morristown and Newark schools and facilities, as well as the acceleration of changes in the contrasting urban and suburban environments, progressively exacerbated the tensions existing within the Abbey. In the mid-1950s, as the St. Benedict's student population approached the eight hundred mark it would eventually reach a few years later, and as Delbarton's passed two hundred, the Abbey again confronted the issues raised by the separate communities. At this time also, Abbot Patrick's single-mindedness helped him accomplish his goal but it hardened the opposition of those who disagreed with him. Through this period, nonetheless, the monks of St. Mary's Abbey and their abbot maintained in the end their characteristic faith and generosity.

Visitators again precipitated the crisis. In 1949, the abbot visitators recommended "complete union" of the Newark and Morristown communities. The separate monastic locations, they sensed, could not, in time, be maintained in one abbey, given the distinct and growing demands on each community. Nothing came of this recommendation.

In June of the following year, 1950, the community entertained the resolutions of the Newark committee of 1947 that an auditorium complex be built at St. Benedict's Prep. In 1950 the Abbey held a debt of $100,000, yet the appropriation for the auditorium was set at $200,000. In the discussion before the vote, one of the older monks remarked that if St. Mary's Abbey could spend $600,000 in a ten-year period for Manchester and Morristown, it was not too much to ask that the Abbey carry a debt of $300,000 incurred for the Newark building. Apparently the community agreed, because the secretary of the Chapter recorded a community vote overwhelmingly in favor of the proposal. As in 1941, 1943, and 1947, however, no construction occurred as a result of the proposal. The Chapter minutes are silent on the reasons why.

> "The monastic family must be brought together, the whole family. We are not living the life of the Jesuits or of the Dominicans. The one thing you must do is to make such provision that the family can be brought together and live together."

The abbot visitors arrived again in 1952. In their closing statement to the visitation, they referred to the recommendation for "complete union" made by the visitors of 1949. But the Abbey once more neglected to address the question in an extended open forum. Yet, in lieu of open discussion, many monks in both Newark and Morristown through the 1950s participated in informal small-group sessions considering "union" or "separation". Although still only a minority identified with separation, and these were predominantly Newark monks, the concept gained increasingly vocal support. Consequently, the visitors of the triennial visit of 1955 felt they had to take a forceful position. In the recessus, or closing statement, of 1955, they wrote:

*"Today we find little change in the conditions that existed years ago.
The monastic family must be brought together, the whole family.
Any other condition can be only temporary. It cannot be permanent, nor would
Rome permit it to continue indefinitely. We are not living the life of the Jesuits or
of the Dominicans. The one thing you must do is to make such provision that the
family can be brought together and live together. It is up to you as a
Community to determine where that shall be, where that family shall live, and it is
up to you as a community to see that it is accomplished."*

The visitors then required that within a year the community submit a report detailing how it proposed to achieve union. On May 17, 1955, referring first to the community discussions of 1947 and then to the closing statement of the visitation in 1955, Abbot Patrick addressed the community:

*"It hardly seems necessary to remind you that a few years ago we held several
chapter meetings on the future of St. Mary's Abbey. It is the mind of the visitors
that these discussions be continued until the thinking of the community is crystal-
lized in a definitive plan for the future. This definitive plan must result in a St.
Mary's Abbey that will have all the constituent parts of a monastery under one
roof – Abbot, priests, clerics, and brothers. How we will attain the organization –
or reorganization – of St. Mary's Abbey is the problem of the Capitulars."*

Abbot Patrick then appointed a committee, chaired by Father Philip Hoover, O.S.B., to investigate the Newark Housing Authority plans for an area adjacent to the site of the Abbey. He and the community felt that before they could address the question of union or separation they required knowledge of the work and projections of Mr. Louis Dansig of the Housing Authority and the relationship of the Abbey to possible future redevelopment in Newark. Father Philip's committee reported back to the community on October 4, stating in a long report: "The present site (in Newark) is adequate for any expansion of school or monastery, and that such a project would be justified in view of the city's redevelopment." They further recommended consideration of:

1) the formulation of a long-range master plan for redevelopment at the Abbey.

2) the probable needs of the pupil population in the light of the increasing numbers of future applicants; the desirable size of the school; the probable size of our future faculty and staff.

3) the financial implications attendant upon any project for growth at this site.

On October 18, the Abbot appointed a second committee, chaired by Newark's prior, Father Matthew Hoehn, O.S.B., to pursue study of the above recommendations. This committee, however, received the abbot's permission to undertake a broader study, including a survey of the capitulars on five questions related to separation, closing one or the other or both locations, and establishing the abbey at a place other than Newark.

In the meantime, Abbot Patrick visited Archbishop Boland of Newark to inform him of the Abbey's deliberations. The Archbishop told the Abbot that he wanted the Benedictines to remain in his archdiocese but that he agreed that the High Street location was not appropriate for training young monks. In turn, he recommended that the community consider moving the Abbey to a site in West Orange. Later, in December, sites in Scotch Plains and Livingston were also recommended for this purpose.

Father Matthew's committee reported to the Chapter on December 19 and announced the results of the questionnaire returned by eighty-two capitulars. At this meeting also, Abbot Patrick called on all present to state their positions, if they wished, on choosing a new site for the Abbey and St. Benedict's Prep. Subsequently, at a Chapter meeting on February 23, 1956, with Father Matthew presiding, members were called upon to express their views on separation. A third meeting was held on May 24. At this time, Abbot Patrick invited all to speak on two proposals: union of the Abbey at Newark and transferal of the title of the Abbey to Morristown.

Since no votes were taken on any of the proposals discussed at the December, February, or May meetings, the mind of the community on these questions cannot be precisely determined. In addition, although internal and external evidence confirms that the Chapter notes were both complete and objective, they cannot be said to reflect precisely the mind of the community because it is axiomatic that what monks say in Chapter does not always conform to the way they vote in Chapter. Finally, the secretary of the Chapter specifically warned the historian against interpreting the mind of the community through the Chapter minutes when he wrote in his notes on December

19, 1955: "The following summary of the comments made at this meeting is given without any reference as to the relative merit of the comments and without any indication as to how many concurred in making these comments." Consequently, after cautious interpretation of the Chapter minutes and judicious use of participants' recollections, the historian can ascertain only the following about the mind of the community prior to Abbot Patrick's speech on May 24, 1956. In the first place, few of the capitulars seemed to agree with the visitators that the two communities abandon one or the other or both locations and assemble at one place. Arguments from the viewpoints of history, tradition, economy, and from the value of a particular apostolic work were presented against closing St. Benedict's Prep or Delbarton School or one or the other of the monasteries. Secondly, both separation and the proposal to move the Abbey to Morristown received the support of significant minorities within the community. If either position was held by a majority of the capitulars before Abbot Patrick's speech, the available evidence does not confirm this.

At the May Chapter meeting, however, Abbot Patrick announced his choice – one apparently consistent with his views since 1937 – and thus affected the final resolution of this phase of the question in the Abbey's history. He said that he again visited Archbishop Boland, who agreed with him that the best solution, given the "impossibility of training young monks in Newark" and the unlikelihood of purchasing additional land there, was to move the title to Morristown. After discussing this visit and stating his own view, Abbot Patrick closed the meeting.

The capitulars assembled in early June, 1956, for a vote on the abbot's final proposal, the transferal of the Abbey to Morristown. In a lengthy introductory statement Abbot Patrick reviewed the history of the Abbey in Newark. He reflected more his faith (and what were probably the understandings of the majority of the community), than historical accuracy. He made statements which, in the light of current research, were either incorrect or unverifiable. He said:

> "Archabbot Wimmer purchased the estate in Denville, N.J. with the intention of locating the Abbey there – but, Abbot Hilary disposed of the property when the request came from Bishop Denis M. Bradley to establish a College in Manchester, New Hampshire...When St. Anselm's Priory in Manchester was elevated to an Abbey, Abbot Ernest purchased the Delbarton estate and he had every intention to transfer the Abbey from Newark to this new site...It's incumbent on me to do what my predecessors intended to do."

He added that many abbots advised him to move the Abbey to Morristown. Most likely from rural abbeys, they apparently shared Wimmer's views of the 1850s.

> "During the past years, I consulted with at least ten Abbots and the Abbot Primate. All were unanimous in their belief, that a Benedictine Abbey could not function properly in a large city. All likewise expressed the belief that the Abbey should be transferred to the Delbarton estate."

Abbot Patrick then concluded decisively with his resolution and request:

> *"I propose that St. Mary's Abbey, now located at High Street, Newark, should be*
> *transferred to the property now owned by St. Mary's Abbey in Morris Township,*
> *New Jersey. I am seeking at this meeting a vote of acquiescence and of confidence*
> *from the Chapter of St. Mary's Abbey to petition the Holy See to effect the transfer*
> *as soon as possible....May I, as your Father in God, appeal to you all for*
> *agreement. I seek for harmony and peace, which is the legacy of Our Father*
> *St. Benedict. I seek accord, in the name of Mary Immaculate Mother of God;*
> *your mother and mine, whose glorious name our St. Mary's Abbey bears and*
> *whose name our Abbey will continue to bear, in the new location.*
> *"Mary, Seat of Wisdom, pray for us"."*

The community gave Abbot Patrick the vote of confidence by a small majority, and in July the Holy See responded favorably. Thus, Newark's child in Morristown became the motherhouse of Newark.

In spite of the fact that a significant minority in the Abbey voted against Abbot Patrick's proposal, all Newark and Morristown monks seemed to support the early phase of his extensive building program of the next decade. Again, faith and generosity, and for some, perseverance, characterized the New Jersey Benedictines.

The Abbot and his counselors organized building committees according to the design of the Newark and Morristown committees of 1947, with monks resident in both locations sitting on the same committees. As it happened, the union of the two communities evident in these committees provided the planning stages of the building program with both a balance of views and a maximum of expertise available in the communities. In addition, union allowed St. Mary's Abbey to fund the program by borrowing against the combined assets of Newark and Morristown. As a result, from 1956 to 1966, the monks built more than $5,000,000 worth of facilities at the two locations. These buildings included: in Newark, an auditorium and classroom building (1958) finally erected after its need was first announced in the early 1940s; in Morristown, an addition to the gym (1956), the classroom building called Trinity Hall (1959), and the abbey church and monastery complex (1964-1966).

In 1961, the community engaged Victor Christ-Janer as architect for the Morristown church and monastery. He and his staff queried the monks and worked with the building committee before finally drawing the plans in 1963. In early 1964, a few months before construction began, a group of nearly twenty monks submitted a request for separation and independence from Newark. Although the majority of the capitulars of St. Mary's Abbey probably agreed with the Newark petitioners that the issue was no longer "premature", many, especially those residing in

"I propose that St. Mary's Abbey, now located at High Street, Newark, should be transferred to the property now owned by St. Mary's Abbey in Morris Township, New Jersey. .....May I, as your Father in God, appeal to you all for agreement."
– Abbot Patrick O'Brien, O.S.B.

Father Peter Meaney, principal celebrant at a concelebrated Mass in the Abbey Church,
spring, 1967, the year the Church was dedicated.

Morristown, probably agreed with the Abbot that the request was "inopportune." In any event, Rome responded to the request almost immediately, denying it as "inopportune."

Abbot Patrick M. O'Brien, an octogenarian in 1966, lived to see the completion of the St. Mary's Abbey church. He regarded the opening of the church in 1966 as the most important achievement of his thirty years as Abbot. Although he suffered from cancer since before 1965, he chose to maintain his office until his strength left him and until he had seen the church completed, the realization of his goals first suggested in 1937. Abbot Patrick resigned his office in October, 1966, and died on March 30, 1967, revered and loved by his community for his faith, piety, and generosity, and admired for his single-mindedness. His death saved him from witnessing an event he feared, separation and independence for Newark, which a strong majority of his capitulars approved under his successor, Abbot Martin J. Burne. In the fall of 1968, Rome finally judged such a decision opportune.

Under Abbot Patrick's successors, Abbots Martin, Leonard Cassell, and Brian Clarke, O.S.B., the church he and his men built expanded the work of the Morristown monks into areas of Christian education and prayer not previously realized by the community. Even as it became the focus of the monks' worship, it made it possible for them to respond more fully and generously to the needs of the Church in a new age. Of this, Patrick O'Brien would have approved; for, in fact, it is the fulfillment of his prayer. On a spring afternoon in 1966, while walking through the still unfinished church with one of his young priests, Abbot Patrick said that his fondest hope was that the abbey church become "a powerhouse, a major influence for good and virtue, a dynamic center of prayer and study" for his monks and for the people in the area. After stopping for a few minutes of silent prayer, he concluded: "I pray that the monks who worship in this church will be as open to the Holy Spirit and to the needs of God's people as Mary was."

XIII

Newark Dies and Rises:
THE PASCHAL MYSTERY
OF NEWARK ABBEY

Newark made Morristown! Evident throughout these pages is the fact that the Benedictine monks on High Street, St. Mary's Abbey, Newark, sacrificed through their entire history for the Church, for other foundations and Morristown, for the poor, and for Catholics throughout northern New Jersey. Yes, the monks in Newark put off development of St. Benedict's Prep on High Street, first to establish and develop the abbey and college at St. Anselm's in Manchester, New Hampshire. Then, often in each generation of monks, 1930, 1937, 1947, 1956, and through the early 1960s, the monks of St. Mary's Abbey in Newark stretched to build the burgeoning community at Delbarton in Morristown. Both Morristown and Newark were one abbatial entity, but every effort that was made to purchase Morristown, to develop it as a monastery, to begin the seminary there, to start Delbarton School and later help it recover from a major fire in 1947 put off necessary physical improvements and expansion at St. Benedict's Prep and at the monastery in Newark. Vote after vote of the capitulars of St. Mary's Abbey, most of them stationed at St. Benedict's Prep in Newark, acceded to the needs of Morristown and obeyed the promptings of Abbot Ernest Helmstetter and Abbot Patrick O'Brien in favor of the foundation at Delbarton.

That, however, was only part of it. Newark made the suburbs! Newark made New Jersey! The sacrifice that the Newark monks made for the community at Delbarton prefigured and later provided paradigms for what the city of Newark was doing for the northern suburbs and the State of New Jersey. Shortly before the Second World War, and indeed, after the Second World War, the commercial and industrial promise of Newark enriched the suburbs and northern New Jersey. Over time in the late 1940s and through the 1950s and early 1960s, a great deal of manufacturing left Newark. In addition, much of the educated and financial base of the city moved to the suburbs, an exodus often referred to as "white flight." A new ghetto-ization occurred to the point that in the mid-1960s Newark was regarded as one of the poorest cities in America. Historians and sociolo-

Aerial View of Newark, Jersey City, and New York
(Greater Newark Development Council), circa 1964

gists have commented about the classic tragedy affecting the city of Newark, bringing it from a proud and stately urban center of the 1930s, to the poverty-stricken and dangerous inner city of the 1960s. The riots in the summer of 1967 were inevitable.

POPULATION BY COLOR 1920-1960				
	1920	**1930**	**1950**	**1960**
State of New Jersey				
Total population	3,156,000	4,041,000	4,835,000	6,067,000
White	3,037,000	3,829,000	4,512,000	5,539,000
Non-white	117,000	209,000	319,000	515,000
% Non-white	3.7	5.2	6.6	8.5
City of Newark				
Total population	414,000	442,000	439,000	405,000
White	397,000	403,000	363,000	266,000
Non-white	17,000	39,000	75,000	138,000
% Non-white	4.1	8.8	20.7	34.1

Demographics for State of NJ and City of Newark, 1920-1960

(Photo and Chart Courtesy of *Where Cities Meet: The Urbanization of New Jersey, The New Jersey Historical Series. Published by D. Van Nostrand Co., Inc., Princeton, NJ, 1964.*)

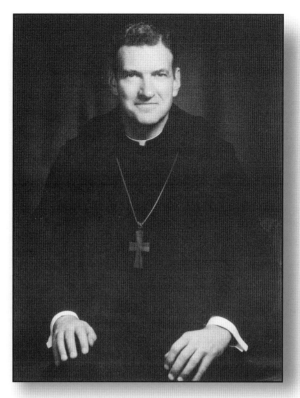

Abbot Martin Burne (Abbot, 1966-1971)

The city hit "rock bottom" at about the same time St. Benedict's Prep and St. Mary's Abbey faced a painful crisis. Abbot Martin Burne, a valiant proponent of separation between the Newark and Morristown communities in the late 1950s and early 1960s, was elected fifth abbot of St. Mary's Abbey to succeed Abbot Patrick in 1966. Abbot Martin experienced five years of agony as leader of St. Mary's Abbey until he resigned. Surely he could count among his greatest achievements that of creating a stable and admirable monastic life in Morristown where he resided. Faithful monastic observance in all its details was important to Abbot Martin, and he let his monks know that. His first love of Newark and St. Benedict's Prep was evident nonetheless. Though he lived and died as a monk of St. Mary's Abbey, Morristown, his twin concern to improving monastic observance was bringing about the independence of the Newark community.

After a number of quick votes of the Newark and Morristown monks, shortly after Abbot Patrick's death, Abbot Martin succeeded in convincing the Holy See to grant abbatial status to those monks who wished to stay in Newark under the title, "Newark Abbey." These were agonizing months and years for Abbot Martin, a time during which, according to his prior, Father James O'Donnell, he privately threatened to resign four times. In his fifth year as Abbot of St. Mary's Abbey, he finally did resign, only to be promptly elected to the office of president of the American Cassinese congregation, a post he held for the next twelve years.

Abbot Martin was a decorated Navy chaplain during the Second World War and a very important German and music teacher at St. Benedict's Prep prior to the title of the Abbey being moved to Morristown. After that event, Abbot Martin came to Morristown to serve as novice master of the community and to teach Scripture at Delbarton School, which he continued to do for more than thirty years. The number of devotees he had among Delbarton students and graduates surely equaled the number he enjoyed in Newark because of his many years of teaching at St. Benedict's Prep. He will be remembered also by his many confreres as a leader of the civil rights movement in New Jersey and beyond, as a gadfly in developing scholarship programs for disadvantaged youth at Delbarton, and as a confessor and spiritual director for many of the monks in his own community and laymen throughout northern New Jersey. (See Appendix 1)

For the men at Newark, their experience of separation and independence was not the end of their experience of the passion of Christ; indeed, it may be regarded as only the beginning. The 1960s were fruitful years for both of the major Benedictine schools, St. Benedict's Prep and Delbarton. Both Schools had waiting lists of students; they were eminently successful in athletics and college placement, and their excellent reputations grew apace.

At St. Benedict's, however, the impact of the demographic and economic changes in Newark began to play a role in the monks' vision of the future of the School. Indeed, the riots in the summer of 1967 might be regarded as something of a turning point in the history of St. Benedict's. From then until 1972, a division was obvious within the monks at Newark Abbey. On the one hand, some in the community felt that the demographic changes might make the existence of St. Benedict's as they knew it, untenable. Furthermore, this group felt that were St. Benedict's to accommodate itself to the urban poor and African-American population more than the School had done before, it might be lowering its standards and creating another type of school that the monks were neither trained for nor willing to serve in.

Another group adhered to the importance of staying and addressing the needs of the people of Newark, particularly the people in the immediate environs of St. Benedict's on High Street, the people of the Central Ward and elsewhere in the growing inner city. These monks felt that the history of St. Benedict's affirmed that they had a moral imperative to stay, work and dedicate their lives to the poor there.

Through the late 1960s and into the early 1970s, this division of opinion within the community became all the more obvious in Chapter votes and community group discussions, although, as a credit to the monks, people outside the community were not aware of the fissure. In 1972, the leadership of St. Benedict's, including its abbot, Abbot Ambrose Clark, O.S.B., the first abbot of Newark Abbey, began to articulate clearly that the School should close. Finally, in agony, the entire community of Newark witnessed the closing of the School in the spring of 1972.

During the spring and summer of 1972, the monks of Newark Abbey, brothers to the monks of St. Mary's Abbey of Morristown, hit bottom. The deep fissure and crisis within continued. It felt all the more bitter and catastrophic because the one source of funding and youthful life for the community, St. Benedict's and its students and parents, no longer existed. Most of the men in the community then agreed to find jobs in a variety of places in order to support the community. This

Abbot Leonard Cassell (Abbot, 1971-1975)

led to a response from the monks of St. Mary's Abbey, Morristown. Shortly, upon the closing of St. Benedict's Prep in June, 1972, Abbot Leonard Cassell, Abbot Martin's successor, telephoned Abbot Ambrose to indicate that the monks in Morristown would be happy to receive the elderly and infirm monks of Newark, should the Newark community no longer be able to care for them.

Then, first in a trickle, but later in greater numbers, several of the monks of Newark Abbey asked to transfer their vows to St. Mary's Abbey, Morristown, because they felt that the responsibility of working for a living outside the monastery was not what they expected of monastic life and that the monastic observance in Newark, because of the difficulties the monks faced prior to and after the closing of the School, had become too much to bear. It should also be noted that most of the men who asked to come to Morristown lost all faith in conducting a school in the Central Ward of Newark. The kind of school and mission they were used to served white suburban youngsters and families.

Regardless, whether the intentions of the monks leaving Newark were because of frustrated monastic ideals, disillusionment, or escaping an unfriendly environment, the monks of St. Mary's Abbey, Morristown, received willingly and fraternally thirteen monks from Newark Abbey in the summer of 1972. In addition, at the same time fifteen young men in the sophomore and junior classes of St. Benedict's Prep transferred to Delbarton School.

While the monks who remained in Newark might have considered the exodus of their thirteen confreres to Morristown a great tragedy, in fact, it served as a marvelous opportunity for them to create one of the Church's most successful secondary schools. The monks who remained in

Modern view of Newark Abbey with the City in the background.

Newark demonstrated remarkable heroism in the life of poverty they had to live over the next couple of years, as well as in the creativity they revealed in crafting an educational philosophy that would meet the needs of the young people, mostly African-American, in the Newark inner city.

The end of the institutional Paschal Mystery that Newark Abbey experienced occurred in 1973 when Abbot Melvin Valvano, O.S.B., succeeded Abbot Ambrose Clark, and Father Edwin Leahy, O.S.B., a young, vibrant and enthusiastic monk, was appointed headmaster of the new St. Benedict's. With the magnificent support of Fathers Albert Holtz, O.S.B., Philip Waters, O.S.B., Boniface Treanor, O.S.B., Theodore Howarth, O.S.B., and so many of the other Newark monks, a miracle occurred on High Street. As will be indicated later, the Benedictine sources from which Father Edwin and Father Albert drew to recreate St. Benedict's Prep in the mid-1970s were not unlike the Benedictine sources that their brothers in Morristown used in the 1970s and 1980s to create the school the St. Mary's Abbey monks ran at Delbarton.

Once more, however, so many of the themes of the history of the northern New Jersey monks were repeated in the series of events in the late 1960s and 1970s in Newark and in Morristown. For one thing, if it is true that many of the monks left Newark after the original St. Benedict's Prep closed in 1972 did so for the sake of a more stable monastic observance in Morristown, their actions echoed the thinking of Abbot James Zilliox and Abbot Hilary Pfraengle. Furthermore, the exodus from Newark in 1972 benefited Delbarton School significantly in that Delbarton enjoyed the addition of seven full-time monk teachers on its faculty. Again, Newark sacrificed for the sake of Morristown.

Following the movement of the title of the Abbey to Morristown and independence for Newark in 1968, Abbot Martin Burne and later Abbot Brian Clarke recognized the need to divest the Abbey of some of its parishes. After independence, Newark Abbey kept St. Joseph parish in Maplewood, having held the mission since 1914. St. Mary's Abbey in Morristown, however, kept the following parishes: St. Benedict's in the Ironbound section of Newark; Sacred Heart in Wilmington, Delaware; Sacred Heart in Elizabeth; Blessed Sacrament in Elizabeth; Notre Dame of Mt. Carmel in Cedar Knolls; and St. Elizabeth in Linden. St. Mary's Abbey relinquished four of those parishes from the late 1960s through the mid-1990s. To some degree, these decisions were made in the tradition of Abbot James Zilliox, when the superiors felt that the community should be less involved in parochial ministry. In addition, it was becoming increasingly obvious to Abbot Martin and Abbot Brian that age and sickness in the community as well as the importance of work at Delbarton, made the monks increasingly unable to conveniently staff the parishes.

The first parish the Abbey turned over to the Archdiocese of Newark was St. Benedict's in the Portuguese and Spanish section of Newark. In 1966, Father Hugh Duffy, the pastor, was in failing health and needed to return to the Abbey. Abbot Martin, recently elected co-adjutor to Abbot Patrick, recognized that he would soon need a successor as master of novices in the Morristown community. Father Brian, stationed in Wilmington, met the criteria and shortly returned to Morristown while Father William Norman, O.S.B., stationed at St. Benedict's, replaced him in Wilmington. After 107 years of Benedictine pastoral service to St. Benedict's Parish, Newark, the

Abbot Brian Clarke (Abbot, 1975-1995)

monks returned to the Abbey in 1966, and the community officially relinquished the parish to the Archdiocese in 1970. Father Hugh died shortly after returning to Morristown, and Father Brian followed Abbot Martin as novice master in 1967.

In addition, when Abbot Brian H. Clarke was elected seventh abbot of St. Mary's Abbey, he recognized that at least two other parishes the Abbey staffed ought to be turned over to the Archdiocese, namely Sacred Heart in Elizabeth and Blessed Sacrament, also in Elizabeth. At that time, the St. Mary's Abbey community did not have monks who could adequately serve the Spanish and Portuguese population along Rt. 1 in Elizabeth. In addition, a Portuguese parish that worshipped nearby in an inadequate facility, Our Lady of Fatima parish, needed a church. As this Portuguese parish was growing, the traditional American community of Sacred Heart parish was diminishing. Consequently, with Father Gilbert Crawford, O.S.B., serving as the Abbey's last pastor at Sacred Heart, and after 112 years of monastic parochial service there, the parish was relinquished to the Archdiocese of Newark in June, 1983. For similar reasons, the community left Blessed Sacrament in Elizabeth. A growing Spanish community which few if any of the monks of St. Mary's Abbey could adequately serve caused Abbot Brian to relinquish Blessed Sacrament also. After 67 years of Benedictine service there, and with Father Kevin Bray, O.S.B., as the Abbey's last pastor, the pastoral care at Blessed Sacrament in Elizabeth was returned to the Archdiocese in 1987. The Abbey, however, continued to staff and maintain the large parish in Linden which it had served since 1910, St. Elizabeth's of Hungary, as well as the parish in Cedar Knolls, Notre Dame of Mt. Carmel, which it had staffed as a mission of St. Christopher's in Parsippany since 1926 when Father Norbert Hink became its first pastor.

The Abbey left the parochial ministry of its fourth parish in forty years when Sacred Heart in Wilmington was closed by the Diocese of Wilmington. Benedictines from St. Vincent Archabbey and later from St. Mary's Abbey served the German Catholics there since 1874 and ran a college there until 1885. Since then, the parish flourished and grew under the parochial ministry of the men from St. Mary's Abbey, Newark. Industrialization of the city around the parish and the gradual decline in the number of parishioners caused the diocese to close the parish, and the community to seek an alternative use for the buildings. In 1995 a Franciscan priest and social workers bought the property from St. Mary's Abbey and, with Father Bruno Ugliano, O.S.B., as its closing pastor, St. Mary's held the farewell liturgy in June, 1996.

In addition to those parishes, the combined community of St. Mary's Abbey of Newark and Morristown, before independence for Newark, responded to the appeal of Pope John XXIII in 1963 to send monks as missionaries to South America. Consequently, on September 6, 1963, Father Edmund Nugent, O.S.B., and Father Kevin Bray departed for Brazil where they began the Abbey's missionary work in the town of Anapolis in the state of Goias. Father Kevin was recalled from Brazil in 1964 to become the pastor of Sacred Heart church in Elizabeth. In 1966, Father Columba Rafferty, O.S.B., set sail for Rio de Janeiro to reinforce the Brazilian mission; he served there until 1985 when illness forced his return home. Father Sebastian Joseph, O.S.B., left for Rio de Janeiro in 1967 to join Father Edmund and Father Columba in the Brazilian mission. In January, 1971, Father Sebastian Joseph suffered a heart attack and died shortly after. His body was returned to the St. Mary's Abbey, Morristown cemetery. Father Columba Rafferty returned to Morristown because of ill health in 1985 after nearly twenty years of missionary work in Brazil.

Father Edmund Nugent then was the only member of the St. Mary's community in the mission. He died in August, 1995, in the town of Silvieris, and his body was returned to Morristown where he was buried. With Father Edmund's death, the St. Mary's Abbey Brazilian venture concluded after thirty-two years. Fortunately, the growing number of indigenous Brazilian vocations ordained to the priesthood at the time made the loss of the community and the cessation of the work of other American communities in Brazil and elsewhere in South America less of an impact to the faithful there.

PART THREE:

THEMES OF THE ABBEY AND SCHOOL IN MORRISTOWN

XIV
ABBEY CULTURE AND ADMINISTRATIONS

The young monks and their professors at St. Mary's Abbey School of Theology from the late 1940s through the late 1960s lived a tranquil life. Most of them were unaware of the talk of separation, independence for Newark, the closing of St. Benedicts Prep, and its reopening. Young monks enjoyed little contact with the outside world, other than occasional automobile trips to Morristown, walks to Mendham Road after dinner, watching Delbarton School games, and, during their theological studies, teaching one course a year at Delbarton. Instead, their lives were circumscribed by the monastic horarium, by contact with their teachers who also served as their superiors, and by their study of Scripture and theology.

The St. Mary's monks from the late 1930s through the early 1970s took different paths before beginning theology in Morristown. Some of the future Benedictines announced their desire to become priests and sought entrance to the Community immediately after high school. A few of these young collegians in the 1940s lived in the new monastery and took classes from some of the early clerics there and attended other area Catholic secondary schools such as Bayley Ellard. The more common route was that taken by more than a generation of young monks who, after being admitted to the scholasticate as young collegians, went to a Benedictine college for their first two years, then to novitiate, and then back to the same Benedictine college or to another one prior to arriving at the St. Mary's Abbey School of Theology.

Typically, when the young monk returned to the Abbey for the summer or was studying theology there, he rose with his confreres, in the monastery building built in 1939 under the leadership of Father Vincent Amberg, at 5:30 a.m. and arrived on time for morning office, without fail, at 6 a.m. If he were late, the junior master for many years, Father Adrian McLaughlin, would assign him to ring the monastery bells indefinitely or at least until the next person was late for office. The Liturgy of the Hours was celebrated in Latin until the mid-1960s in the chapel in the south section of what is now Vincent House. Even without air conditioning, the eight large windows and

Celebration of the Eucharist in the old monastery chapel (Vincent House) in 1964.

spacious exit kept the surroundings pleasant, and Brother Benedict Meyer's, O.S.B., soft organ playing maintained the pace of recitation and the beauty of the singing. For many of those monks of the 1950s and early 1960s, their time studying theology and worshipping at the monastery was idyllic.

On hindsight, some might disagree. The young monks who entered the community in the late 1940s, '50s, and '60s were bright and well educated. They were also a product of their age: they questioned adults, they were mostly liberal Catholics, and some were a little cynical. Consequently, though everyone grudgingly loved Father Bede, the prior for a time, and the long-term dogma teacher, he was found by some of the clerics to be too conservative, too much "by the book". The young Father Austin Queenan, who had recently arrived from Rome to teach history in the early 1960s, was interesting and friendly; Father Leonard Cassell, opened their eyes to the historical critical approach of scripture; Father Christopher Lind added a breath of fresh air with a modern look at moral theology; Father Stephen Findlay, impressed them with his knowledge, although he often had to miss assigned classes because of his work at Delbarton; and earlier, Father Vincent Ambrose, Father Augustine Verhaegen, Father Michael Ducey, Father Hugh Duffy and others covered the necessary material. Later, on the eve of the close of St. Mary's Abbey School of Theology in 1970, Father Gerard Carluccio, from St. Paul's Abbey in Newton, as well as a number of distinguished professors from Drew University, challenged the monks who would be ordained in the early 1970s. All the while anywhere from three to ten monks from St. Paul's Abbey in Newton attended classes with the St.

> "The young monks who entered the community in the late 1940s, '50s, and '60s were bright and well educated. They were also a product of their age: they questioned adults, they were mostly liberal Catholics,...."

Mary's Abbey monks each day. When the student body was at full complement, at least six places at each of the four tables in the monastery north library, sat before the professors.

Life in the monastery for the young monks included faithfulness at office, attention to their responsibilities in the sacristy, caring for the sick and the elderly, driving the monks and in regularly picking up Father Bede at the railroad station, returning from Benzingers Publishing House every evening, to teaching a class in a school each day, if one was two or three years away from ordination. This School experience, which often included attending the games of the students, served as a positive experience for the young monks.

In addition to that, life in the monastery included a beer or soda at haustus, and often a smoke, each late afternoon, as well as a softball game on the south Abbey field or a restful conversation after dinner. The late 1950s and early '60s, however, were heady, almost exhilarating times. The Church then was moving towards major change in the areas of social justice and liturgical renewal. Most of the young monks looked forward to the change from the use of Latin to the vernacular, and rejoiced at Pope John XXIII's opening of the Council. During recreation and after evening prayer, clerics read and discussed many of the latest articles in *Commonweal, America* magazine, and other liberal periodicals of the day. More importantly, so many of them shared with each other the results of their reading outside of class. Sometimes bored and even offended by what they might have regarded as pedestrian instruction or "teaching down" to them, they often found their stimulation in reading theology and scripture independently of their teachers. Most memorable to the classmates Father Giles Hayes and Father Melvin Valvano, in 2006 the Abbots of St. Mary's Abbey and Newark Abbey respectively, was their enthusiastic study of St. John's Gospel after the publication of Father Raymond Brown's two-volume work on that Gospel. Night after night would find them running from room to room excited about the latest insight they gained on the Gospel. In turn, the young monks were often stimulated by confreres who were not their theology instructors but were working at the School, such as the former prior, Father Hugh Duffy.

The late 1940s, the 1950s and 1960s were exceedingly busy times in the School. With the student body growing from as few as 20 to as many as 300, the monks involved in the School had all they could do to meet the needs of the students. This was especially the case for the eight to ten monks who served as prefects in the main building and in the Brothers' House. Consequently, that fairly large group of ordained monks was able to spend very little time during the school year at the monastery on top of the hill. With the exception of Father Thomas Confroy, for a time the dean of discipline, who attended Divine Office every Sunday morning at the monastery, and Father Peter Meaney, who often celebrated Sunday Mass for the students and the monks, very few of the priests who prefected and worked full time in the School frequented the monastery on the hill during the school year. Consequently, they became known as "School fathers" to the students at St. Mary's School of Theology and, probably, to some of their teachers. Whether real or not, during the 1950s and 1960s, there was a perceived division between the monks who lived in the monastery on top of the hill and those who worked full time in the School. With the opening of the new Abbey church in 1967, the election of Abbot Martin Burne as the fifth Abbot of St. Mary's Abbey/Delbarton in 1966, and the phasing out of the boarding school in the late 1970s, the idea of "School fathers" disappeared. Most of the monks after that time lived and worshiped in the monastery, whether they were working in the School or not.

The title of St. Mary's Abbey was transferred from Newark to Delbarton in Morristown on July 23, 1956. On November 21, 1968, the St. Mary's Abbey community in Newark became an independent Abbey under the title Newark Abbey. A year later, the St. Mary's School of Theology in Morristown ceased to admit students, yet continued its legal existence. The young monks who chose to belong to Newark Abbey began their study of theology at Woodstock in New York City or elsewhere, while those who chose to join St. Mary's Abbey in Morristown, continued or began their theological studies at Drew University, Immaculate Conception Seminary at Seton Hall University, St. Vincent Archabbey Seminary, St. John's Abbey Seminary, and Catholic University.

Using a business analogy, if the abbot of the monastery is the CEO, the prior is the COO. He handles the daily operations of the community, including arranging the horarium in ways consistent with the direction of the abbot. St. Benedict wrote in Chapter 65 of his Rule:

"The prior, for his part, is to carry out respectfully what his Abbot
assigns to him, and do nothing contrary to the Abbot's wishes or
arrangements, because the more he is set above the rest, the more he should
be concerned to keep what the Rule commands."

Clerics at the Divine Office in 1957: (read counterclockwise) Fraters Marius Meehan,
Karl Roesch, Rembert Reilly, Germain Fritz

Before Newark became an independent community, St. Mary's Monastery in Morristown had only four priors: Father Vincent Amberg, Father Bede Babo, Father Hugh Duffy, and Father Michael Collins. In the earliest days, Abbot Ernest Helmstetter rarely came to Morristown, and only in his last days of the early and mid-1960s did Abbot Patrick reside in Morristown for more than a day or two at a time. He spent most of his time residing at the Abbey in Newark. Consequently, he depended greatly on his four priors and on Father Stephen Findlay, who worked closely with Fathers Vincent, Hugh, Bede, and Michael on the temporal and personnel needs of the Morristown community. For most of that time, in fact, Father Stephen had the title of subprior and served as superior for the monks who resided in the School. The abbot and the chapter of St. Mary's Abbey held the ultimate authority over the monks in Morristown, but in the absence of the abbot, Father Stephen held discretionary power regarding Delbarton School, and the priors were the principal day-to-day authorities for the monks in Morristown.

Morristown was poor; there seemed to be little ready cash available. The $1,000 per month allowance the Morristown community of 20 to 30 monks received from the Abbey in Newark in the 1940s, 1950s, and 1960s proved wholly inadequate. In so many areas, the monks in those years had to "make do." The rather simple life that the clerics and the brothers lived lightened up with home movies made by Father Alfred Meister or Father Bede Babo, with game-playing, cards, and anything that didn't cost money. Rarely, if ever, except with his parents, did a young monk go to the movies or go out for dinner. As he did in the 1930s and 1940s, Father Vincent Amberg, in the 1950s and 1960s, made frugality the order of the day. In this way the monastery existed adequately, though simply, on a very low budget. Building and occupying the new monastery between 1962 and 1967, at a time which paralleled the fervent discussions on independence for Newark, made the life of the priors more complicated and life in community more expensive.

Abbot Martin, in those turbulent days, appointed Father James O'Donnell to be his prior. After Newark Abbey became an independent community on November 21, 1968, physical developments in both Newark and Morristown began. Once Newark overcame the crisis of closing the school and then re-opening it, an entirely new campus was built on both sides of Martin Luther King Boulevard over the next 30 years. Virtually the same thing happened in Morristown; the independence of Newark allowed Morristown to develop physically without restrictions and the need to compromise.

On September 22, 1969, the chapter of St. Mary's Abbey in Morristown approved construction of a new dormitory, Schmeil-O'Brien Hall, the building which is currently the Abbey's retreat center. This building was completed in May, 1970, just two months after the Abbey cemetery was created and opened on a southern slope of the property.

Abbot Martin resigned as Abbot on July 1, 1971, and Abbot Leonard Cassell was elected on August 2. Facility development continued apace with the creation of three additional tennis courts and a baseball and football field close to the pond on Route 24 in June, 1974. More development occurred in the summer of 1975 with the creation of an athletic field south of the monastery

The St. Mary's Abbey community on the occasion of the election of Abbot Brian Clarke,
June 13, 1975.

adjacent to the National Park. Then all development ceased temporarily because of the old
monastery fire of December 12, 1975.

Abbot Leonard resigned as Abbot because of ill health on May 1, 1975, and was succeeded by
Father Brian Clarke, who became the community's seventh Abbot. Abbot Brian had served as prior
to Abbot Leonard and was the COO, or the person in charge of Abbey operations when, in the
summer and fall of 1972, the community received a transfer of 13 monks from Newark Abbey,

Mr. Frank Lynch breaking ground for the Patricia and Frank Lynch Athletic Center,
1982. Left to Right: Father Stephen, Abbot Brian, Mr. Lynch and Father Giles

seven of whom then began to teach in the School. Others were elderly or ill, and still others helped the community significantly in pastoral and convent work. But Abbot Brian received his baptism in crisis with the fire that destroyed a major portion of the old monastery, called Vincent House after 2000, and caused major damage to the valuable monastery theological library. The fire was started because of a cigar smoking accident, and the community was lucky not to have lost any of its members. Thanks to the quick work of Father Rembert Reilly, O.S.B., and Father Justin Capato, O.S.B., both of whom lived on the second floor and who noticed heat and smoke around 4 o'clock on the morning of December 12, all of the monks were awakened and led to the roof off the bedrooms of the monks who lived on the second floor, north end. In addition to waking as many monks as possible, Father Justin also made it

*Father Bruno Ugliano, Headmaster
1985-1990*

to the third floor where he was able to help two Vietnamese refugee visitors to safety. Two or three of the monks suffered smoke inhalation and a number of the monks have felt that the eventual death of Father Cornelius Sweeney, O.S.B., occurred because of that fire. Father Beatus Lucey, O.S.B., Father Richard Cronin, O.S.B., and Father Cornelius served as Abbot Brian's priors from 1975 through 1995. Father Cornelius served for thirteen years.

Major changes in School programs and the development of important new physical facilities occurred during Abbot Brian's twenty years. Following the repair of the old monastery in 1977, the Abbey voted to remove the Bernini statues, known as Flora and Priapus, to the Metropolitan Museum of Art where they were exhibited on loan and later purchased. A one million dollar fund resulting from the purchase became a part of the Abbey and School endowment. After Abbot Brian's insistence, the Chapter passed a proposal on March 6, 1982 to build a health center to care for the aged and infirm of the community. This was completed in 1985. At the same time, the proposal to build a new gym, which is now called the Abbot Brian Clarke Gymnasium of the Frank and Patricia Lynch Sports Facility, and the refurbishing the St. Joseph's Gym, were approved by the Chapter. This, too, was completed in 1983 and opened with a New York Knickerbockers basketball exhibition program given for the Delbarton athletes and all of Delbarton's basketball opponents and neighbors. On December 12, 1983, the Chapter also approved construction of the two South Gate soccer and lacrosse fields called the Shoemaker Fields.

In the spring of 1985, Father Bruno Ugliano was appointed Headmaster to succeed Father Giles Hayes upon completion of his five-year term. Father Bruno quickly continued the development of

*The combined communities of Newark Abbey and St. Mary's Abbey on the occasion
of the communities' celebration of the 100th anniversary of the raising of
St. Mary's to abbatial status, 1984.*

the physical plant, but first engaged with the Chapter's permission, the architectural firm of H2L2, from Philadelphia, to produce a master plan for the entire campus. The plan was approved in the next year, 1987, and became the design followed faithfully for nearly twenty years. Two important retirements occurred in that same year, the first by Coach William O. Regan, after having worked at Delbarton for 41 years. He surprised Father Bruno by retiring from both of his posts, that of athletic director as well as that of head coach of football. After consultation with School administrators and faculty, Bill Regan's understudy, John Kowalik, a graduate of Williams College, and a successful teacher and coach at Delbarton, became both the new athletic director and the football coach.

Father Stephen Findlay then retired as director of development, leaving a major void in the School's fund raising and public relations programs. This was filled temporarily by Father Giles Hayes, who spent a year in development before returning to his post as director of college counseling, which he had assumed in 1985. Later in 1988, the School hired two succeeding non-Delbarton laymen as directors of development, Dr. Thomas B. Hanson and Stephen McLaughlin, until Delbarton's seasoned alumni director, Craig Paris, Class of '82, assumed the post in 1995. In 1988 as well, one of Father Bruno's dreams for the lay faculty, the condominium housing complex at the south end of the property, was completed. This set of housing units provided relatively inexpensive housing for more than twenty lay faculty members.

Finally, on September 3, 1991, in the last few years of Abbot Brian's tenure as Abbot, the Chapter agreed to have the Brothers' House demolished, the building on the east side of campus which was originally a caretaker's house and later a student dormitory, as well as its adjacent garages, and the construction of parking lots A, B, C, and D and the loop road from the west or the Mendham side of the campus to the lower entrance on the east side of campus. Other utility work, such as changing all of the underground water lines on the campus and converting from oil to gas, made the developments of the late 1990s and of the years after 2000 possible. Two consequences of these far-reaching facility developments of Abbot Brian's period were the building of the Father Stephen Findlay Science Pavilion in 1993 and of the arts facility in 2006. The master plan of 1987 and the Campaign for Delbarton, which followed it, promoted the further development of Delbarton's athletic facilities, academic programs, and the restoration of Old Main. Delbarton School and St. Mary's Abbey, after Abbot Brian's administration and the headmaster terms of Father Bruno (1985 to 1990) and Father Beatus Lucey (1990 to 1995) were poised to make even greater strides in Benedictine living and education.

XV

LIFE AT THE SCHOOL FOR DAY AND BOARDING STUDENTS

Day students were a distinct minority at Delbarton until Trinity Hall opened in 1959. Prior to that, the ratio of day to boarding was usually one to three. While onerous to all at the time, Saturday school from 8:30 until noon was less difficult for the boarding students who did not have to commute. For most day students, the DL&W, now New Jersey Transit, from the Oranges to Morristown or from Dover to Morristown, represented the most common means of travel. Busing of day students began in the 1960s, but even then many students chose to take the trains because the boys could sleep longer.

In fact, the day students, often called "day hops", enjoyed the train rides. For one thing, they were accompanied part of the way by the girls from Oak Knoll and St. Elizabeth's Academy. Many valued the social life on the DL&W. In addition, if one had to study, he could easily separate himself from the rest and study. There was a certain stability to day hops' traveling the trains in that the DL&W always arrived at 14 after the hour or 44 after the hour. Furthermore, the students always enjoyed the early morning wit and wisdom of the monastic bus drivers of more than twenty years, Father Frederick Muench, Father Kenneth Mayer, Father Arthur Mayer and Father Wilfred Schultz, O.S.B..

The day hops were also not above committing a few adolescent pranks. Most of them regretted the fact that Delbarton, with more than 60% of the student body living on campus, rarely if ever had "snow days." Since boarders had only to wake up, roll out of bed, go to breakfast, and then attend class, all in the same building, the School administration was rarely concerned if there were a blizzard. Consequently, on an occasional snowy morning, but never more than once a year, when the day hops would arrive at the station on the 7:44 train, one of the fleet-footed seniors would exit the train quickly, run under the tunnel, come up into the station master's office without the bus driver's seeing him, enter the corner telephone booth, make a quick call to the station master and identify himself as Father Cletus Donaghy, and then ask the station master to quickly tell the

A 1950s photograph of Old Main

Delbarton students to get back on the next train to the Oranges because there was no school. Instantaneously, after getting that call from the alleged Father Cletus, the station master would rush down to the tunnel to tell the boys to get back on the east-bound train to the Oranges, just then arriving at the station. Meanwhile, the priest driving the bus parked in the west parking lot never saw the boys emerge from the tunnel and assumed they did not board the train in the first place because of the snow.

Recreation Room scenes in the basement of Old Main, late 1940s.

From the 1940s to the 1960s, the day students and boarders lived together in peace. While their lives differed and a day hop club was founded to help represent day students' interests, the School seemed to be one brotherhood from its beginning. All students shared common interests in athletics especially, and since Delbarton teams were usually undermanned but never outclassed, all students showed positive School spirit. They also shared in the 1940s and 1950s the basement of the main building where smoking was allowed for older students and where the Tuck Shop was located. Even as late as 2006, the wooden wall in the basement still stands where hundreds of student names from the early days of the School are carved.

The Tuck Shop was visited often by the boarders before and after evening study hall for candy, soda, and ice cream. The younger boarders lived in the Brothers' House or the old farm house which dated back to pre-Revolutionary War days. Even in the 1940s this building showed its age. The relatively small rooms accommodated as many as six or eight 7th through 9th graders and three prefects. In Old Main, the rooms in the back, most of the rooms on the third floor, and one or two rooms on the second floor, were used for housing 10th through 12th graders. Again, while the rooms were slightly bigger and the ceilings much higher than the rooms in the Brothers' House, each Old Main room housed four or six students.

The values of the monastic community intertwined with the lives of the hundreds of Delbarton boarding students from the 1940s through the 1960s. Often during the day, a boarder would see a monk saying the Divine Office in a quiet moment, or be called upon to serve his Mass in the student chapel or at Mallinckrodt Convent, Villa Walsh, or Carmel in Morristown. For these young men, conversation with priests became commonplace and easy. "Joking around" with the priests, as well as with the other students, became part of the School's culture. However, there always

Evening softball game between the young monks and the senior boarders, May 28, 1964,
Seniors 5, Monks 4. In a rematch the following week, the monks won, 9-7.

The Benedictine Sisters who worked at Delbarton in the 1950's. Left to Right:
Sisters Christina, Anastasia, Delphina, Helen, Aurelia, Ottilia.

seemed to be a clear line of authority from the faculty beyond which a student should never go. Talking back or assuming too much was not tolerated. And just as the students lived their lives independently, the monks were always allowed their privacy.

German Benedictine nuns from Ridgely, Maryland were also very much a part of the fabric of life at Delbarton from the 1920s through 1956. Up to six of them lived in the convent, a few hundred yards southwest of the monastery building and a quarter mile from Old Main. They assumed responsibility for the monks' cooking and laundry and later prepared the meals for the students at Delbarton. They arrived early in the morning and returned to their convent after dinner, while using their great physical strength, good humor, and compassion to feed the 80 to 100 boarders and 20 to 30 monks. As the years passed, fewer and fewer sisters from the Benedictine Sisters from Ridgely or elsewhere chose to do such domestic work, so the last nuns left Delbarton in 1956.

While the sisters were beloved by the monks and the students, they sometimes provided unsavory fare. Most students found it difficult to identify the thin, "well done," brown pieces of beef which they called "mystery meat." Few complained too loudly, however, because with the "mystery meat" the sisters usually provided a super abundance of mashed or boiled potatoes and very thick gravy and bread. If the potatoes and gravy weren't satisfying enough, the Tuck Shop was always available. Or, for those boarders at Delbarton when Father Lucien Donnelly was in residence, there was often his 11 p.m. raid of the kitchen for whatever food could be found, when he would take along eight or so juniors and seniors.

Stories abound about boarding life. Few boarding students could forget the Sunday afternoon "tea dances" at various area girls' schools. In the 1950s and early 1960s virtually all of the boarders and as many day students as could be gathered together made four or five tea dances a year, thus satisfying, Father Kenneth Mayer thought, the students' need for social education. To prepare for the tea dances and the prom, Father Kenneth and Father Arthur Mayer created a dancing school to which students went to learn the waltz, the jitterbug, the fox trot, and later more daring dances. Typically, the buses left for Sunday afternoon tea dances around 4p.m., arriving at Tuxedo Park or at a number of other New York State girls' schools around 5:00p.m. At that point, the boys and the girls were paired off according to age and size as pre-arranged by the presidents of the student councils from each school. Often a Delbarton boy, out of courtesy to the girl with whom he was paired, would give her but a dance or two before searching for another date.

Also, some of the student smokers had to feel guilty in later years about the many days they snuck out to the "lost city," or the quarry where the extra columns and statues of an unused Greek temple were kept, in order to enjoy a few cigarettes in peace. Freshman initiation, a mixed blessing, offered too many opportunities for disrespect from the 1940s through 1964, as did student joking with and about faculty members at the Christmas parties of the early years. And, looking back from the vantage point of the post civil rights era, what Delbarton student would not be embarrassed by the black-faced "day-hop" minstrels which Father Arthur Mayer and Father Frederick Muench directed in the 1940s and 1950s. Perhaps all these experiences were characteristic of their age, but they also stand as reminders of Delbarton's human weakness in a time of significant promise.

Prom under a tent in the Formal Garden, early 1960s.

Father Kenneth with an outdoor work crew of boarders, early 1950s.

Father Kenneth Mayer served as dean of discipline through most of the 1950s, to be followed by Father Thomas Confroy and later Father Arthur Mayer and Father Karl Roesch. Except for the truly major transgressions, those which touched violating the law, everyone knew that Father Kenneth was quite compassionate, even soft, but he probably didn't think that the students knew that. The principal instruments of discipline before the reform of the mid 1970s were the demerit, detention, and the "D book" listing of all the infractions. Younger students were allowed more demerits before probation and expulsion; older students were allowed fewer. If the truth were known, however, except for those major infractions, not too many students were ever expelled for exceeding the prescribed number of demerits. In fact, during the 1950s, deals were made with Father Kenneth, who also had the unenviable job of supervising the maintenance of Old Main. In a typical deal, Father Kenneth would agree to remove demerits from the offending student if he promised to mop the bathroom floors or wax the first-floor hallway. Other work, including outdoor work, all of which helped him fulfill his other responsibility of maintenance, was frequently done for the sake of having a transgression forgotten. And when that didn't work, wily students, often the student council president, would negotiate with Father Kenneth, or, if even that failed, the student or president would fashion a small hook out of paper clips and fish the demerit notices out of the opening on the top of the demerit box outside Father Kenneth's room.

XVI

BENEDICTINE PHILOSOPHY AND VALUES IN EDUCATION

Family is everything. Community is everything. More than that, family and community are Christ. Even more, the Divine life resides within each one of us. As St. Benedict always taught, the stranger should be treated as though that person is Jesus Christ; a sick person is to be treated as though that person is Jesus Christ; the elderly person is to be treated as though that person is Jesus Christ. All who come into our lives should be treated as though they were Jesus Christ: the stranger, the sick, the elderly, and also the child, the student. These values represent the foundation of Benedictine education. But there is more.

The monk's vows incorporate him into the life of Christ of which he is constantly reminded by his praying the Liturgy of the Hours and his taking part in the Eucharist as the centerpiece of his day. Benedictines take three vows, but these are all interconnected with the concept of community: the vow of obedience to an Abbot and to one's fellow monks; the vow of *"conversatio morum,"* or the resolve to live a life of commitment to each other in community, which leads the monk to continual conversion of life; and the vow of stability to the community and to the place, a vow which proclaims that this place is holy, this community is sacred, and there is no retreat from entering more deeply into the mystery of Christ.

> ... Family is everything. Community is everything. More than that, family and community are Christ. Even more, the Divine life resides within each one of us.

Monastic communities which conduct secondary schools or colleges work hard to incorporate the above values into the structures and systems of their schools. This reality becomes automatic when the students are so closely connected to the monastics. For example, in the early days at Delbarton, before the expansion of the School in 1959-60, the School enjoyed the constant presence of twenty Benedictines, while the number of students fluctuated between a few dozen and one hundred and seventy-five. A ratio of one monk to five or six students, at a time also when two-thirds or more of the students lived at the School and saw the monks all day long, made

Dinner for boarding students in the Old Main dining room, now called the Gallery, 1952

communicating the values of Benedictine life to the students very easy. In those early days one didn't have to talk too much about family, community, the vowed life, Eucharist; these were obvious everywhere and a very part of the fabric of life at Delbarton. Students in those days of the 1940s and the 1950s generally confirmed this to be the case. When the School began to expand, however, from approximately 250 in the late 1950s to nearly 500 by the early 1980s, the leaders of Delbarton had to consciously create systems and practices which proclaimed these Benedictine values of education.

Father Stephen Findlay managed to create a personal relationship with all of the students, as did the monks who were prefects of the boarding school in those days, including: Fathers Kenneth Mayer, Arthur Mayer, Felix Pipen, William Norman, David Conway, Lucien Donnelly, Frederick Muench, Adrian McLaughlin, Peter Meaney, Rembert Reilly and a number of other monks who worked full time in the School during the 1940s, 1950s, and early 1960s.

Many monks attended the students' games and activities on a regular basis. Some coached the teams and devoted a great deal of time to leading the students' activities. And often, whenever a parent or family invited one or two monks to their home for dinner or to socialize in any way, Father Stephen would insist that the party be held for all of the monastic teachers in the School. The message was always, "It is not about me, it is about us." And this same attitude of unity and togetherness informed the life of the students and became part of the foundation for that fiery School spirit and School loyalty characteristic of Delbarton students.

More importantly, the way of life of the monks helped the students believe and internalize the School's spiritual values which convinced so many of the graduates to pursue lives of service and leadership in society, particularly in law, government, and medicine. A number in the 1940s and 1950s also entered seminaries. For example, from among the one hundred graduates of Delbarton in the 1952-1956 period, four became Roman Catholic priests: Father Robert Lilly, '52, Maryknoll; Father Anthony Tomasulo, '53, an Augustinian; Father Robert Hoffman '54, the Diocese of Paterson, and Father Giles Hayes, '56, a Benedictine.

..."It is not about me, it is about us."
– Father Stephen Findlay, O.S.B.

Young Catholic men (and the School was 99% Roman Catholic in those days) found a congenial faith community at Delbarton. In the 1940s and 1950s, the entire student body prayed the Rosary daily during the month of May. Mass was available daily in the Old Main chapel, and until the Abbey church was completed in 1966, Mass was often celebrated for the entire student body in St. Joseph's gymnasium, and if a boy were a boarding student, the chances were good that one of the monks would awaken him before 6:00a.m. so that he could accompany the priest as his altar server to a nearby convent chapel.

The Second Vatican Council and the various international and domestic crises of the 1960s challenged the monks and the lay teachers to take stock again of who they were and use all of their resources to make the School in every way true to its Benedictine roots. The generation of

Students praying the rosary at noon in May around the statue of the Blessed Virgin on the east lawn of Old Main, a custom of the 1940s and 1950s.

Father Francis O'Connell, Headmaster, 1967-1972

Delbarton leaders after those questioning 1960s worked in a systematic way to incorporate their understanding of the Benedictine philosophy of education into many of the practices of the School. The sense of urgency to become more Benedictine heightened as the School grew from 250 students in the early 1960s to more than 500 students in the late 1990s. At the same time, the faculty grew from twenty-five to seventy-five, while the number of monks on the faculty fluctuated annually in those days between seventeen and twenty. The decrease in the percentage of monks in the faculty and administration also challenged the School leadership to integrate the lay and monastic faculties as much as possible and to clearly proclaim the Benedictine ways of educating so that the lay faculty might not be merely informed but also would live out these values. School leadership in the last third of the 20th century labored to insure that Delbarton would be fully Benedictine regardless of how many monks taught in the School.

The frustration so many in America felt with the assassination of President Kennedy, the protracted war in Vietnam, the nationwide recognition of our wounds of racism and poverty, the urban riots and assassinations of the mid to late 1960s, the growing generation gap, and the general feeling among American educators that our schools were not working, created in concert an uncomfortable environment in which to teach. Many teachers nationwide became depressed and wondered whether things would ever get better. At Delbarton, the determined leadership of three successive headmasters, Father Francis O'Connell, Father James O'Donnell and Father Gerard Lair, O.S.B., sought to be proactive and to engage the issues of the day. As a result of the School's facing up to the difficulties of the 1960s and 1970s, and encouraged by the Vatican Council's recommendation that religious communities should be more faithful to their roots, Delbarton leaders worked creatively at developing Delbarton's unique Benedictine character. As a result, the School, in the 1990s and beyond, began to be recognized as a national and even international leader in Benedictine education.

Father James O'Donnell, Headmaster, 1972-1975

Father Stephen Findlay celebrated his twenty-fifth anniversary as headmaster of Delbarton in 1967, and he followed that with passing the baton to his successor, young Father Francis O'Connell. Abbot Martin Burne, who had succeeded Abbot Patrick as the fifth abbot of St. Mary's Abbey in 1966, invited Father Stephen to either continue on as head into his next quarter-century or step aside for a younger man and throw his valuable energies completely into the office of director of development. Father Stephen chose the latter assignment and proceeded to build on the work he had begun in the early 1940s when he founded the Delbarton Mothers' Guild and the Delbarton Fathers and Friends. In the next few years he further strengthened the Delbarton Alumni Association and founded the Delbarton Parents of Graduates Association.

In 1951, with the blessing of Abbot Patrick, Father Stephen established Camp Delbarton. Father Stephen wanted to provide a camping program for boys of the area, utilizing the School's faculty and facilities. The pastoral setting of the School would lend itself perfectly to the operation of a day camp. He knew that it would not only be a wonderful opportunity to keep young boys actively involved in wholesome activities over the summer months but also provide possible newcomers to the School a chance to have a taste of life at Delbarton. Father Stephen also felt that interaction with these youngsters would give the young clerics an opportunity to gain experience in teaching, coaching, and mentoring, abilities they would need in the coming years.

In the early years the Camp program provided fairly simple activities such as swimming, hiking, games, crafts, story-telling, nature study, sports, and movies. By the mid-1960s the Camp experience grew to include major sports such as tennis, golf, wrestling, baseball, horseback riding, archery and others. Along with these activities there was still time for arts and crafts, nature study, and games. The Camp has evolved over the years to include all the major sports such as soccer, lacrosse, football, and offers courses in a variety of academics as well.

*Father Stephen and Father Cletus dining with members of the Fathers and Friends,
December, 1956. Rod Keller is in the foreground.*

Father Stephen understood that organizations and programs such as these would develop cadre
of parents, alumni, and parents of graduates who, in their volunteer roles, would provide
important supplementary funding for the School as well as community building social organizations. His genius, earlier as a headmaster and later as director of development, lay in tapping the
talents of others and freeing them in such a way that the work would get done. Annual fashion
shows and spring fund raisers by the Mothers' Guild, annual golf outings and scholarship dinners
by the fathers, regular organizational activities by the alumni and now by parents of graduates,
have, along with the annual fund, not only generated more than $25,000,000 for the School over
the years, but have created an esprit de corps among Delbarton men and women, young and old,
that binds them firmly in one extended and supportive community.

Father Stephen actively supervised the lay leadership of the organizations and initiated and
conducted a number of capital campaigns to build the School's facilities: a campaign that raised
$125,000 built the St. Joseph's gym after the devastating Chapter House fire of 1947; a
$2,000,000 campaign that funded the building of Trinity Hall which opened in 1959; a campaign
for nearly $2,000,000 also funded the building of the Abbey church and the monastery on top of
the hill between 1964 and 1966; a $1,000,000 campaign resulted in the construction of the
Schmeil-O'Brien Hall in 1971, formerly a boarding school dormitory but now a retreat center, and a
$2,500,000 capital campaign funded the building of the Abbot Brian Clarke Gym of the Frank &
Patricia Lynch sports complex. In addition to overseeing the funding and much of the construction
for these projects, Father Stephen assumed responsibility for the repair and refurbishing of all the
School facilities. More than any other single individual Father Stephen was responsible for much

of Delbarton School. Father Stephen died on February 16, 1994, and in 1995 the new Rev. Stephen Findlay Science Pavilion was dedicated in his honor.

Continuing to promote collaboration with laymen for conducting the School, Father Stephen and Father Francis O'Connell, shortly after Father Francis took over as headmaster in 1967, founded the lay board of trustees, an advisory board of friends of the School with whom the headmaster and the monks could consult on important matters. Father Stephen wrote the constitution and by-laws of the organization and appointed committees to work on ways and means, education, and legal matters. The board committees met three times a year, and the Board itself twice a year. The same pattern endured through the 1970s and 1980s. In the late 1960s, the board leadership included Mr. John Cross, Mr. Mario Formichella and Mr. Louis Thebault, all leaders in northern New Jersey corporations. In those early years of the Board, the members numbered one dozen to twenty, but as the board expanded in the 1980s and 1990s, the numbers grew to twenty-five through thirty-five, including an increasing representation from the Delbarton alumni.

Father Francis also concerned himself with a number of important academic reforms at the School, all consistent with the Benedictine concept of the dignity of the individual. Sadly, Father Francis began to suffer from cancer only four years after he began his work as headmaster. He required a confrere to serve as acting headmaster during his nearly two-year battle with the disease. He died in 1972 and was followed immediately by Father James O'Donnell, who stayed on as headmaster until 1975.

Father Francis and Father James had much in common, which made them valued leaders during their time at Delbarton. Both were well educated theologians; both were educated in Rome;

Father Francis O'Connell, Headmaster, at dinner with members of Delbarton's first
Lay Board of Trustees, May 1967.

Parent and grandparent supporters of the School and Abbey since the 1950s,
Dorsey and Lou Thebault with Father Stephen in an undated photograph

and both served at Delbarton under Abbot Martin Burne, Father Francis as headmaster and Father James as Abbot Martin's prior. Those three influences strengthened their legacy left at Delbarton. The insistence by Abbot Martin that students be seen as other Christs born in the image and likeness of God, a value he lived by, thus guaranteeing the respect and love he received from the students, was the motivation for many of the changes in the Father Francis/Father James era.

Since Delbarton in its early days resembled boarding schools, and the greatest percentage of its students were boarding students, like most boarding schools Delbarton held classes on Saturday mornings. Delbarton eliminated Saturday school early in Father Francis's administration. In addition, motivated by a number of education reforms of the late 1960s, as well as by a need to be more personal in the faculty's relationship with students, Father Francis began and Father James continued a careful work with Delbarton's evaluation or grading system. The School also began to experiment with alternative daily schedules to remove some of the tedium from the horarium.

In addition, the administration and faculty began to reflect in those days on the School's discipline system. The ten years paralleling the war in Vietnam and many other national crises, roughly 1965 to 1975, saw much of the anger and protests over the war seep into school life. Traditional schools like Delbarton had difficulty in those days dealing with long hair, the generation gap, violation of the dress code and protests against the war and the bombing of Cambodia. Under the leadership of Father Francis and Father James, Delbarton weathered these storms out of sensitivity to the students and their parents, and even allowed and encouraged "teach-ins" by faculty on the war and Cambodia. Following the example of many college student bodies after the bombing of Cambodia and the shootings at Kent State in 1970, more than half of the student body and faculty walked out of classes as a sign of protest. Rather than punish or remonstrate with the offenders, the School administration scheduled "teach-ins" on the war for the next week.

The end of the war in Vietnam and its accompanying end to the draft caused the nation to experience a massive sigh of relief. Individual and collective anger subsided dramatically. This was especially seen at Delbarton. 1975 was also the year that Father Gerard Lair began a five-year term as headmaster. On June 18, 1975, Abbot Brian Clarke had been elected as the seventh abbot of St. Mary's Abbey to succeed Abbot Leonard Cassell, who resigned because of ill health after following Abbot Martin Burne and serving for nearly four years. Abbot Brian, with his advisors and the Chapter concurring, decided to appoint headmasters for Delbarton School for five-year terms, with their selection involving consultation with all of the monks and the lay teachers in the School.

Father Gerard Lair took advantage of that national sigh of relief and introduced sweeping changes in the School, all intended to make the School even more reflective of the values of the Rule of Benedict. In the first place, he addressed the discontent many faculty felt about Delbarton's discipline system by discontinuing the traditional program of demerits, detention, and the office of the dean of discipline. He introduced a rotating six-day cycle of classes and discontinued the ringing of bells to signal the beginning and end of classes. He pleased both students and faculty by eliminating the requirements of jackets and ties and instituting a more casual dress code. He continued the work begun by Father Francis of changing the system of student evaluation and

Father Gerard Lair, Headmaster, 1975-1980

began a discussion on ending the boarding department at Delbarton. Father Gerard also initiated a discussion on the desirability and feasibility of co-education at Delbarton, subsequently recommending to the Chapter that the issue be tabled. He began the custom all headmasters after him followed of actively recruiting young men and women from the most competitive small liberal arts schools to teach and coach at Delbarton. This began the influx of nearly one hundred bright and youthfully enthusiastic teachers and coaches to the Delbarton faculty, many of them scholar-athletes from Williams College, a factor that has done much to improve teaching and increase the reputation of the School.

Changing the discipline system might well be the most far-reaching change in Delbarton's history and the change most consistent with the teachings of the Rule of Benedict. Father Gerard and a number of young monastic and lay faculty members led principally by Father Jerome Borski, O.S.B., had become familiar over the years with the work on moral development by Dr. Lawrence Kohlberg of Harvard University. Kohlberg and his critics, in the 1970s, published a large corpus of work on educational philosophy and teaching methods designed to promote the leading of students to higher levels of moral reasoning. Benedictines could not help but be intrigued by the similarities between Kohlberg's findings and the teachings of the Rule of Benedict. According to Kohlberg, on whose teachings Father Jerome educated most of the faculty, an individual progresses in moral development through six stages: in the first two stages, the lowest level of moral reasoning, an individual does the right thing because otherwise he would be punished; in the third and fourth stages, one does right because it is the law; it is the social convention; but in stages five and six, one does the right thing because it is the right thing to do. By Kohlberg's measure, fewer than 25% of individuals reach the highest level of moral reasoning, and it should be the work of families and schools to get as many people as possible into that highest level.

How is that done? According to Kohlberg one is drawn from a lower level to a higher level through a process called "conversation"; one is drawn by another's urging, preferably a friendly adult or even a peer, often a slightly older peer. For an individual to move from one stage into a higher stage of moral reasoning one is taking a risk. Consequently, the environment in which the individual lives must be conducive to that risk-taking. For example, the individual must trust the one who is leading him to a higher level of moral reasoning; he must feel accepted and comfortable in his environment; there ought to be a certain élan or positive spirit about that environment; and there ought to be positive peer modeling of the kinds of behaviors he is being invited to internalize at the higher level of moral reasoning. Similarly, St. Benedict writes about the good zeal that monks ought to have, a zeal which creates an environment for personal development in goodness and holiness:

> *"This then is the good zeal that they must foster with fervent love: they should each*
> *try to be the first to show respect to the other, supporting with the greatest*
> *patience one another's weakness of body and behavior. No one is to pursue what*
> *he judges better for himself, but instead what he judges better for someone else."*
> Rule of Benedict, Chapter 72.

The School leaders in 1975 merged this thinking of two experts on human development, though 1500 years apart, and created Delbarton's "discipline by conversation," a system which would incorporate into School life a well accepted secular model as well as the tried and true Benedictine experience. In addition, "discipline by conversation" resembled the monk's vow of *conversatio morum,* in that verbal conversation between the young person being invited to a higher level of moral reasoning and better behavior led that young person to conversion of life, to a literal change in behavior that would help him mature even further.

Out went demerits and detentions along with jackets and ties! The School even eliminated the office and concept of the dean of discipline. At this time the assistant headmaster was appointed to supervise a number of class moderators whose work was to organize the social events of a class, develop class spirit, as well as follow up immediately on undesirable behavior by leading a young person with patience, support, and conversation to better behavior.

Discipline by conversation has been eminently successful at Delbarton and continues at the School. With the passage of time and with the fine tuning that comes from administration to administration, the School has raised the profile on student behavior with the creation of the Prejudice Reduction workshop, the Drug and Alcohol Task Force, and Students Against Destructive Decisions, all student-led and student-manned committees.

Lead by Father Gerard, the Chapter made the decision to discontinue the boarding program after a great deal of discussion in 1978. This decision followed only seven years after opening a new boarding facility, Schmeil-O'Brien Hall. The monks who prefected boarders from 1939 through the early 1980s recognized by the late 1960s and 1970s, that this commitment of twenty-four hours a day to young students became increasingly difficult. They understood the importance of monastic prayer, silence, the common life, and the need for free time for study and human development. In addition, during those same years, the School faced increasing difficulty in recruiting boarding students. Noble efforts were made, often by word of mouth, to bring in students from Latin American and South American countries, and some of the younger monks even made recruiting trips to parishes in Bergen County and the New York suburbs to interest families in sending their sons to Delbarton. The School aligned itself with the A Better Chance (ABC) program which helped boarding schools recruit disadvantaged youths from urban centers. As a result of that program in the 1960s and 1970s, half-a-dozen to ten of Delbarton's boarding students came from the inner cities. None of these efforts resulted in substantial numbers of boarding students enrolling. However, the Chapter felt that the most important reason to eliminate boarding at Delbarton pertained to the demographic changes in northern New Jersey.

The demographic changes affecting Newark after the Second World War and into the 1960s echoed into the suburbs. A great deal of industry moved out of the Oranges and into western Union County and Morris County. With the industry moved the workers, particularly the executives. Predictably, those same years saw the planning of route 80, the northern New Jersey east-west artery; route 287, a north-south artery; and route 78, an east-west artery further south of route 80.

(Photo courtesy of New Jersey: A Mirror on America by John T. Cunningham
Afton Publishing Co. Florham Park, NJ - 1978)

Delbarton was ideally located in the middle of the intersection of these routes, and many of the new industries moving into the area of Morris County began populating the suburban towns immediately east and west of 287, from Short Hills on the east to Chester on the west. Students from these towns could quite easily commute to Delbarton. This resulted in a very significant press for day enrollment in the mid-1970s.

Finally, the nature of the families moving into the Delbarton area increased the number of day candidates. As the demographers taught, most of the companies along the 287 artery, such as insurance companies, chemical companies, financial firms, technology and telephone companies tended to develop immediately after the Second World War and employed, therefore, the newly educated veterans or first-generation college-educated young men and women, young people who tended to be from certain ethnic groups which were heavily Catholic, many of whom themselves attended single-sex Catholic secondary schools like Seton Hall Prep, St. Benedict's, St. Peter's, and other single-sex Catholic secondary schools outside of New Jersey. For many of these employees of corporations recently moved to Morris County, Delbarton was ideal for their sons. Therefore, the Chapter made the decision to discontinue boarding in 1978, deciding that those who were currently boarding at the School could remain until they graduated. Consequently, the last boarder left Delbarton in June, 1983.

The administration of Father Gerard Lair from 1975 through 1980 set the tone for developing the Benedictine philosophy of education at Delbarton for the next thirty years. Father Giles Hayes succeeded Father Gerard as head of School in July, 1980, and appointed as his assistant headmaster,

Father Manus Duffy. Both Father Giles and Father
Manus were seasoned Delbarton graduates, 1956 and
1960, respectively. In addition, Father Giles appointed
Mr. William Crane, who had been an experienced and
devoted Delbarton faculty member since 1963, as dean
of faculty. The monks surrounding him as guidance
counselors and moderators collaborating with him to
build on Father Gerard's work, were Fathers Frederick
Muench, Peter Meaney, Andrew Smith, Cronan Tyms,
Jerome Borski, Luke Travers and many members of
the lay faculty, especially Mrs. Shelley Levine, Mr.
Giacomo Pagano, Mr. John Sanfacon, Mr. Wayne
Gardiner, and others. This team of administrators and
faculty worked tirelessly to bring Delbarton to a

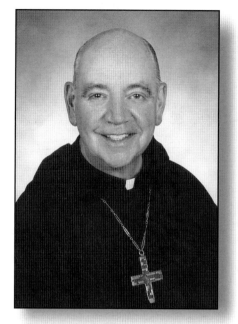

Father Giles Hayes, Headmaster,
1980-1985; 1995-1999

View of St. Mary's Abbey, Morristown, in the 1980s

stronger position among secondary schools throughout the State and nation, but also to a level
even more faithful to its Benedictine and Judeo-Christian roots.

Interestingly, the School leadership at Delbarton in the early 1980s communicated frequently
with the school leadership of the new St. Benedict's Prep, especially Father Edwin Leahy, the
headmaster of St. Benedict's, Father Albert Holtz, and Father Philip Waters. Father Manus was
close in age and experience to both Father Edwin and Father Philip and often brought ideas back
to Delbarton from the experiences of the monks at St. Benedict's. These young monks at both

schools often studied their common roots in the Rule of St. Benedict to create the systems and practices in their schools that were most consistent with the values of the Rule. Often enough they shared their ideas, and in the case of Delbarton School, they borrowed generously from St. Benedict's when they established the deanery system and the Council of Seniors.

Building upon the advances of Father Gerard's administration, faculty and students felt in the late 1970s and 1980s that the School needed more school spirit, a greater sense of community, justice, and integrity within the body, and a greater sense among all that everyone at Delbarton is "our brother's keeper." In 1980-81, therefore, the School administration, along with student leaders, began to study the development of peer counseling, peer leadership, and support systems in schools in the northern New Jersey area. They spent time at some of these schools, notably St. Benedict's, and sent representatives to various leadership institutes, such as those at Princeton Day School and the International Student Leadership Institute at Notre Dame. In all of these places they saw excellent programs developing, programs which, in part, they wanted to replicate. But they had to go further in developing a sense of community which gave pride, dignity, responsibility, and care to all of its members, all characteristics stemming from the recognition that St. Benedict wanted his followers to see Christ in each other. These activities resulted in the early design of what Delbarton now calls its deanery program.

Chapter 21 of the Rule of St. Benedict, in which St. Benedict invites the abbot to enlist the more mature members of the community to assist him in the leadership of monks, serves as a model for the deanery program and the many opportunities for shared leadership at Delbarton:

"If the community is rather large, some brothers chosen for their good repute and
holy life should be made deans. They will take care of their groups of ten,
managing all affairs according to the commandments of God and the
orders of their abbot."
Rule of Benedict, Chapter 21.

The School administration decided, therefore, to call upon students, particularly juniors and seniors, to fill leadership roles in the Council of Seniors, a Benedictine term used for leaders in the monastic community. These leadership roles include serving as peer counselors or deans in charge of small groups of students, campus ministers, coordinators of community service programs, captains of teams, leaders of retreats, officers of clubs and classes, and as members of School and joint faculty committees. In the early 1980s, as the School continued to grow to nearly 500 students, a deanery program was established to maintain the sense of a small community and to facilitate the concept of shared leadership as espoused in the Rule of St. Benedict.

The founders of the program, both administrators and senior leaders at the School, wanted each deanery of roughly fifteen students to include representation from each grade. This enabled students from different ages and interests to get to know one another. A junior and a senior dean led each deanery in regularly held discussion groups on important topics that were pre-selected by the deans as a group. In addition, by having the juniors and seniors in families including seventh and eighth graders, the likelihood was great that the younger students would not get lost, would not "fall through the cracks."

All students were invited to apply for dean positions. A committee comprised of faculty, administration, and senior deans, selected a new group of deans each school year. Deans, as well as all other students called to leadership roles, received then, as now, extensive formal and informal leadership training to prepare them for the rigors of leading their peers. This training included monthly or bi-monthly organizational meetings as well as leadership retreats, often two or three times a year.

The model for the School's deanery system, another example borrowed from St. Benedict's Rule, became the central component of student life at Delbarton. In addition to serving as forums for discussion groups, the deanery structure was utilized by other organizations in the School. For example, the campus ministry program began to operate many service projects through the deaneries. Furthermore, the deanery system supported many of the School's principal values: extending a sense of belonging and brotherhood, working collaboratively, being accountable to others, demonstrating leadership, and participating in the running of the School.

> "If the community is rather large, some brothers chosen for their good repute and holy life should be made deans."
> – Rule of Benedict, Chapter 21.

The values of Father Gerard's administration, which broke down the divisive concept of the "generation gap" of the 1960s, continued into the School leadership of the 1980s and 1990s. Each administration gave seniors a great deal of responsibility, affirming them as valued collaborators in the education of the younger students at the School. This trust and affirmation created over time an important sense of unity between the faculty and the students at Delbarton. Three students, called "Warlords", ran the deanery program with the help of a faculty member, and another thirty students in the Council of Seniors, under the executive officers of the Council, had the responsibility for every area of school life except curriculum and the athletic department. In the late 1970s, early 1980s, down to the present, the students literally ran the entire social life of the School, many clubs, most of the social action programs, the retreats and spiritual programs of the campus ministry department, student elections, and many other areas of School life. The Council of Seniors also took the responsibility for Spirit Week in February, and with the Faculty Social Action Committee, they organized the annual Prejudice Reduction workshop in collaboration with the B'nai B'rith Anti-Defamation League, and a variety of other programs.

This organization of deaneries with junior and senior deans, of the warlords and Council of Seniors, soon led to an organized program of leadership training for all students involved in leadership. The importance of training Delbarton students for leadership, however, was not new to the School officials in the early 1980s. Indeed, it had been a primary goal of Father Stephen and his stalwarts as early as the 1940s. The Benedictines then understood that many of their students came from family environments which would promote leadership in political life, the church, and in academic life. Consequently, Father Stephen often spoke to the students about preparing to

Assistant Headmasters at Delbarton School, like the Priors at the Abbey, supervise the
daily operations and discipline at the School, Left to Right,
Brother Paul Diveny (1985-1990), Father Bruno Ugliano (1975-1980),
Father Manus Duffy (1980-1985)

assume important leadership roles in society after they graduated from Delbarton and college. The boys who listened to his frequent sermons and speeches at Mass or convocations often heard him talk about the "pursuit of excellence" in the classroom, in their values, and in assuming roles of significance among their peers now and in society. A canon lawyer himself, he often held up the law and political life as important arenas for Delbarton graduates to exercise their influence. He often tapped attorneys of significance in the State of New Jersey and beyond, jurists of the Superior and Appellate courts, as well as senators and governors, to deliver the graduation addresses to the boys. All of this was not lost on his successors in the office of head of School.

In the early 1980s, the School leaders created a systematic program for leadership training. Dozens of students each year were sent away for instruction in the techniques of group dynamics and t-group training. As the years progressed, School leaders recognized the need for an academic component to strengthen the experiential component of leadership training which developed systematically within the School. Tenth graders began to be formally trained to assist in the orientation of incoming freshman, and juniors and seniors began to be trained by faculty members as "buddies" and mentors for seventh, eighth, and ninth graders. In addition to that, beginning in 2000, all seniors, as a requirement for graduation, had to take a twelve-week academic course in leadership. This curriculum included the reading and discussion of several well respected books and articles, role-playing exercises, public speaking instruction, and training for living morally in college and beyond.

XVII

COMMUNITY SERVICE AND CAMPUS MINISTRY IN THE DELBARTON OF MODERN TIMES

The Abbey Players, a student drama group, performed Kurt Vonnegut's *Happy Birthday, Wanda June* on February 23, 1978. While that event bruised the reputation of the School for a number of months, it was the catalyst for the beginning of an exemplary program for community service and campus ministry. The event of February 23, 1978, and the steps that the School leaders of Delbarton took to respond to it, assured the development of its community service and campus ministry programs. But the seeds for these programs were evident long before that day in 1978.

Mature people, especially those with spiritual roots, put others ahead of themselves. The scriptures of every faith require the giving of oneself to others, especially if one has been blessed. Delbarton students have had a long history of community service and social action. President Kennedy's call of 1960 that individuals should consider how they should serve their country, and Dr. Martin Luther King, Jr.'s teachings through most of the 1950s and 1960s, that we should promote equality of all human beings regardless of our differences, certainly affected life at Delbarton. Both monks and students recalled the leadership of Father Martin Burne on the March on Washington of 1963, the peace march in Newark in 1968, and his many homilies about social justice during his period as abbot of the monastery and school, and of how his example influenced many of the initiatives of community service in the 1960s and early 1970s.

Members of Delbarton's Class of 1969 were principal leaders of early service activities. Student government President Jim Nugent, and his friends Rinker Buck, Brian Thebault, Doug Satzger, and others founded a program called RUSH, Rescue Underfed Starving Humans, which resulted in collecting a number of eighteen-wheelers of food and clothing for the poor in Beaufort and Jasper counties in South Carolina. The leaders of the Class of 1969 with the encouragement of many of the

*Father Hilary O'Leary meeting with some Delbarton students who
participated in a tutoring project at Sacred Heart Parish,
Elizabeth, 1973.*

monks, including Father Gerard and Father Giles, established relationships with the African-American community in Morristown which resulted in the founding of "IT," a social organization which held an arts festival in Burnham Park in Morristown. "IT" brought together the young people of private and public secondary schools, especially Morristown High School and Delbarton. In addition, Father Hilary O'Leary, Father Germain Fritz, and others regularly involved students in serving the poor, especially those in Newark and Elizabeth, New Jersey.

Long before the 1980s, then, community service held a high priority in the life of the monks and students at Delbarton. As the war in Vietnam concluded, however, many young people lost their interest in community service projects throughout the nation. Delbarton seemed to be no exception in the mid to late 1970s. Then, on the afternoon of Thursday, February 23, 1978, the Abbey Players held their rehearsal for the first showing that evening of their play *Happy Birthday, Wanda June.* Community service and campus ministry changed dramatically after that.

Kurt Vonnegut's *Happy Birthday, Wanda June* is an anti-war play set in Germany during the Second World War. Two minor characters are Gestapo soldiers dressed in authentic Gestapo uniforms including realistic looking plastic guns, riding crops, and caps. It was performed at Delbarton on the weekend of February 23, 1978, by the Abbey Players. Immediately following the Thursday afternoon dress rehearsal, the two boys who were dressed in Gestapo uniforms went to the American Rabbinical College on Sussex Avenue in Morris Township to have their picture taken by one of their girlfriends next to the entrance sign of the Rabbinical College. As their picture was being taken, an automobile entered the property containing a driver and three passengers, all rabbinical students, the passengers having recently arrived from Europe and North Africa. Since the car belonging to the Delbarton students blocked a portion of the entrance, the rabbinical student's car could not proceed, which caused the rabbinical students to leave the car in an excitable state. The boys, recognizing the wrong they had done, then began to call to the rabbinical students to move their car so the students could exit, at which point a third automobile containing Neo Nazis passed the entrance on Sussex Avenue. The Neo Nazis stopped their automobile, exited their car, and allegedly threw stones at the rabbinical students shouting anti-Semitic epitaphs in German.

At mid-morning the next day, while Father Gerard Lair and some of his colleagues were enjoying a coffee break in the Trinity Hall sitting room, a confrere entered with a copy of the day's *Daily Record,* the Morris County newspaper, which included an account of the event dominating the front page. Assuming that the young men in the Gestapo uniforms were members of the cast of the play of the night before, Father Gerard immediately telephoned the county prosecutor, Mr. Peter Manahan.

In a week's time, the police understood all of the details, including the fact that the Neo Nazis were not connected with the Delbarton students. Father Gerard responded with appropriate discipline for the boys, and he encouraged the faculty to discuss the incident among themselves, express their outrage, and to take steps to address the issues of anti-Semitism, racism, and prejudice in the curriculum. Abbot Brian Clarke made a special visit to the superior of the American Rabbinical College to offer an apology from the School and monastic community. The incident caused great harm to the rabbinical students and it also reflected the virulent anti-Semitism simmering in American society only a generation after the Holocaust. For Delbarton, however, the incident caused a great deal of embarrassment that two of its students could have acted so thoughtlessly. It resulted in a public relations nightmare for the School for a number of weeks and caused many at the School to search their souls and wonder why two otherwise good young men, neither of whom had been in disciplinary trouble, could commit such a horrific anti-Semitic act. Father Gerard stated, "We abhor this incident as senseless, flagrantly irresponsible and insensitive to the feelings of others. We apologized to the faculty and students of the Rabbinical College of America and our neighbors in the community for such gross, inexcusable behavior." Many of the faculty questioned what more could a School like Delbarton do to forestall events like that.

> "We abhor this incident as senseless, flagrantly irresponsible and insensitive to the feelings of others."
> – Father Gerard Lair, O.S.B.

The deanery system, a logical result of the values that Father Gerard's administration embraced, as discussed in an earlier chapter, was created in part as a result of February 23, 1978. But this event also led to the creation of Delbarton's unique community service program. Delbarton of the early 1980s, during the time when Father Giles Hayes served as Headmaster (1980-1985), was very much the School that the demographers of the early 1970s said it would become. Ninety-three percent of the student body and ninety-nine percent of the faculty were white Caucasians, and seven percent of the student body were either African-American, Latino, or Asian-American. The tuition in 1983 was $4,300, compared to the $1,500 tuition, room and board of the 1950s and the $20,000 tuition of the post 2000 years. That 7% of African-American, Latino, and Asian-American students in 1983 compares to the 1% of those groups in the early 1950s and more than 17% of those groups after 2000. Delbarton had 125 students in 1952, 490 in 1985, and 540 in 2005. The faculty of the School in 1983 numbered 67 members, including 20 monks and 6 female teachers. Most had joined the faculty from the mid 1960s through the late 1970s and had experienced those initial days when Benedictine values were being institutionalized into the School life. They advocated the deaneries, expansion of campus ministry, and the full development of community service. Furthermore, they took active roles themselves in advancing the concepts of justice, compassion, integrity, and brotherhood. For example, the faculty in the last years of Father Stephen Findlay's service as head of School started the Headmaster's Fund for the Disadvantaged and contributed regularly to scholarship funds for disadvantaged students. In the early 1980s, then, they were ready to respond fully to the February 23, 1978, incident.

Faculty members formed a Social Justice Committee in the fall of 1980. Led by Mrs. Shelly Levine, Father Germain Fritz, Mr. Giacomo Pagano, Mr. John Sanfacon, and Father Giles Hayes, the Committee sought to discern the characteristics of the student body that the School should address with respect to the formation of the boys. The Committee created the survey of student values, anonymously completed by the boys and evaluated by the Committee. After the survey was calculated, Father Giles invited two psychologists, one a School parent and the other a professional from Morristown, to explain to him the meaning of the results and interview a few willing students and parents for their own impressions. This process took a number of months.

Left to Right: Mr. Michael Domas (math), Mr. Giacomo Pagano (Spanish),
and Mr. John Sanfacon (French), 1964

Students bringing gifts to children of the Perkins family,
Royalton, KY, December 1987.

The study of Delbarton's student body in 1980 revealed that the boys had a great deal of knowledge about social issues. They knew the scriptures and the values of the Judeo-Christian background of the School. They understood the teachings of the monks and the faculty members on values often given in church, in religion class, or in classroom and athletic field conversations. They knew the meaning of and the sources of racism, prejudice, and anti-Semitism. In their knowledge about every topic but one, they received high marks. The topic on which they scored low, however, was poverty. They generally agreed with the statement that "The poor are the authors of their own misery." They showed little knowledge and emotional connection to the causes of poverty and the culture of poverty wherever it might be. The Social Justice Committee understood at that time that such a conclusion of the students would be expected since, overwhelmingly, they were children of the "managerial class." The question for the Committee, then, was how to help the students become more sensitive to those who were not like them, especially the poor. Father Giles, in 1980, received an answer to this from a surprising source.

Father Giles' sister, Sister Mary Florence Hayes, SND, Ph.D., was a professor at Trinity College in Washington, D.C., and a member of a committee of the United States Catholic Conference of Bishops dealing with questions of social justice. Specifically, Sister Mary and one of her colleagues on the committee, Father Donald McNeill, CSC, in the late 1970s, studied ways of improving social justice education in Catholic institutions. They discovered that in the early to mid-1970s, much of the social action of young people decreased, in part because of "burn-out" after the war on poverty, the civil rights movement, and anti-Vietnam war activity, as well as the frustration of volunteers at not realizing success in their efforts.

Sister Mary and Father McNeill learned that it is beneficial for the social justice education of young people to have a long-term, "hands-on," experience with those who are not like themselves, an experience which can bring about an emotional connection and a sense of responsibility to others in the student or the volunteer. With this in mind, at the Center of Social Concern at the University of Notre Dame, Father McNeill founded the "Urban Plunge." In this program, he had students live for a week within the slums of Chicago or other urban centers and do the kind of work that would give them personal exposure to the poor, where they would come to know and love the poor. The "Urban Plunge" was unique to social action programs everywhere, but the concept since the early 1980s has become rather common and is experienced in one form or another in social justice programs at many Catholic institutions.

Father Giles, however, was fortunate to have learned about it from his sister and Father McNeill, after which he discussed it with Delbarton faculty members and Abbey personnel. He received strong support for this concept from his assistant headmaster, Father Manus Duffy, and from the School administrators and faculty. So, with the concept accepted, all the School needed to do now was execute it.

Delbarton's version of the "Urban Plunge" experienced a few false starts. In the School's first attempt, Father Giles arranged with the pastor of a parish in the Bronx to have a dozen members of Delbarton's senior class live in the school and tutor children for ten days to two weeks. At the last minute, the pastor felt that this might have been too much responsibility for him to assume, so he withdrew his consent. The School then sought to establish relationships with an inner city parish in Paterson, but was turned down. In the third false start, the School had arranged to do a residential social justice program in an inner city parish in Harrisburg, Pennsylvania, but a week before the students were expected to leave, religious leaders from that Harrisburg community told Father Giles it would be too dangerous for the Delbarton students to be there.

Immediately after receiving the denial from Harrisburg, Father Giles found himself walking through the refectory at the Abbey where he met an old priest friend he hadn't seen for years. They sat down to share a cup of coffee, and the priest said: "Giles, what are you up to?" Whereupon Father Giles spoke of his frustration with these false starts. The priest then asked: "Have you spoken to Monsignor Ralph Beiting of the Diocese of Lexington? He's the acknowledged apostle to Appalachia and eastern Kentucky." Immediately after that conversation, Father Giles found Monsignor Beiting's telephone number, called him to discuss the project he had in mind, and on the spot, Monsignor Beiting invited the Delbarton students to eastern Kentucky and promised to provide volunteer dormitory space for their work among the poor.

Initially, the Delbarton students went to Kentucky in groups of five to ten at Thanksgiving, before Christmas, and during the summer. By 1984, the number of annual trips dropped to two, and Father Giles moved the Delbarton volunteers from Monsignor Beiting's facilities in Floyd County to abandoned homes and an old small motel in Magoffin County. There Delbarton's area guide and mentor became Victoria Doucette, the head of the Kentucky Social Services in Magoffin County and a recent convert to Roman Catholicism. Vicky has continued working with the Delbarton students and Father Giles for more than twenty years.

Habitat for Humanity project, Magoffin County,
KY, spring, 1989.

*Chris Shoemaker and Tom McCabe, with their "little
brothers" in the Big Brothers program, Fall, 1986.*

With the help of Father Benedict Worry, O.S.B., Father Giles and the Delbarton volunteers
were able annually to fill twelve or thirteen 18-wheelers with food, clothing, and toys for the
pre-Christmas trips. In the mid-1990s, because of the difficulty of that work, the number of
18-wheelers delivered to Kentucky annually numbered six or seven. The number of student
volunteers, however, grew significantly. From 1989 to the present, more than 50 Delbarton
juniors each year lived and worked for a week among the poor in eastern Kentucky. A dozen to
fifteen adult volunteers accompanied them and Father Giles, including a number of parents of
the students working in Appalachia as well as fathers of students who have graduated, including Mr. Pat Luciano, Mr. Sam Mantone, Mr. Lawrence Whipple, Judge Daniel Coburn, Mr.
Seldon Clark, Mr. Frank Skidmore, Mr. Thomas Pecora and others. By 2000, more than 1,000
Delbarton graduates had lived and worked among the poor in the "hollers" and mountains of
eastern Kentucky. In addition to the more than 150,000 volunteer hours given to the poor of
Magoffin County and nearby counties, the School has also collected and delivered to
warehouses or directly to the homes of the poor over 1,500,000 tons of food, clothing, and toys
since 1981.

With the beginning of the Delbarton Appalachian project in 1981, other social action programs began which centered on direct contact with the poor or with those who are not like the Delbarton students. For example, in the 1981-1982 school year, initiated by a senior at that time, James Petrucci, the Delbarton Big Brothers program began. This was the paradigm for other Big Brother programs to be begun throughout the United States where the big brother was a junior or a senior in high school, rather than an adult male. Organized by Jim Petrucci, who convinced the Morris County "Big Brothers - Big Sisters Program" to accept this, a number of students were entrusted with the responsibility of being big brothers to boys who did not have a male "significant other" in his family. The Delbarton big brother would meet with his little brother at least once every two weeks and connect with the little brother by phone or by another meeting each week. This has proved to be a beneficial program, not only for the little brothers, but also for the Delbarton big brothers. In addition, since the program was initiated in 1981-1982, five of the little brothers have attended Delbarton. Also, more than 400 graduates of Delbarton have had the training and the experience of having been a big brother at the School.

In the early 1980s, a number of other "direct-contact" programs were founded by Delbarton students, including the Mendham Core Group Gap program, intended to improve relationships between the students at Delbarton and Mendham High School, and the Harding Township Core Group, which provided Delbarton students to care for the poor and elderly in southern Morris County. Again, the leadership came from students, principally in these programs, Andrew Hurley, Craig Flinn, and Robert Doherty. A variety of other programs were established during the early 1980s, including those at the food bank, Christmas collections and Thanksgiving food collections at the Neighborhood House in Morristown, at St. Rose of Lima parish in Newark, and other programs working with physically and emotionally challenged youngsters at the Madison YMCA and other service organizations. Since programs like this often needed seed money to fund their activities, the parents and friends of James Nugent, a 1969 graduate and a New Jersey State prosecutor who died while working on a case in the New Jersey Attorney General's office, established the James E. Nugent Foundation. Since 1982, this Foundation has provided several thousand dollars a year for seed money to help fund such programs as the Delbarton Appalachian project.

Through the 1980s and 1990s, Delbarton continued to follow the model of community service exemplified by Father Don McNeill's "Urban Plunge." After 2000, nearly 100% of Delbarton students have participated in one or more community service projects while Delbarton students and well more than a majority have participated in multiple projects. Indeed, more than 32 service programs are available to students and most of them provide direct contact with the poor, programs that have often been described as "total immersion" projects. Appalachia might well have involved the majority of Delbarton's students, but the School also has a total immersion program in Camden, New Jersey, and has been carefully planning others. The Logos Tutoring Program, the Neighborhood House Tutoring Program, and similar efforts fit the model.

Father Elias Lorenzo, Campus Minister, celebrating the Eucharist, early 1990s.

One of the most significant experiences for Delbarton students, however, was developed on the initiative of Father Benedict Worry in the late 1980s and continued through the 1990s and later by Father Elias Lorenzo, O.S.B., the "Operation Smile" program. By virtue of this, over a period of years, students are involved in training for medical missions with plastic surgeons under the direction of Dr. Bill Magee who founded "Operation Smile." Students who participate on missions spend two and a half to three weeks in a foreign country working closely with poor children who are receiving reconstructive facial surgery from volunteer plastic surgeons from the United States. Since the late 1980s, dozens of Delbarton students have worked with these plastic surgeons in Vietnam, the Philippines, the Gaza Strip, China, Bolivia, Kenya, Romania, Russia, Honduras, Mexico, Nicaragua, Paraguay and other foreign lands.

Finally, a variety of other changes in the systems of Delbarton from 1975 through 1985 helped to create a positive culture at the School. During the administration of Father Gerard Lair, for example, the School discontinued the use of bells to announce the beginning and the end of class periods. By doing so, the School created a certain calmness and a sense of responsibility among the students to pass from class to class without coercion. In 1980, all classrooms were outfitted with a handmade wooden shrine affixed to the front wall of each classroom, on which the Holy Bible was placed. After 1980 class began each day with a reading from Sacred Scripture, readings that were organized according to themes, such as social justice, prophets, leadership, compassion, community building and other Biblical themes that supported the values of the School. In Father

Gerard's administration, the school day was given a rotating schedule so that each class over a six-day period would have a different academic schedule. Also, after 1980, the School administration added special names to each period and each day to remind the students of different themes and values. The six-day schedule and periods between 1980 and 1985 included such names as: Erasmus, Francis of Assisi, Gandhi, Archbishop Romero, Andrei Sakharov, George Fox, A. Philip Randolph, Albert Schweitzer, Leo Tolstoy, Martin Luther King, Dorothy Day, Pope Leo XIII, Pope John XXIII, Thomas More, and Dag Hammarskjöld. Not often, if ever, did students before attending Delbarton have an opportunity to go to class during Martin Luther King period or Dorothy Day period; but when they did after attending Delbarton, that kind of hidden curriculum, day after day, surely had a positive effect on them. In the early 1980s, the "hidden curriculum" in other areas of the School included putting up signs with the words "integrity", "brotherhood", "justice", and a variety of other graphic descriptions of Biblical quotations and values. In addition, during assemblies which were held two or three times a week, the phrase "Does anyone else have anything to say?" was often heard.

As indicated earlier, most important in that decade from 1975 to 1985 was the extraordinary student leadership supporting the administrations of Father Gerard Lair and Father Giles Hayes. Gone were the days of the generation gap of the 1960s and early 1970s. Rather, student government presidents and leaders of community service activities and campus ministry were regarded as allies of the School administration. Since the program of the deaneries and "discipline by conversation" required positive peer modeling of older students for the younger, the adults depended upon the juniors and the seniors for their example and leadership. Consequently, many of the older students rose to the occasion provided by Father Gerard, but most notable were the Council of Seniors presidents: Paul Yearwood, Steven Yevak, Kevin Kenny, Stephen Faber and Donal Mastrangelo. Father Giles was blessed as well by the leadership of the seniors, including: John Hanlon, Joe Chernik, Andrew Anselmi, Glenn D'Angerio, Peter Petino, Andrew Hurley, Jim Petrucci, and Bob Doherty, to name a few.

Area educators in 1984 nominated Delbarton for the Exemplary School award from the United States Department of Education because of the developments at the School over ten years and because of the School's response to the Rabbinical College incident of 1978. Along with fifty other public and private secondary schools throughout the country, Delbarton received the award from President Ronald Reagan on August 4, 1984, presented on the occasion of President Reagan's televised speech on education at the opening of his second presidential campaign. Fortunately for head of School, Father Giles, and the two student leaders who accompanied him to Washington, D.C., to receive the award, Peter Petino, Council of Seniors president, and John Facciani, Middle School president, Delbarton had a graduate on President Reagan's White House staff, Bill Sittman, '67. Bill arranged for the Delbarton visitors to have a special tour of the White House and to meet with President Reagan personally before receiving the award. Two especially memorable moments were associated with that meeting.

*Father Giles, Headmaster, introducing student leaders, John
Facciani (Middle School President) and Peter Petino (Council of
Seniors President) to President Ronald Reagan on the occasion
of Delbarton receiving the Exemplary School Award from the
United States Department of Education, August 4, 1984.*

After President Reagan finished his preparations for the speech, he took Father Giles aside and asked: "Father, did you know that I was baptized a Roman Catholic?" To which Father Giles responded: "Yes, Mr. President, I had heard that." President Reagan then said:

> *"I was a Catholic until I was 15 or 16, and I learned all the Catholic prayers,*
> *the Hail Mary, the Act of Contrition, and others, and I still say them today.*
> *In fact, the morning after I was shot, the doctors came into my hospital room and*
> *told me that in the previous evening they thought I was going to die, but that this*
> *morning they could tell me that I am going to live. After hearing that, I asked*
> *everyone to leave the room, the doctors and the Secret Service agents, because I*
> *wanted to pray. They left for about ten minutes and I said my prayers over and*
> *over again, thanking God. And then, before they came back into the room,*
> *I promised the Lord that everything else I would do as President of the*
> *United States I would do for the Lord."*

President Reagan's candor and sensitivity evident in that remark, as well as the close attention he gave to the Delbarton group, all characteristics which have helped label him the "Great

Communicator," were reflected in the next memorable moment related to that August 4, 1984, meeting. On the evening of November 4, 1984, after three months of intense campaigning throughout the nation and probably thousands of meetings with constituents since that August 4 introduction to the Delbarton trio, President Reagan held an election eve dinner at the J.W. Marriott Hotel in Washington, D.C. for CEO's of major American corporations. Daniel Nugent, President of ITT and a Delbarton parent of four boys and a major benefactor of the School, attended the dinner. As it happened, Dan Nugent arrived late for the dinner and as he entered the hall, a Secret Service agent stopped him at the door and told him to wait because the President was on his way in. President Reagan then walked to the entrance and stood at Mr. Nugent's right, when the Secret Service agent asked him to wait a minute until the agents completed their safety precautions in the dining hall. Finding himself immediately to the left of the President of the United States, Dan Nugent spontaneously offered his hand and said, "Mr. President, my name is Dan Nugent, and I'm from Delbarton!" Dan reported later that he did not know why he said "I'm from Delbarton" because he could well have said "I'm from ITT", or "Morristown, NJ", his hometown. Regardless, after that introduction, the President turned directly to Mr. Nugent, put his hands on each of Mr. Nugent's shoulders, and smiling broadly said, "Mr. Nugent, I met your headmaster and a number of your students recently!" More than 70 years old at this time, and three months after that initial meeting, President Reagan remembered it. Between dinner courses, Mr. Nugent excused himself for a minute to telephone Father Giles about the incident, to which Father Giles said that he knew whom he was going to vote for the next day.

XVIII

ACADEMIC/ARTISTIC GROWTH AT DELBARTON

Father Stephen Findlay enjoyed the company of many gifted faculty as he was developing the School. Some of these were members of communities other than St. Mary's Abbey. For example, in the early years of the School, Father Stephen, and his predecessor, Father Augustine Wirth, had the services of a Scottish monk, Father Ninian MacDonald. He also had volunteer help from Affligem Abbey, Belgium, in the person of Father Augustine Verhaegen. In 1950, Father Cletus Donaghy of the Archdiocese of Baltimore, joined Father Stephen at Delbarton and stayed with him until Father Cletus' death many years later. Father Cletus initially served as Father Stephen's dean of studies, and taught physics and calculus. As he aged, Father Cletus joined the Abbey and was professed on his deathbed in 1983.

A number of monks came from St. Anselm's Abbey, Manchester, NH, to help the Morristown monks with the new school. Among them was Father Felix Pepin, who was one of Father Stephen's deans of discipline in the early 1950s and an important teacher of mathematics and baseball coach. In 1952-53, Father Stephen also received the assistance of Father Egon Javor, a refugee from St. Stephen's Abbey in Pannonhalma, Hungary. Father Egon stayed on at Delbarton until 1956 when he went to California to establish the Woodside Priory School of the Hungarian congregation.

All of these men and others contributed to the development of the academic program at the School during the 1940s and 1950s. The bulk of the teaching, guidance, and coaching during those early years came from Father Augustine's and Father Stephen's stalwarts, as well as from the many young clerics studying theology at St. Mary's Abbey School of Theology. Father Stephen convinced his confreres of his vision for Delbarton, a school which he felt could become one of the best in the State. Consequently, the visitors, including Father Ninian MacDonald, Father Felix Pepin, Father Augustine Verhaegen, and Father Cletus Donaghy, and others, as well as the many clerics, and Father Stephen's "stalwarts", Fathers Kenneth Mayer, Arthur Mayer, Peter Meaney, Adrian McLaughlin, Lucien Donnelly and Frederick Muench, came to be the significant teachers of the remaining middle school students and the growing secondary school student body.

The earliest records of the School indicate that the curriculum included many basic courses including English, mathematics through Algebra II and Trigonometry, Western European and American history, biology and chemistry, Latin, German, French and Spanish, as well as religion, handwriting, public speaking and other courses. The faculty specialized in the "basics" and did it well. Since Delbarton's earliest days, the 15-to-30-person senior classes earned average SAT scores in the 1150-to-1250 range, which positioned the ability and academic achievement of the boys well within the norm of the Eastern United States independent secondary schools. Father Stephen and Father David Conway handled the college selection process in the 1940s and 1950s, followed by Father Karl Roesch, Father Gerard Lair and Father Cronan Tyms, who did this counseling from the 1960s through the mid-1980s. Average combined SAT's of the senior class in the late 1950s totaled 1200; in the 1980s and 1990s, 1350; and after 2000, between 1350 and 1420. The college selection results reflected that development of the ability of Delbarton seniors. Of the 880 Delbarton graduates from 1948 through 1969, 6% matriculated at Ivy League colleges, with Princeton and Brown the favorites; 29% matriculated at the five favorite Catholic colleges, Georgetown, Villanova, Notre Dame, Holy Cross and Boston College, in order of preference. Of the next 880 graduates, including the classes from 1970 through 1983, 10% attended Ivy League colleges with Princeton and Yale the favorites, and 21% attended the above Catholic institutions, with Notre Dame and Villanova the favorites. Since 1983 the Ivy League colleges attracted annually an average of 20% of the graduates, and the above Catholic colleges approximately 30% annually. In a major trend since 1980, more small liberal arts colleges (e.g. Williams, Amherst, Bowdoin, Middlebury and Colgate) became attractive, as did more pre-professional training in medicine, engineering, and technology. Finally, since 1980, a growing percentage of boys in each graduating class chose their college because of opportunities for performance in the arts or athletics.

Delbarton students in the 1940s and 1950s did what was expected of them. They listened to the lectures, generally completed their homework, took notes, and recycled the material for the tests. Such was the educational approach of the 1940s and 1950s in America. Very few of the Delbarton students then complained about the pedagogy they faced and most seemed to benefit by it. Genuine stimulation greeted them in the classroom in the late 1950s and early 1960s when a number of young monks recently graduated from St. Vincent College began teaching in the School. Typically, a young monk studying theology, in most cases, taught the subject of his interest and expertise.

Prior to ordination to the priesthood, then, the young clerics who studied theology would teach four years at the School, at least one course each year. In the late 1950s and early 1960s Father Gerard Lair and Father Regis Wallace, O.S.B., taught English; Father Christian Caspar, O.S.B., Father Benet Caffrey, O.S.B., and Father Thomas Confroy, O.S.B., taught the classics. Father Karl Roesch taught math; Father Rembert Reilly taught history; Father Beatus Lucey taught English and art; Father Germain Fritz taught music.

Certain more experienced teachers stood out for their mastery of the material and their intellectual stimulation. Any Delbarton student who had Father Stephen Findlay in senior English cannot forget his eloquence, his mastery of the language, and his facility in teaching writing and vocabulary. Father Lucien Donnelly kept chemistry exciting and none will forget his bus rides back and forth from the chemistry lab; Father Kevin Bray made botany particularly interesting by taking the students on walking field trips throughout the four-hundred-acre Delbarton campus and teaching them about the flora and fauna there; Father Christian Caspar was particularly adept at interesting his students in Latin and Greek; and many a sleepy-eyed student of Father Adrian McLaughlin quickly came to know his accuracy with an eraser. Mr. William Regan himself could spin an enjoyable tale about American history while sitting at the edge of his desk in history class; and the younger monks who often taught but one course a year prior to their ordination were often most enjoyable to have as teachers for the impressionable Delbarton teenagers.

Admission to the School in the 1940s, 1950s and 1960s was somewhat selective, but not nearly as selective as it became in the 1980s and later. Until 1952, Father Stephen Findlay occasionally admitted post-graduates, who, for a year, improved their academics at Delbarton while helping to make the School's teams more competitive. Scholastic aptitude test scores in the 1940s and 1950s surpassed those of area public schools, but never reached the high levels of their younger Delbarton brothers in the 1980s and beyond. Occasionally, a student in the early days was identified through his National Educational Development Test as a National Merit Scholar, but not until 1968 did 10% or more of the graduating class receive that honor.

Father Eugene and Brother Benedict leading "Glee Club" practice in the late 1940s.

Christmas performance in Old Main, December, 1953.

The last years of Father Stephen's administration and those of Father Francis O'Connell and Father James O'Donnell, 1959 through 1975, saw a dramatic expansion of the curriculum at the School. This was made possible first by the completion of Trinity Hall in 1959, which was followed by the dramatic growth in the student body to more than 300 students after 1970. The addition of more than a dozen new classrooms as well as much more adequate science facilities resulted in a significant decrease in the size of classes as well as the addition of more advanced programs. Father Cletus Donaghy, the chairman of the Science Department, added additional laboratory courses in biology, chemistry, and physics. Larger applicant pools in the 1960s made increased selectivity possible in admissions, which required the School to improve its honors curriculum. Father Karl Roesch, the young monk who in the 1960s succeeded Father Stephen and Father David Conway in guiding seniors to college, also assumed responsibility for introducing the Advanced Placement program at Delbarton. With the help of his successor in college counseling, Father Gerard Lair, initially two or three Advanced Placement courses were offered, and then a large assortment of AP courses by the mid-1960s. Through the 1970s and as early as the 1980s, Delbarton became one of the leading proponents of Advanced Placement courses among secondary schools in the United States, and for two years in the late 1990s, it had the highest percentage of students nationally taking Advanced Placement courses and becoming AP National Scholars.

Finally, the fine arts at Delbarton might well have been the principal beneficiary of the opening of Trinity Hall in 1959-1960. The rooms at either end of the second floor in Trinity Hall became studios for art and music. Father Beatus Lucey and Father Germain Fritz took responsibility for initiating and developing very strong programs in studio art, art history, music history, and music performance. After 1966 and the opening of the new cafeteria at the lower level of the Abbey church, more facilities were made available for the arts in the old kitchen and the monks' dining room, called Duffy's Tavern, in the back of the main building. The gradual decrease of boarders as the late 1970s progressed into the early 1980s also made rooms in Old Main available for classes which, in turn, invited the expansion of the size of the School from 250 in 1959 to 490 in 1984.

During the 1960s and 1970s, a number of significant groups of performers characterized the growth of music at Delbarton. As examples, the Townsmen performed regularly from 1963 through 1967; the Delbarton Baroque Ensemble performed regularly from 1971 through 1983.

Father Germain Fritz, the energetic founder of the Delbarton music program, established the Townsmen in 1963. This group of guitar players and crooners included Ron Goeke, Rudy Marchesi and Hugh McBride, from 1963 through 1966. Hugh graduated in 1966, and was replaced by Les Toeplitz, until the Townsmen disbanded with the graduations of Ron and Rudy in 1967. This group put Delbarton music on the map! They performed in more than 100 concerts during those four years, including a number of performances before the entire Delbarton student body. They created tapes and disks, used some of their own music, and entertained throughout northern New Jersey with their mellow and rhythmic rock and country style music.

In 1970, Mr. Roy Horton joined the faculty to complement Father Germain Fritz, chairman of the music department. There began a partnership between the two musicians which lasted 35 years, until Mr. Horton's untimely death. As a result of that partnership, Delbarton's music program began to be recognized as one of the best in New Jersey. First they organized small *ensembles and a capella* singing groups and then orchestras at the intermediate level and the

The Townsmen, Father Germain, Rudy Marchesi, Hugh McBride, and Ron Goeke,
performed in 100 concerts from 1963-1967.

Delbarton Baroque Ensemble: Blake Patterson,
Father Germain Fritz, Ann Donner, Roy Horton,
George Donner, represented Delbarton throughout
the metropolitan area in the 1970s.

Delbarton Brass ensemble at Canterbury Cathedral, England, Spring 1979. Father
Germain Fritz and Mr. Roy Horton towards the center, Mr. David Sampson, right

Delbarton's "Raels," Paul Bowyer, John Wlader, Mike O'Mara and Tom Graham,
performing at the Creative Arts Festival, May, 1981.

Teachers Tim Scherman and Ernie Sandonato jamming at the 1986 Creative Arts Festival
with seniors Ned Cooper, Jeff Gora, and John McCann.

Dr. Roy Horton, 1970-2005

Abbey orchestra level, which included in the 1990s, 70 or 80 instrumentalists, along with the Wind Ensemble, which included 30 or 40 instrumentalists.

Together they established the Delbarton Baroque Ensemble. The professional musicians of this ensemble, playing harpsichord, violin, flute, and piano, performed throughout the New York-New Jersey area when professional musicians were needed to grace a social event. In the early 1970s, the Delbarton Baroque Ensemble performed at more than 75 concerts as professional musicians. Most important among the professional musicians at Delbarton, however, was David Sampson, a talented trumpet player with the New Jersey Symphony and other professional organizations. David joined the adjunct music faculty at Delbarton in 1974, and with the advantage of working with a grant from a professional sponsor, he stayed on at Delbarton from 1975 to 1979 teaching the Delbarton students, writing original music and holding concerts, most of which were entitled "Hardly Any Sampson." David's presence in the early days of the music program at Delbarton enhanced the foundation for the School's very strong Abbey Orchestra and Wind Ensemble. In addition, his professionalism and expertise created a base of fans for the Delbarton Abbey Orchestra which has led to the support of that group through the end of the century.

The same happened with studio art and art history with the arrival in 1977 of Diane Lopez as a full-time complement to Father Beatus in the arts. Soon exceedingly strong studio art and art history courses could be offered which became successful and well appreciated Advanced Placement courses. As time passed, additional teachers joined both the music and the art programs, including a number of alumni such as Father Edward Seton Fittin, O.S.B., Brian Ferriso,

*Spring, 1986, performance of Pirates of Penzance, starring Stefan Howells (left)
and Peter Dinklage (right).*

and Jonathan Dinklage. With the foundations for the arts at Delbarton securely laid in the 1960s
by Father Germain and Father Beatus, the academic courses in the arts at the end of the century
became among the most popular Advanced Placement programs in the School.

One of the results of this expansion of programs devoted to the arts was the student-led
development of the Creative Arts Festival, first organized in 1971. On a budget of $1000, three
seniors, Fred Hartley, Terry Regan and Joe Daly, with Father Beatus' help, organized the five-day
event. They brought 25 guest speakers, professional and non-professional musicians, art exhibits
and a variety of creative activities to the campus. Many of the exhibits, recitals, and plays occurred
simultaneously and students participated in any one or more of these activities. The Creative Arts
Festival remained an annual event of two or three days in May until the early 1990s.

The School offered few courses in drama, but many opportunities for performance. The Abbey
Players, founded by Father Arthur Mayer and Father Frederick Muench in the 1950s, with musical
assistance from Brother Benedict Meyer, offered two or three principal shows a year. The
repertoire of serious drama, comedy, or musical drama expanded significantly in the 1970s.
Occasionally, shows-in-the-round were performed in the gymnasium under the leadership of Mr.
Dennis Malin, but gradually the music and art departments preferred the gallery in Old Main, in
spite of its small size. There, with Diane Lopez handling the choreography and much of the acting
instruction, and Roy Horton handling the music, the Abbey Players and the Schola Cantorum
treated the School to annual Gilbert & Sullivan programs and a variety of dramas. Student interest

expanded through the 1980s and early 1990s, causing the School leadership to commission the arts faculties with the responsibility of two fall dramatic productions, at least one major musical drama, and three to five student-authored and student/faculty-acted one-act plays. In addition, music orchestral performances included three concerts a year by each of the major groups, the Intermediate Orchestra, the Abbey Orchestra, and the Wind Ensemble. Later a Jazz Ensemble was added which also held regular performances. Assisting Father Germain Fritz and Roy Horton in the second generation of music leadership was Mr. Gregory Devine, and later, to fill Roy Horton's shoes as director of the music program, Mr. David Blazier.

In the early 1970s the Schola Cantorum became a fixture of the Delbarton arts program. Mr. Horton, taught generations of young men at Delbarton not only how to love music but also how to live. Beginning with a small handful, Mr. Horton developed the Schola to an outstanding group of more than 30 voices. Towards the end of his life, in the 1990s, he enjoyed the important help of the vocal coach, Dr. Jerry Foderhase, who provided weekly training in voice for each member of the Schola. Mr. Horton's excellence in music education, his proficiency as an organist and a pianist, as well as a harpsichordist, and also his compassion and wisdom earned him the love of many of the young men who had their first experiences with music from him.

A survey of the Delbarton graduates who studied music and art with these gifted teachers suggests that a very high percentage continued their love of the arts long after they left Delbarton. Many Delbarton graduates have had important careers in film, the music industry, acting, and music performance, including: Academy Award winner Kary Antholis, music industry leaders Peter Clancy and Michael Bloom, playwright Chris Durang, actors Daryl Bell, Peter Dinklage, his brother in music Jonathan Dinklage, and opera singer Paul LaRosa.

Schola Cantorum, 1977

Daryl Bell and David Newcomb in Neil Simon's God's Favorite, May 1981.

Delbarton publications in the early years of the School, the 1940s through the 1980s, when print media exercised an important influence on the delivery of information and shaping opinions were quite significant in the life of the School. As the internet and the use of information from computers became more important, Delbarton publications may have become less significant in the daily life of the students and faculty. This is illustrated, to a degree, in the attention given to publications by the students. From Since 1948 through the mid-1960s, the Delbarton *Archway* had been an important instrument of daily life at Delbarton as well as an essential source of information for the historian.

From the mid-1960s through the 1970s, however, editors and moderators of the *Archway* concentrated more on the quality of the photography than the frequency of the text. In fact, in a number of the *Archways* between 1966 and 1973 there is no text, no listing of the students participating in the photos, nor is there any discussion of the activity or sport being photographed. On the other hand, the photography from the late 1960s through the early 1970s was quite extraordinary. The School administration suppressed the 1969 yearbook, presumably because some of the photos were considered, in those days, to be anti-American, and others, such as a young man being hung on a crucifix, were considered to be blasphemous. Regardless, the 1969 yearbook, along with a few before it and a few after it, might well be the most creative yearbooks that the students have published.

After 1975, the *Archway* identifies each person in a photograph and gives information and records about activities. In the 1980s and the 1990s, more color photography was used, and professional photographers were introduced. Text regarding clubs and sports abounded in those days, as did creative approaches to reflecting on School values, faculty characteristics, and social concerns.

Beginning in 1948, the editors of the *Courier* provided a great deal of expository writing during the early days of the School. The dominance of the internet and on-line news information of the late 1980s and 1990s contributed to diminishing the importance of print media, which was evident

Members of the Class of 1970 clowning around for the 1969 yearbook photographer.

in the attention the students gave to publishing in the *Courier*. For example, rarely did the *Courier* fail to come out less than once a month during the 1950s and '60s. In fact, as technology began to permit, a four-to-six page copy of the *Courier* was published every two or three weeks in the 1960s. Indeed, because the editors would count the letters in articles and the space that those articles would fill, athletic contests that occurred on Saturdays could easily be read about in the *Couriers* that were published and distributed among Delbarton students on the following Mondays.

Unfortunately for the editors of the *Courier* and its moderators, however, since the newspaper was paid for by the School, it was subject to censorship by the moderator and the Headmaster. Therefore, during those angry days of the 1960s and '70s, the *Courier* rarely printed material that could be misinterpreted and result in criticism of the School, whether material that could be interpreted as offensive to the Church or to stances of the federal government regarding the war in Vietnam. The *Courier,* consequently, became a bit stodgy in the late 1960s and early '70s, a reputation it had difficulty stripping itself of later. In the 1980s and '90s, the design of the *Courier* increased in size to something similar to *New York Times,* with six to eight pages, and fewer publication dates. During some years of the 1980s and the '90s only two or three *Couriers* were published.

The *Delta,* the student intellectual magazine which included creative and non-fiction articles, suffered the same fate. While in some years *Delta* editors were particularly assertive in publishing the *Delta* two or three times a year, in other years, particularly in the 1980s and the 1990s, the *Delta* was rarely published more than twice a year. Since most of the articles in the *Delta* were oriented towards the creative, the paucity of issues may reflect the fact that the students had more difficult work to do for their classes, the kind of work that would prevent them from publishing their creative work in the *Delta*.

The perceived inadequacies of the School's publications provided fertile ground for protests at Delbarton from intellectually gifted and creative students. Consequently, a tradition of the "underground press" began quite early in Delbarton's history. For example, the *"Jersey Japper,"* founded by an anonymous member of the Class of 1957, possibly Art Condon, anchored the School's underground press tradition. As with the other underground papers, the *Jersey Japper* was not distributed to faculty but was usually made available to a group of friends and classmates who would understand the humor and the sarcasm. An article in an early 1957 issue follows:

GRAFT AND CORRUPTION MARK STUDENT COUNCIL ELECTIONS;
JAPPER EDITOR RECOMMENDS AN INVESTIGATION OF
TWEETY AND COHORTS.

In a typical scene at the Del, student council elections were held last week. As usual, Tweety was there seeing to it that the candidate that he backed got to power. This year it was John, who by immense corruption, managed to defeat reform candidate Frank; it is this type of political bribery that the Japper seeks to eliminate. In the election for vice president, again the Japper candidate, in its move for good clean government, was defeated. The Japper candidate, Big Jim, stood a good chance of election, and was it not for the miss-led votes for seemingly unknown Alfred E. Neuman, Big Jim would have won for sure. The rest of the elections also ran true to form, with the machine's Dan and Tom getting into office. Japper editor Condon demanded an impounding of the votes for a recount. He stated there was evidence of people voting more than once. "I ought to know; I voted for my man nine times," said Condon.

While those who wrote for the Japper more or less maintained their anonymity, the authors of an underground newspaper in 1964, the *"Dark Glass,"* identified themselves: Ed Binkowski, Frank Arlinghaus, James Huebner, David Dines, Kern Buck and Beriau Picard. Here is a sample of their lead article of No. 4, Vol. 2 published on November 11, 1964:

"Recently a teacher (an English teacher on our distinguished lay faculty who is connected closely with the Abbey Players and shall remain anonymous by request) remarked that by our non-appearance over the last few weeks we were becoming more like the Courier. He also might have added the Delta in his comparison, for our similarity to both in this respect is for the same reasons—lateness of articles and trouble with printing. The tardiness of this publication, contrary to popular belief, is not due to an inefficient staff as is the case with the Courier and the Delta, but rather to the apathy of the student body. The Courier and the Dark Glass have been largely able to overcome this hurdle, but at the present time, the Delta is in rather desperate straits. Stories and essays are in anxious demand and anyone possessing such is asked to hand them in to the editor, Jerome Doherty."

Old Main, circa 1985

Another underground paper with anonymous editors, *"The Fifth Column,"* surfaced in the late 1960s, in part to make fun of various areas of Delbarton life but also to ask serious questions through humor and sarcasm. One of the issues of *"The Fifth Column"* available in the archives has the following label and an interesting article:

"This is copy number eight of a thirty copy, limited edition printing of the Fifth Column. This copy is not for public release nor is it for sale under this or any other cover. It is to be considered a private memorandum for selective release.

The Sub-Culture Exposé

Since the Tet offensive in Vietnam in 1968, it has been known that Father Giles Daze operates an underground railroad from Delbarton to somewhere north. It was believed that Father Giles aided C.O.s with the assistance of the youth sub culture. Father Giles' buddy in 1968 was a noted crusader Stinker Buck. Since Stinker owned an airplane, it was logical to assume that the C.O.s contacted Father Giles, who in turn secured them passage northward on Stinker's plane. The story ended here until now.

After three years of hard work, key code words used by the sub-culture were deciphered. Father Giles has always referred to his close friends as "buddy." What exactly is a buddy? Battle, Useless, Demented, Detached Youth (BUDDY). Who is Stinker Buck? Stay truly involved and nebulous by kibitzing every reform (STINKER). What about the present buddy, Lenny get-to-ban go? Let my egotism nauseate non-involved youth (LENNY). And Father Giles himself? Get involved like every Socialist (GILES).

A recent breakthrough in decoding has provided a key piece in the sub-culture \puzzle. While everyone was facing north watching Father Giles' operation, no one bothered to look south. Down south was RUSH. RUSH is not Rescue Underfed Starving Humans. RUSH deciphered means "Reforms United Secure Harmony."

In 1980 a short-lived underground paper emerged from the senior class called <u>Concerned Seniors of Delbarton,</u> including "all the news that should be printed." Once more some of the writers objected to the Courier:

"Having been at Delbarton for four years I have seen many things, both good and bad. However, the articles in the Courier have discovered new definitions for the word "awful." I feel that this is due to a lack of interest by the School, and a lack of adaptability by the Courier staff. There are many changes needed and many of the changes have fallen on deaf ears. For example: there is no longer a senior forum because it is felt that it does not interest a broad enough spectrum of Delbarton School. On the other hand, constant articles on wild life at Delbarton are hardly of interest to students. The Courier is presently a paper that includes almost every article that can be written (no matter how ridiculous) and is in desperate need of change. I hope that this change is easily facilitated by the cooperation of all students, and that the Courier raises its level of writing and general interest about 150%."

Then, in 1987, the Delbarton Underground appeared. On November 23rd, in issue number two, an anonymous author wrote:

The Reward of Antiquity

AP Latin CL 50 has gotten off to a pretty good start this year under the leadership of Brother Paul, who has lived up to the amazing task of doubling as a Latin teacher and the building principal. The class boasts an average attendance of 3.87 persons, thereby eclipsing the old school low of 3.92, which was set by the AP Latin class of 1985-1986. All four of the students in the class have been taking Latin for five years, and three of the students still can't tell their agricola *from their* agricolae. *The one student that stands alone from the others is Brian Maher, the Underground's "Latin scholar of the month." On Friday, October 30th, Brian was awarded the certificate proclaiming his excellence in Latin. When asked what he thought of the honor he simply replied, "Veni, Vidi, Vici." So there you have it, from the world of antiquity....look for AP Latin articles in the future issues of the Underground.*
Signed, Sarcastiticus Aehems.

PART FOUR:

ATHLETICS AND SCHOOL SPIRIT

Chapter XIX

EARLY ATHLETIC ADMINISTRATIONS

The concepts of family, community, and brotherhood are intrinsic to the Benedictine way of life. Benedictines help, complement one another, especially when in service to a community. Every individual has unique skills and talents that may be employed to serve the greater good, the greater community. A remarkable illustration of this is the special relationship that Father Stephen Findlay and Mr. William O. Regan shared during their many years serving Delbarton School.

Bill Regan played football at the University of Notre Dame on those storied teams from the 1938 through 1941 seasons. He also coached semi-professional football. When Coach Regan started his career at Delbarton, there were only four teams at the School – football, baseball, basketball, and track. Like Father Stephen, who was charged with guiding Delbarton towards high school status, Coach Regan knew that in order for Delbarton to succeed as a premier secondary school, it would have to expand its athletic department. Under his tenure the School went from four sports to fourteen by 1986, and eventually to more than twenty. Regan recognized that support from the students' families, alumni, and friends was of paramount importance for expanding the athletic program and building the necessary facilities for those sports. He also knew that it was important for Delbarton teams to be able to compete under the New Jersey State Interscholastic Association and worked hard to make that finally happen in 1981. But perhaps even more basic, especially in the early days, was the willingness to take a "hands-on" approach and get the job done. A story is related of how when Regan first started, he asked Father Stephen about goal posts, and Father Stephen answered him by saying, "There's the barn. The tools are in there." And Regan "got the job done."

Coach Regan left active coaching and teaching in 1987 and, after 11 years of retirement, died in June, 1998. As coach of the Green Wave football team, Regan's record 236 wins, 83 losses, 10 ties, and 33 winning seasons is the best in Morris County and fifth best among New Jersey coaches. He

*Coach William O. Regan, Delbarton's athletic
director and head football coach, 1946-1987.*

was a founding member and first president of the Morris County Football Coaches Association and a former president of the New Jersey Independent School Athletic Association. He was the recipient of many awards including the State Football Coaches' Hall of Fame, the 1995 Distinguished Coaches award, and the Delbarton Hall of Fame. On October 7, 2000, the new William O. Regan field was dedicated.

If Father Stephen was known as the "Father of Delbarton," then Bill Regan might very well have been its uncle, the uncle always willing to join his "nephew" in an impromptu game of touch football, the seemingly tough guy with a heart. Both men were highly skilled leaders. Both were keen observers of people, and could assess the talents, skills, and abilities of those around them and tap into those resources. They possessed the singular facility for identifying a need, focusing on what it would take to meet that need, and then come up with a plan of action.

When Father Stephen died in 1994, the chairman of the Lay Board of Trustees, Tom Ferguson, said:

> *"I would watch the way he would organize (people) in a meeting to get the task at
> hand done, and no one would know he was the maestro behind it. You could see
> the man just knew how to handle the diversity of talent over there."*

Bill Regan Jr. offered these thoughts in 1984 about his father:

> *"He understood boys and how to get them to grow up to be young men. More importantly, he knows when to pat him on the back, when to chew him out and when to build up his self-image. He's been a father figure to many who have gone through Delbarton."*

What do these wonderful traits in these two dedicated men add up to? A family. A family where it is recognized that each individual can participate, can add value. That even the youngest, the oldest, the infirm, has something to contribute, because Christ resides in each of us. This is fundamental to the Rule of St. Benedict. When one falls, another is there to pick him up. When one fails, another is there to lend a hand. Together we build a community.

The Beacon interviewed Father Stephen in 1992, and he had this to say:

> *"I'm not the kind who picks up his marbles and leaves if things don't go his way. I got into community because that was what I wanted so I abided by community decisions."*

On the approach of his 25th anniversary with Delbarton, in 1970, Bill Regan was interviewed regarding his longevity with the School and was asked for his reflections. He made a very telling statement when he said:

> *"But even though I wanted to "go college" there was still that feeling that I would be giving up not a job but a way of life. The family spirit generates with the Benedictines and seems to work right on down the line. I couldn't let that cooperation which I had received over the years pass me by."*

Many of the School's leaders over the years had been athletes. The School's first Headmaster, Father Augustine Wirth, played high school, college, and professional baseball. Two of his assistants, Father A. Paul Foley, O.S.B., and Father Philip Hoover, both played high school and college sports. The disciplinarian in the early 1950s, Father Felix Pepin, played high school and college baseball, and others, including Fathers Kenneth Mayer, Arthur Mayer, Thomas Confroy and Karl Roesch, all played high school sports; and while students at Delbarton, Father Giles Hayes and Father Manus Duffy, regularly played two or three seasons each year. Emphasis on athletics in those early years, therefore, was inevitable.

Father Stephen and Coach Regan saw athletics as an important teaching instrument of values. In addition, for Benedictines who believe in the development and education of mind, body, and spirit, who realize how everything is connected in life, understand that what happens on the ballfields can positively affect what happens in the classroom. Rarely, if ever, at Delbarton in the early days was a student forbidden to play a sport because he experienced difficulty in the classroom. On the other hand, an athlete would be benched if he committed any offense against sportsmanship. Father Stephen, in his 25 years as Headmaster, would constantly remind the students about the importance of their pursuit of excellence, a pursuit which had to be undertaken in one's behavior as a person, an athlete, and a student. A man of impeccable integrity himself, Coach Regan never tolerated unsportsmanlike behavior. While he rarely had to throw a player off the team, all of his athletes knew that he would, if a transgression occurred, and they respected him for it. It was said of Coach Regan, that he taught his players how to win as gentlemen and how to lose with one's head up and pride maintained. "He made us all feel like winners," said John F. Conner, co-captain of the 1952 football team.

"....Benedictines who believe in the development and education of mind, body, and spirit, who realize how everything is connected in life, understand that what happens on the ball-fields can positively affect what happens in the classroom."

Father Paul Foley was the first part-time director of athletics when he served under Father Augustine Wirth. A number of other monks, including Father Adrian McLaughlin and Father Kenneth Mayer, served as part-time organizers of the athletic program after Father Stephen became headmaster, but the first full-time athletic director at the School was Bill Regan. Following his retirement from coaching, teaching, and his position as athletic director, he stayed on at the School as a member of Delbarton's Board of Trustees until shortly before his death. Consequently, Coach Regan's influence spanned more than a fifty-year period at Delbarton, as did Father Stephen Findlay's. Mr. John Kowalik assumed both the responsibility of head football coach and director of athletics when Bill Regan retired in 1987. He was followed in 2000 by Mr. Brian Fleury. It is a credit to the popular influence of both Father Stephen and Coach Regan that the goals of Delbarton's athletic program, as illustrated by Mr. Brian Fleury in 2000, reflected so clearly the continuity between the goals and intentions of the 1940s and those of the present. Coach Fleury's text follows:

> *"The Delbarton School Athletic Program is committed to the values that are consistent with the mission and overall objectives of the School. Recognizing that athletics are key in the development of a student, the School provides athletic programs that are comprehensive and varied, offering athletic opportunities to all of its students. In deference to the School's Benedictine mission to develop a student's "Mind, Body, and Spirit," the Athletic Program specifically pursues excellence in competition through personal development and team work, admires responsible and ethical behavior on the field and off, and nurtures leadership and strength of character. Above all, Delbarton promotes the long lessons inherent in athletic achievement and good sportsmanship—that a student-athlete demonstrates humility in victory and grace in defeat."*

Regan, Kowalik, and Fleury enjoyed a worthy predecessor in Father Augustine Wirth. All four of these founders and keepers of the athletic tradition at Delbarton had a grand vision of sports at the School. Father Augustine's early dreams were reflected in the July 20, 1940, report on Delbarton's new facilities in the *Maplewood News*:

> *"Extensive alterations on the athletic campus at the Delbarton School for Boys will result in one of the finest set-ups in the state. Though the institution is only for boys from the 6th through the 8th grades, the work is being done with an eye to the future when high school classes will be included. At that time, Delbarton will be represented by many interscholastic teams. The golf course has been increased from three to six holes. The fourth hole will be almost 500 yards with a par 4.*
>
> *The gridiron is being resodded and is being permanently laid out. When needed, temporary bleachers can be put up to accommodate over 500 spectators. The diamond is being leveled off, and will have a smooth playing surface. In addition to these improvements, a volleyball court and croquet set with sideboards had been built. All of these improvements will fit in with the intramural plan of the Headmaster, the Rev. Augustine Wirth, O.S.B., who desires to have all students take part in the program."*

The facilities the newspaper commented on were those 200 yards to the north of Old Main and just to the south of the current bleachers overlooking the William O. Regan football field on the very north of the campus. Currently, those facilities that Father Augustine built are used by the middle school for baseball and for the varsity football team practice. At that time, the current football field to the north of the property and the baseball field further to the north on the edge of Route 24 were woods and brush. Shortly after Coach Regan's appointment to athletic director of Delbarton, Father Stephen, with money given to him by the Delbarton Mothers' Guild from their annual Lawn and Garden Parties held at the School, built the Regan Field and baseball diamond. The construction of these fields began in June, 1946. On August 25, 1946, the *Morristown Daily Record* commented:

> *"This new field, which is planned to accommodate the vast athletic program to be inaugurated this coming season, will be completed sometime in September. The field will be one of the best in this section of the country and will compare favorably with the accommodations provided by the other large preparatory schools in the state."*

FOOTBALL

While these fields were being built, Bill Regan was receiving an honorable discharge from the United States Air Force after four years of service through most of World War II. For much of this time he was training the troops for combat as well as keeping them physically fit. His experiences with Notre Dame football taught him well, and Father Stephen recognized the gifts that he could bring to the Delbarton students. Indeed, through his 40 years of coaching at Delbarton, his fellow coaches and newspaper commentators respected the fact that the Delbarton teams were in better physical shape than their opponents and could play at the end of the fourth quarter as energetically as they did at the beginning of the game. Bill Regan had mastered the techniques of speed training and calisthenics long before the more technically oriented physical trainers of the latter part of the century did. "His approach was timeless," said Daniel R. Honeker, '87, a co-captain of Regan's last team in 1986. "If he wasn't happy with what you were doing in blocking and tackling drills, even at an advanced age he would turn his hat around, get down on all fours and say, 'This is how you do it!'."

Legend has it that John Brodhead, the *Morris County Daily Record's* sportswriter, gave Delbarton's teams the nickname "Green Wave." Monks have passed on from generation to generation the story Brodhead included in a September, 1947, issue of the *Record*, that while he stood at the crest of the hill overlooking the football field before the beginning of Delbarton's first varsity football game, he saw the team in borrowed green uniforms running down the hill to the field. Impressed by the green uniforms against the background of the vast green lawn in front of Old Main, he labeled the team the "Green Wave."

It took no more than one year for Coach Regan to establish Delbarton as a prominent football team in the State. "We were completely untalented," remembers Edward F. Broderick, Jr., '50, who played on Regan's first team, "but we looked like the Green Bay Packers!" Six members of the 1948 season team made the State All-Prep School First Team, including Ed Connolly, Peter Good, John Spinale, Joe Hillock, Joe Cartier, and Jay Cuff. A few years later, Cartier became one of Mr. Regan's first full-time assistant coaches. According to the Delbarton *Archway,* the 1948 Delbarton football team was rated "one of the most powerful grid machines in the State." The Green Wave was also given the Class B Catholic football crown. John Spinale, a guard, won a place on the All-State football team. Peter Good, right tackle, placed on the second team All-State.

While football existed at Delbarton in the nine years prior to this 1948 team, competition then was mostly with elementary schools and middle schools. The 1948 season represented the first time that the School received State recognition at the varsity level. Father Adrian McLaughlin continued as Mr. Regan's assistant coach until Joe Cartier came to the School in 1953, and Father Kenneth Mayer helped Mr. Regan with the junior varsity teams. At the end of the 1940s and into the 1950s, winning seasons of seven victories and one defeat, or eight victories and two defeats, were common. In 1949, 1950, and 1951, the following names appear in the *Archway* and the *Courier* as significant players on these victorious football teams: Milbauer, Saul, Wry, Austin, McMenanin, DeInnocentes, Donahue, Bogan, Fornaro, the brothers Standen, Hillock, Broderick, Foley, O'Brien, Mealey, D'Agostino, Farmer, O'Hara, D'Alia, Havas, Connors, Good, Callahan, and Geraghty.

Coach Regan rarely used superlatives. The Pingry game on Friday afternoon, November 13, 1953, however, he called "The Game!" From 1946 through 1953, perhaps no single athletic contest at Delbarton was more exciting. In addition, this victory over Pingry, on top of another victory over

Newark Academy, gave Coach Regan his first undefeated season. Furthermore, for the first time in Delbarton's history, a number of players on that 1953 team went on to distinguished athletic careers at colleges, including Boyd Sands, Arthur Doyle, Donald Landry, Tom Sanfacon, Joseph DeDeo, Harry Tappen, and Richard Riley. Prior to the members of this team, few Delbarton football players competed at major colleges, with the exception of Vince Jazwinski, who played football at Brown and then in the National Football League.

Coach Regan and Delbarton enjoyed the friendship of significant sports-writers and editors of the *Morris County Daily Record* from the late 1940s through the 1970s. Chief among them were John S. Brodhead, the sports editor of the *Record* and his successors, Ray Goin and Ray DeGraw, who manned the sports desks at the *Morris County Daily Record* well into the 1970s. The unquestioned integrity of Bill Regan and the dignified approach to the public by Father Stephen guaranteed that newspaper reporters and sportswriters would treat the School kindly. A typical report, among the many of John Brodhead, appeared in the October 30, 1954 edition of the *Record*. Brodhead wrote:

> "…..not….. to detract from Regan's ability—but we must confess that Bill (Regan) not only gets the best of equipment of any school in the Ivy League but he gets the best of cooperation from his superiors and co-teachers."
> – John S. Brodhead

"To Bill Regan we must again doff the cap in winning his fourth straight Ivy League flag and going undefeated in the league over that period of time. His undefeated record is now twelve in a row and his teams have lost but one contest in the last twenty. Taking it back still further, Delbarton has lost only twice in the last twenty-eight times out and Regan's career record at Delbarton is forty-three wins, two ties, and six defeats for a nifty .878 record, by far the best in the county. Perhaps it would be wise here to stop for just a moment—not in any attempt, mind you, to try to detract from Regan's ability—but we must confess that Bill not only gets the best of equipment of any school in the Ivy League but he gets the best of cooperation from his superiors and co-teachers.

Gingerly threading through the mud at "the opponent's field," was Delbarton Headmaster Father Stephen Findlay, rooting just as hard as any of the students, and with him was just about the whole faculty of the School. Spirit like this is difficult to deny. Even the old grads can't stay away. Paul Ferguson, our choice as the county's outstanding player two years ago, rarely misses a game."

To be sure, in the 1940s, '50s, and '60s, very few monks teaching in the School, if any, missed the games the students played. The morning after each game, an athlete at Delbarton was sure to hear some praise or an encouraging word from a number of the monks teaching at the School. There were monks present at all the athletic contests and, indeed, at all of the co-curricular events of the Delbarton students. Father Stephen encouraged their presence, insisting that: "It is not about you or me, it is about us."

Always the master of the game, Bill Regan brought a number of football innovations to Morris County, which helped account for his popularity among his fellow high school coaches and for the respect given him by sportswriters. As a 1943 graduate of the University of Notre Dame, Coach Regan played his football under Frank Leahy. When Leahy arrived at Notre Dame in 1941, he abandoned Knute Rockne's box formation for offense and introduced the T-formation used by some professional teams. Having used that offense with his teammate and quarterback, Angelo Bertelli, Coach Regan knew it well and introduced it to the Delbarton team in 1946. That year, then, became the beginning of the end for secondary school use of the single wing and box formation in Morris County.

John S. Brodhead and his successors at the *Daily Record* commented often about the physical conditioning of the Delbarton athletes. Coach Regan insisted that a major portion of each practice be devoted to running and calisthenics, and often, particularly in the early years, he personally led those workouts. He took pride in the speed and conditioning of his linemen and rarely, if ever, used fewer than six men on the line in defense. He favored the six defensive linemen backed up by three linebackers and two scat back safeties. Occasionally, he poured it on the opponents with a seven-man line.

When Bill Regan joined the Delbarton faculty, the student body numbered fewer than 100 boys. 125 students were enrolled in 1952, and 175 in 1956. The School grew quickly, and athletics grew apace. In 1948, peer private schools in northern New Jersey, including St. Bernards, Montclair Academy, Newark Academy, Morristown Prep, Eastern Christian Academy, and Montclair College High came together to form the Ivy League. Delbarton took the Ivy League trophy in football in 1949 and won every game in the Ivy League in football from 1951 through 1959, when the League disbanded. Newark Academy tied Delbarton in 1954, and the games with Newark and Morristown Prep provided much competition. In order to fill the schedule, Oratory, Pingry, Hun, Tower Hill in Delaware, and two public schools, Mountain Lakes and Dover, were added periodically through the 1950s and 1960s.

While membership in the Ivy League helped the School organize athletic schedules in all sports, strong voices from among the Delbarton parents and even sportswriters led the School to seek other competition. John Brodhead wrote boldly about this on November 2, 1954:

> *"Delbarton had better get out of the Ivy League for its own good before it's too late. The local institution is a growing school, a mighty good one, too, that is rapidly getting ahead. Its progress is being deterred by its association with the Ivy League . . . the boys from Sugarloaf as well as the School, are going no place in a hurry in the Ivy. They've taken fifteen out of twenty-eight trophies offered by the League since 1949; and won every football game since 1951."*

The Stephen Findlay partnership with William Regan benefited Delbarton athletics tremendously. Coach John Bauer of Randolph High School, a long-time friend of Coach Regan, often kidded his friend about all of the football conventions Coach Regan was able to attend. Even as Coach Regan brought the T-formation to Morris County, he brought a succession of other advances in coaching football from the many conventions he attended. Father Stephen would somehow find a way to make sure Coach Regan had funding to advance his own knowledge and skills through continuing education. "He lived, ate and slept football," said Edward F. Broderick, Jr., '50.

The Delbarton football team won 32 games from 1946 through 1951 and lost or tied eleven. During the remainder of the 1950s, they dominated their opponents, winning 56 games, losing three and tying three. From 1953 through 1959, Bill Regan enjoyed five undefeated football seasons. In the 1960s, with the Ivy League behind them, the team had three undefeated seasons and two more in the 1970s. Star players in the 1940s included John Spinale, Jay Cuff, Peter Good, Joe Cartier, Joe Hillock; and in the 1950s, Vince Jazwinski, Boyd Sands, Tom Sanfacon, Paul Ferguson, John Conner, Joe DeDeo, Richard Riley, Ted Mercolino, Jim Corroon, Lee Trumbull, Bill Clark and Daryl Russell, all of whom won multiple All-State and All-County honors.

Coach Regan's assistant coaches in the 1950s and 1960s included Buzzy Flynn, Joe Cartier, Mike Barry, Father Adrian McLaughlin, Don Grevara, Dan Barron, Ron Matakitis, and later in the 1970s, Tom Sweeney, Brian Regan (Coach Bill Regan's son), Carmen Palladino, Earl Dorber, and Jack Regan (Coach Regan's nephew). Towards the end of Bill Regan's reign, Ken Heaton, Chuck Ruebling, and John Kowalik served as his assistants.

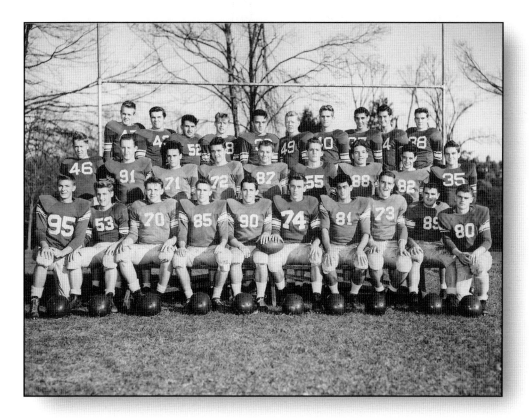

Delbarton's first undefeated football team, 1953.

*Tom Sanfacon, '54, leaping over a Pingry tackler in "The Game," Nov. 1953, when
Sanfacon scored two touchdowns, including a 102 yard run, to seal the 18-6 victory over
the favored and undefeated Pingry team.*

Until his retirement and beyond, Coach Regan was careful not to identify his best teams or his best athletes. Every once in a while, however, he slipped. As indicated above, he often identified the Delbarton-Pingry Game on Friday, November 13, 1953 as "The Game." Both the Big Blue of Pingry and Delbarton at that time were going for undefeated seasons, in the case of Delbarton, its first undefeated season. "The Game" occurred on a rainy and cold Friday afternoon. Pingry annually had been Delbarton's most competitive opponent, so the hype for this game was intense. Coach Regan indicated to a number of his closest friends among the parents that his team of the 1953 season was probably the best he had coached since he began in 1946. The boys demonstrated that on the field that afternoon. While the game was tied in the second half, one of the most dramatic plays in the history of Delbarton football occurred when the Pingry quarterback dropped back for a pass that would have put the Big Blue ahead. Out of the defensive backfield beyond the Pingry goal line was Tom Sanfacon who intercepted the pass and proceeded to run 102 yards for a touchdown, making the score 12 to 6. Tom Sanfacon, '54, who many observers felt was the School's finest athlete in that generation, raced those yards stiff-arming a number of Pingry would-be tacklers in record time. Delbarton clinched the win behind the strong play of Don Landry, Art Doyle, and a second touchdown by Sanfacon, making the score 18 to 6, thus giving Delbarton its first undefeated and untied season in the School's history. In seven games in the 1953 season, Delbarton scored 168 points and gave up only 37. They ended as the State Prep School Champions with All-County first team nominations for Bob Sonzogni, Boyd Sands (a sophomore), and Tom Sanfacon.

Bill Clark, second highest scorer in
New Jersey, 1957

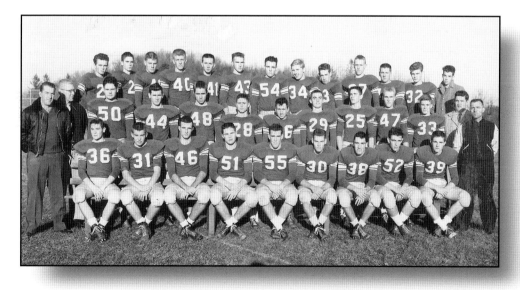

Coach Regan's championship 1958 football team.

Coach Regan encouraging his 1968 Championship team.

Continuing that success, the 1954 team would be Ivy League champs with All-County and All-State honors to Boyd Sands, Joe DeDeo, and Ed Butera. In 1955, Ted Mercolino would rack up 132 points to lead the entire State, private schools and public schools, in points for the year while the team would total 294 points on offense and only 90 against them. Dan McBride, Ted Mercolino, Ed Butera, and Red Green would make the State and County teams.

In the following year, led by Bill Clark, Ted Mercolino, and Lee Trumbull, the Green Wave would have another undefeated season and enjoy the record for the highest scoring team in the State, with 347 points on offense and 38 on defense. Bill Clark, scoring 149 points, would hold the record for the second highest scorer in the State and would be named to the National secondary school All-American team.

The 1958 and 1959 seasons would follow suit, but, after leaving the Ivy League and concentrating on prep school play with teams who had post-graduates and longer histories in their football traditions, Delbarton faced greater competition. The School added to its regular schedule Peddie, Admiral Farragut, Blair, Perkiomen, Hun, Morris Catholic, Bayley-Ellard, Carteret, Croyden Hall, Immaculata, Pingry, Madison, Dover, Mountain Lakes, Whippany Park, Mt. Olive, and Montville whenever they could schedule them.

In the mid and late 1970s, Coach Regan, as athletic director, began to face significant difficulties in scheduling teams, particularly at the freshman and JV levels, since Delbarton was not in a conference. Consequently, he and members of the Fathers and Friends Booster Committees, convinced Father Giles, the headmaster at the time, as well as the monastic board of trustees, to leave the prep school ranks and seek entry into the New Jersey State Interscholastic Athletic Association (NJSIAA). The legal process to effect this movement from the prep schools to the public school league took two years and a number of court battles at the athletic conference, in the New Jersey Administrative Law courts, as well as in the New Jersey State Supreme Court. With the help of a Delbarton parent at the time, Mr. John Gilfillan, and his law firm at Byrne, Bain, Gilfillan, Delbarton won the legal contest to enter the NJSIAA.

While the judicial process moving Delbarton into the public school leagues progressed, urban schools from the former Newark League also sought entrance into the suburban public school leagues. Specifically, Delbarton hoped to enter the Suburban Conference, which included Millburn, Madison, Chatham, and other public high schools that resembled Delbarton demographically. The Suburban Conference rejected Delbarton, and at the same time, rejected the applications of the former Newark League public schools, including West Side, Weequahic, and others. Mr. John Gilfillan represented Delbarton's case as well as the case of the urban public schools, asserting that the total educational program of these schools, including their athletic programs, would be limited unless they were able to join a suburban public school conference. The courts decided in favor of Mr. Gilfillan's argument and the NJSIAA created a new conference, the Northern Hills Conference, to include Delbarton as well as some of those urban schools. In addition, other northern New Jersey

Mr. John Kowalik, head football coach, with assistants Mr. Edward Kim and
Mr. Jerome Rizzo, and the 1988 varsity football team.

suburban conferences were required to take other private schools as well as urban public schools into their conferences for the sake of promoting equality in education.

The 1983 football season for Delbarton included opponents from seven public schools and two private schools, resulting in five wins, three losses, and one tie. Delbarton remained competitive with the public schools during the remainder of Bill Regan's tenure as athletic director, which included 47 wins, 24 losses, and 2 ties. Bill Regan's understudy from the beginning of 1984 was John Kowalik, a young graduate of Williams College where he distinguished himself in football. Subsequently he learned a great deal from Coach Regan when he served as Regan's assistant coach. He took over in the 1987 season and coached Delbarton through the 2002 season, when he became headmaster of the Peck School in Morristown. John Kowalik's record was more than 130 wins and fewer than 30 losses, a record which included two State championships for private and public schools, one in 1993 and the other in 1998. Coach Kowalik was succeeded in 2003 by his offensive coordinator, Coach Brian Bowers, who through 2005 enjoyed 27 victories and 6 defeats.

From the late 1980s through the present, Delbarton's football program has sent dozens of young men to post-season All-State and All-County recognition, as well as to football competition at the Division I AA and Division III levels, especially in the Ivy League and in the most competitive Division III schools like Williams, Amherst, and Middlebury.

Bill Regan kept his peace whenever he was asked about his best players and his best teams. While the memory of the 1953 victory against Pingry and the startling 102 yard run of Tom Sanfacon which won the game never left him, the only other time he expressed his excitement about a team he guided occurred when he was queried by sportswriters as to his best team. Uncharacteristically choosing one among many great teams, he asserted that his team of 1963 was the best. He said to Ray DeGraw of the *Morristown Record*: "This team rates head-and-shoulders above them all because of its excellent balance. In the past, we've always had one or two outstanding players, but on this team, we don't have to rely on just a couple of boys. We have a number of lads who can do a fine job for us." For those coaches, parents, and athletes who believe in good luck, the 1963 season was blessed by a captain, Brian Flaherty, who won every coin toss before every game. Quarterback Mickey Guerriero completed fourteen touchdown passes. Coach Regan's son, Brian, scored ten touchdowns, Alan Guenther received eight touchdown passes, and Dennis Williamson, arguably the best field goal kicker in the State, scored 35 points fulfilling his responsibility. Delbarton went eight wins and no defeats in their fifth undefeated season, and Guenther, Bob Farrell, Dick McGuire, Mickey Guerriero, Bob Chandis, Brian Regan and Dennis Williamson all received post-season All-County and All-State honors. Also in the 1960s, Jack Guerriero, Jack Regan, John Bauer, Steve Regan, Tiny Lansdell, Frank Stynes, Matt Bolger, Ducky Grennan, Bill Turner and Gary Milanesi received multiple All-County and All-State honors.

Following that outstanding team of 1963, Bill Regan's teams of 1967 and 1968 scored 631 points against 57 points and amassed fifteen victories, no defeats, and one tie. In 1967, Jack Regan scored 26 touchdowns and 39 extra points for a total of 199 points, for a new County and State record.

The team did not have another undefeated season until 1977 and 1978 when they enjoyed two consecutive State prep school championships under the leadership of Ken Heaton, Matt Broas, Kevin Kenny, and Matt Monahan. They were State prep champs again in 1980 and 1981, after which they took on more public school teams before entering the Northern Hills Conference in 1982. Even while playing tougher competition in the 1980s and 1990s, often playing public schools two and three times Delbarton's size, they enjoyed winning seasons through the twenty years until 2000, except one. Through the present, the Regan winning football tradition, victorious also in teaching sportsmanship and values, continues each year in the State championship varsity football program.

BASKETBALL

The Delbarton basketball tradition began much like all of the sports at the School: with small teams, part-time coaches and "make-do" facilities. The athletic facility in which Father Anselm Murray and Father Kenneth Mayer coached the teams of the mid-1940s was the old carriage house on the Kountze Estate. It contained a relatively small floor with a hoop at each end. Unfortunately, a devastating fire consumed the carriage house in 1946, which resulted in the Fathers and Friends, the Mothers' Guild and other benefactors constructing what is now known as the St. Joseph Gym. The *Ledger* and the *Morristown Record* in the spring of 1948, when the new gym was completed, touted it as one of the most spacious in the county.

Part-time athletic director Father A. Paul Foley appointed Father Anselm coach of the first team in 1940. The first recorded basketball game in the *Newark News* or the *Morristown Record* ended as a loss to St. Michael's High School freshman team, 30 to 29. A few weeks before that, the *Morristown Record* reported a victory over St. Michael's in football 14 to 0. Many of the same names appear on both rosters: Jack Gillespie, Tom Young, Bill Cannon, Stan Debold, Al Holle, Lou Introcaso, Joe Weiner, Dominick Introcaso, Bill Murphy and Joe Scully. Playing mostly pick-up games with local clubs and area middle schools through the 1940s, the basketball team had its first varsity season in 1948 coached by Mr. Phillip Cummings. In both years, Delbarton basketball won the Ivy League tournament and in its inaugural year it won the Eastern Prep Tournament. Ed Rochford succeeded Coach Cummings and was himself succeeded by Gerald "Buzz" Griffin, a close friend of Coach Regan, a prominent All-State player in his day who later played both basketball and baseball at Notre Dame. Griffin's first teams, led by Ed Velten and Rich Clark, also regularly won the Ivy League title. Coach Griffin stayed on for his two winning seasons, and was replaced in the 1954 season by Harry Stillwell, who joined the School to coach both basketball and his favorite, baseball.

Coach Stillwell remained an important coach and mentor to many Delbarton athletes into the 1960s. One of his earliest teams playing in the 1955-56 season won the New Jersey State Prep School Championship in one of the most exciting basketball games in Delbarton's history, against Newark Academy in the Lawrenceville Field House. According to John Brodhead, Coach Harry Stillwell said "It was the defense that did it!" Newark Academy's premier player, Mike Phelan,

State Championship basketball captains of 1956 with
Coach Harry Stillwell

scored 49 points in the game Newark played just before the Delbarton game. So, Coach Stillwell had Delbarton's premier player, Bob Collins, defend against Phelan keeping him constantly off balance and allowing him to score only one field goal the entire game. While Collins scored his usual double figures, Rich Velten kept Delbarton in the game with his eight points in the first half. Bob Jenco scored six points in the fourth quarter, the last four vital ones. According to Brodhead, "His one-handed push shot from behind the key with 1:28 to play gave Delbarton a 38-37 lead. Then, 30-seconds later on a breaking driving play, he hit from underneath to just about sew things up at 40-37." That victory was Delbarton's first New Jersey State title in any sport and it was, according to Brodhead, the first time in 56 years of basketball competition that a Morris County team won a state basketball championship in any division.

As with football, the later basketball teams continued winning the Ivy League, but Coach Stillwell felt that the best balanced and most experienced and successful team he coached since he began at Delbarton was the 1961 team. According to the Archway, their record of 15 wins and 4 defeats made them a county threat. The first team was composed of five veteran letter winners from the previous year and each complemented the other with his own distinctive qualities. Captain Bob Findlay, George Roth and Jim Farrell regularly averaged in double figures, with Findlay and Farrell making a very valuable back court combination. Daryl Russell led the defense and Frank McGuire was a regular on the reserves. Two sophomores on that varsity team, Jim Stearns and Dan Hollis, would emerge as the team leaders in 1962 and 1963.

Harry Stillwell was succeeded by Bernard Brennan during the 1966-67 season, but Coach Stillwell continued with varsity baseball. A succession of coaches followed Mr. Brennan, including Wayne Schiffner in 1972, Terry O'Brien in 1973, Tom Cruthers in 1977 until Coach Tom O'Brien received the head coaching position in the 1979-80 season, which he kept through the 1983-84 season, to be followed by Mr. Jack Regan in 1984-85 through 1990-1991, when Coach Dan Whelan became the longest and most victorious head basketball coach at Delbarton.

When the School expanded after the building of Trinity Hall, the opportunities for athletics also expanded, including the beginning of the School's popular wrestling program. Swimming and winter track also grew at the time. Possibly because fewer students went out for basketball, the teams from the early 1960s through the mid-1970s had either losing seasons or moderately successful seasons. All of that changed with the arrival of Bobby Kelly to Delbarton as a freshman in 1974. Arguably the finest point guard in the state of New Jersey in the mid to late 1970s, Bobby made the varsity club as a freshman and proceeded with his athleticism to electrify the Delbarton fans and his fellow students. During his last three years, the team had stellar winning seasons, often winning more than 20 games a season as well as the county championship. More importantly for the School, at a time when School spirit during the winter season declined, Bob's presence enlivened winter athletics. When no more than a few dozen students attended the basketball games previously, virtually the entire student body began to attend Delbarton basketball from 1974 to 1978. The spirit of "Kelly's Army" frequently attracted the comments of the high school sportswriters in the *Record* and the *Newark Star-Ledger*. That same spirit continued on in basketball through Coach Tom O'Brien's and Coach Jack Regan's tenure, and became something of a Delbarton hallmark in many of its sports.

One of the characteristics of the 1973-74 team was its academic prowess. Coach Terry O'Brien had access to six or seven National Merit Scholars to put on the court, which would no doubt make the Delbarton team the brightest in the State. That tradition has been maintained in Delbarton basketball, because many of the players after graduation have gone on to play at the most compet-

itive NCAA Division III and NCAA Division I AA teams. Some had the opportunity to play Division I and professional basketball.

Six Delbarton basketball players scored 1,000 points or more: Bob Collins ('56), Dennis Williamson ('68), Bob Kelly ('78), Vin Ferrara ('92), Bill DiSpaltro ('94), and Troy Murphy ('98). Bob Collins scored 440 points in his senior year alone, and while playing professional basketball in Ireland, established the Irish National record for average points per game in a single season, 29.9. Dennis Williamson was well known for his kicking in football at Delbarton, but those who admired his play in basketball regarded him as one of the School's few "pure shooters" who could score on a regular basis from anywhere on the court without hitting the rim. Other fans of Delbarton basketball remember Chris Ward, nicknamed "the dipper" because of the arch in his set shot, and Brian Buchert, who in his career won a number of games for the School on last second 20-25 footers. Bob Kelly went on to play Division I ball at St. John's University; Vin Ferrara attended Harvard where he was the starting quarterback; Bill DiSpaltro stared at Vanderbilt University for four years, after which he played professional basketball with Beneton in Italy; Troy Murphy stared at Notre Dame before he went on to play with the Golden State Warriors.

SOCCER

Bill Regan was a football man! Soccer, then, didn't begin as an organized sport at Delbarton until a number of years after most schools throughout Morris County introduced it. The 1970 season was the first for Delbarton soccer. In fact, though Bill Regan rarely, if ever, made a negative comment about anybody or anything in his adult life, his athletes of the 1960s will remember that when, accidentally, a soccer ball rolled down the football hill on to the lower field, Bill kicked it back up saying, "That's soccer, a round ball game; a football is oval, not round. It is a sport."

Recognizing, however, that soccer could co-exist with football in the fall season at Delbarton, Coach Regan and Father Stephen Findlay asked Mr. William Bandura to introduce soccer at Delbarton. Bill Bandura coached soccer from 1971 through 1977, achieving a record of six wins, thirty-five losses, and three ties. The sport took a while to take hold. In 1977, the School hired Joseph Krakora to succeed Bill Bandura. By 1979, the soccer team won eleven games, lost five, tied one, and beat Newark Academy for the first Parochial School Tournament victory and became the first Delbarton team to finish over 500 in soccer.

Coach Bruce Peckham came on board through 1980 and 1981, when the team won twenty-five games, lost seven, and tied three, behind the play of Wes Bailey, A.J. Connelly, and Ahktar Khan. Anchoring the 1979-1980 defense was Donal Mastrangelo and George Gammond, with Richard Romano and Chris Higgins, and Mark Bixby in goal. Bob Sheridan, Ed Scott, and A.J. Connelly filled the defense gap in the following year along with Peter Gusmer and Paul Faber in mid-field. Wes Bailey, Tim Conway, and Greg Perry finished six years of soccer at Delbarton and contributed significantly in the games of the late 1970s and early 1980s.

*The Delbarton crowd surging out of the stands after the 1984 state
championship soccer victory.*

Delbarton soccer came of age when Coach David Bell took over the program in 1982. He continued as head coach through 1987 and had as his assistants, Mark Koenig and Bill Cook. The combination made for championships. Shortly after Delbarton joined the NJSIAA, the public school conference, Dave Bell brought his team to a Parochial state championship. In 1984, his team won nineteen, lost three, and tied one, but went to the Mercer County Park with almost the entire student body to root them on in playing St. Rose of Belmar, a perennial state champion. With the score tied, on a bitterly cold and rainy mid-November day, the throw-in went directly to the head of Scott Pickering, a six-foot, five-inch forward, who headed the ball to the edge of the net for the winning goal. Bedlam followed, as six or seven bus-loads of Delbarton students who that night traveled from Morristown to Trenton for the game surged onto the field. The Headmaster, Father Giles Hayes, could not help but give the students a day off to celebrate this first

> *... Bedlam followed, as six or seven bus-loads of Delbarton students who that night traveled from Morristown to Trenton for the game surged onto the field.*

public and parochial state championship of Delbarton School in its history. Between 1980 and 1985, the School would win three conference championships, three state championships, and one Morris County championship.

At the end of Coach Bell's tenure, Tom McCabe and Mark Ambrose anchored the defense as captains of the team, making sure that in David Bell's last three years, his team would win more than fifty games, lose no more than thirteen, and tie five. Coach Ken Cherry, then brought

Delbarton to conference championships in 1987 and 1989, to be followed by Ernie Sandonato with his assistants Stu Staley and Ted O'Donnell through 1992. At that time, Coach David Donovan would begin his tenure at Delbarton, which continues to the present. Again, Coach Donovan's assistants were Rick Faubert, Erin Sullivan (who would win a state championship when Coach Donovan was studying for his doctorate) and Jamie Ebersole.

CROSS COUNTRY, WINTER TRACK, AND SPRING TRACK AND FIELD

Few athletic teams at Delbarton have enjoyed more dominance in state competition than has fall cross country and winter and spring track and field. These programs began in 1946 under the leadership of Mr. Joseph Meaney, who, in 1948 became, Father Peter. Immediately, as soon as the School fielded a varsity team in 1948, it led the state prep schools and won the Ivy League in each of the running sports. The stars included long distance runners Robert Spatola and Alain deBerc, with a number of younger runners, including Dick Wolke, Jose Fernandez, Pat O'Donoghue and John Kelly. According to the *Daily Record* in its May, 1948 sports pages, Delbarton came close in spring track against Morristown Prep and Chatham High, but did not win. Jules Spada and Peter Good placed first and second in the field events and Rob Spatola again as well as Alain deBerc, only a ninth grader, were the winners of the mile, but the team came up short in the point scores. That was the last time that Delbarton in the 1940s and '50s would lose a

Father Peter Meaney coaching John "Red" Conner,
Delbarton's strongest high school, college, and masters
level runner.

track and field event. In fact, from the late 1940s through the 1980s Delbarton was the State's winningest team in cross country. The teams created this record under the tutelage first of Father Peter, the head coach from 1948 to 1956; Tony Passarelli, the head coach from 1956 through 1979; and, Coach Passarelli's understudy, Wayne Gardiner, the head coach from Tony Passarelli's death in 1979 until beyond 2000.

Father Peter Meaney and Coach Tony Passarelli helped establish the New Jersey Catholic Track Conference, for which Father Peter served as president. Later, Mr. Gardiner would lead the New Jersey Catholic Track Conference and serve as an important judge in the New Jersey cross country, track and field programs. All three Delbarton coaches over those more than fifty years have received a number of honors from the New Jersey cross country and track and field organizations.

Few Delbarton cross country and track and field teams in competition with their peers could equal the achievements of the 1952-1953 team. Undefeated in cross country, they also went undefeated in spring track and field. This was the first undefeated season of any track team and the first season that the Delbarton track team won all of its conference and state championships. Tom Sanfacon, who later attended Notre Dame, and John Conner who later attended Brown University, were the exceptional stars on the team. But Mark Lilly, a tenth grader, Don Landry, a junior, Bob Zenorini, a tenth grader and Frank McBride, a senior anchored the team. Tom Sanfacon was an important sprinter and middle distance runner, but he earned national prominence as a high jumper. At the high school nationals in Madison Square Garden, Tom Sanfacon high jumped 6'5", which in 1953 was an extraordinary feat.

Arguably the finest runner in the history of Delbarton ever, John Conner completed four years as a sprinter and middle distance person at Delbarton in 1953. During that time he was the New Jersey Prep School's indoor half-mile champion, their indoor quarter-mile champion, the indoor half-mile champion of the New Jersey Catholic schools, the North Jersey Ivy League cross country champion, half-mile champion, quarter-mile champion, and two twenty-yard dash champion. He anchored fourteen relay teams to seven championships and five second places, and established two state records and five Delbarton School records. John ran in ninety-five races in four years at Delbarton and placed first in forty-nine of those races. But, not only did John Conner and Tom Sanfacon achieve in Delbarton track, they also achieved in football, basketball, baseball and other sports. In those days, the Ivy League allowed the student athletes to play more than one sport in a season. So both Tom Sanfacon and John Conner, while sterling members of the spring track team, also played spring baseball. Most memorable in the spring of 1953 was a 400 foot home run hit into the right field hill by Tom Sanfacon, immediately after which he went out to the cinder track and won both the 100 yard dash and the 220 yard run.

Excellence in cross country, track and field continued through the 1950s. The 1956 team won a number of championships. Jim Bowers lead the team in points, closely followed by Art Condon, Red Green, Hugh Lorden, Rich Velten, Ted Mercolino, Paul Bransford, Hank Reinhold, and Karl Zimmerman, and then Rich Holle and Rick Fittin. The text in the 1956 *Archway* stated:

Delbarton's championship cross country team, 1968.

"New records and trophies, medals of all description and plenty of thrilling meets occurred this year. For the seventh time in eight years the Green Wave brought home the Ivy League championship....The Morris County championship saw the Green Wave enter five teams and walk away with three first places and one third. Paul Bransford, Red Green, Art Condon, and Hugh Lorden won the county mile relay crown and lowered the School's record by four seconds. Green led the winners in this race with a 53 second quarter. Also, the freshman relay team composed of Jim Cascio, Ricky Fittin, Mike Slattery and Walter Scott stole the spotlight by winning the county 440 and 880 for a clean sweep of the freshman division. Running in the state Catholic schools meet a week later they placed second in the 880, and lowered the freshman record that had been on the books for six years. Art Condon successfully defended his Ivy League half-mile title and established a new league record. Karl Zimmerman will not be forgotten in the Ivy League meet where he overtook Pitman of Morristown. Hugh Lorden served notice of things to come and the versatile Mercolino jumped, ran and threw for many of the winning points. Paul Bransford, Hank Reinhold and especially Richie Velten will always stand as the trio who sunk Morristown Prep in the league meet with their tremendous leaps in the broad jumps. Walter Mooney in the half-mile, Bill Kearns in the sprints, Bob Bulman in the middle distances and Franz Vintschger in the quarter mile made Delbarton the team hard to beat."

Success at the varsity level in any sport usually means training and excellent performance at the lower level, including middle school, freshman, and junior varsity. After Father Peter Meaney completed his masters degree in religious studies at Catholic University in 1957, he returned to Delbarton to assist Tony Passarelli, the head coach since 1956, in building the foundation of Delbarton cross country, winter track, and spring track and field. He established the first freshman cross country team in 1960, a team which eventually became the first varsity Delbarton team to go undefeated in dual meets in 1963. In 1964 the freshman cross country team won their first junior varsity New Jersey private school cross country championship, and in 1961 Father Peter organized the first freshman spring track and field program. To supplement these sports, he created the middle school cross country team in 1966 and the middle school spring track and field program in 1969. Under his tutelage the freshman cross country team in 1966 won the Morris County freshman championship, as did the eighth grade cross country team in 1966, after going undefeated in all dual meets. The eighth grade cross country team in 1969 also won the Morris County cross country championship. All of these championships and those which followed, guaranteed the extraordinary success that Delbarton cross country, winter track and spring track and field would have in the 1970s. Among the runners Father Peter first coached in the early 1960s included men who shared many championships thereafter: Mike Shale, Bernie Demoreuille, Phil Hoyt, Bill Dunn, Tony Sellito, Jim Fay, Kevin O'Neil, Carl Chapman, Alan Fidellow, Gregory Diebold, Brian Brennan, Bill Joule, Jim McCrudden, and Frank Arlinghaus.

The author of the *Archway* article on varsity cross country gave credit to Father Peter's work with the younger athletes when he wrote: "Next years' varsity squad should be substantially

Penn Relay champions, April, 1969: Left to Right:
David Cole, John Arlinghaus, Coach Tony Passarelli,
Bud Hartman, and Al D'Agostino.

David Cole (L) winning the Morris County quarter mile championship, 1970.

Andrew Verhalen winning a cross country meet, fall, 1972

Coach Passarelli timing Tony Macri,
October, 1973.

strengthened by the addition of several members of an outstanding freshman team well coached by Father Peter. This group of boys, led by Phil Hoyt, crushed all opposition in dual meets and placed third in both the freshman state Catholic and the junior varsity state prep meets".

Delbarton cross country, winter track and spring track enjoyed dominance throughout the state of New Jersey in the 1970s under the coaching of Tony Passarelli. Among his extraordinary championship runners in the early and mid-1970s were: Andy Verhalen, Tony Macri, Matt Leddy, Don Conners, John Gorman, Bill Mullarney, Kevin Kenny, Pat Roche, Kevin Walsh and others. In 1975, Coach Passarelli's twentieth year at Delbarton, the team won for the second time the state prep school championship trophy in cross country. In winter track they won the Morris County invitational, the New Jersey Catholic track conference championship, the state prep title, and enjoyed a number of excellent personal performances. In spring track they won the Morris County relay championship as well as the mile relay in which they set the county record.

Going back more than ten years, Tony Passarelli's teams became known for their relay performances. His mile relay teams, including such extraordinary runners as Alfred D'Agostino, David Cole and others, won several championships at the Penn relays, and in 1968 an all junior team of Al D'Agostino, Rich Hartman, John Arlinghaus and John Bermingham set the national junior class record of 3.22.3 in the mile relay. On that same day an all sophomore team of Jim McDonald, Fred Honold, Richard Lange and David Cole set a national sophomore mile relay record of 3.30.

In 1976, Coach Passarelli's team completed its best dual meet season ever, finishing with 14 victories and no defeats and extended its two year winning streak to 29 in a row to win the state prep title for the second year in a row, and the Eastern States championship for the first time ever. The athletes trained in the early part of the decade came through as juniors and seniors, including Kevin Kenny, Art Rawding, Pat Roche, Barry Enright, Jeff Word, Nigel Delahunty, and Martin Flaherty. In winter track that year, Jeff Word set the county record in the 600 yard run and became the state prep and county 440 champion. Barry Enright and Howard Courtemanche, both sophomores, set indoor school records, thus predicting outstanding performances later.

Wayne Gardiner, a high school state champion from Maine and a college long distance runner from Bowdoin became Tony Passarelli's assistant coach in 1975. Closer to 1979, Coach Gardiner assumed more and more of the responsibilities of the team because Coach Passarelli began to suffer from cancer. Wayne Gardiner learned his coaching skills "from the feet of the master" but he did not develop the lovable quirks of Coach Passarelli. While Tony Passarelli was quite demanding of his runners, the athletes frequently joked about him and learned a great deal from the values and demands he made on them. For example, Tony Passarelli expected far more from his runners than they thought they could give. Consequently, they became better than they ever believed they could be. In his more than 20 years of coaching at Delbarton, at least three or four exhausted runners, lying on the ground after a tough race, would hear the coach lean down over them and yell at the top of his voice, "Get up! If you can hear me, you are not dead; get up." As one anonymous runner wrote in the 1978 *Archway:*

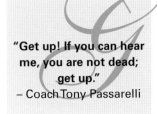

"Get up! If you can hear me, you are not dead; get up."
– Coach Tony Passarelli

"The coach did not usually allow us to go out on our own for practice. Most of the time he sat in his Caddy following us. After finding us engaged in three or four football games he decided it would be necessary to follow us every day. He has an unbelievably loud voice. When he yells at us, everyone in a half-mile radius knows what he is saying. On really tough days, he waits on the top of hill with a stick in hand waiting to thrash us if we slow down. Possibly his hardest work outs come in September. No one is in shape because of summer vacation, and he has us run up and down some very steep hills. Hill work really drains the energy from your body, with each step your legs grow heavier. Gravity pulls and pulls at your arms until they feel like lead. The muscles in your legs begin to stiffen up. Your knees begin to drag. Your heart pounds harder and harder. Then you notice that you are losing your senses. You get a clicking in your ears and you start to lose your vision. Everything becomes warm and your lungs ache. You say to yourself "what am I doing? I feel like I'm going to die. Oh me....I wish the coach's car would break down or something. I really need to stop. This is becoming unbearable." Finally, you reach the top and start your flight down the hill.

With the sweat clearing from your eyes, you begin to see a little better but the constant pounding on the road keeps your ears clogged and your legs numb. You barely feel your toes touch the ground as you seemingly bounce your way to the bottom. Throughout this entire journey away from reality, the coach is screaming at you to pick up the pace.

People asked me why I submit myself to this torture day after day. I have no good explanation other than self-satisfaction. I doubt if any runner knows why they enjoy running. To most people runners are crazy. Subjecting oneself to harsh weather and willingly inflicting pain upon one's body are reasons enough to be committed, true. I have met quite a few runners who I consider insane, but then again, have you ever watched a football team doing practice drills?"

Coach Passarelli earned the love of all of his athletes from 1956 through 1979 with his methods, because they knew that even though he was hard on them, he cared for them, loved them. In his last winter and spring track season his teams again won the county titles.

Anthony Passarelli died on November 6, 1979 after a long bout with cancer. He had been the track and cross country coach at Delbarton for twenty-three years and he left a legacy of excellence

Coach Tony Passarelli embracing Barry Enright '79 after the latter won the New Jersey State Prep School cross country championship. Coach Passarelli died of cancer shortly after Enright's victory.

that everyone will remember. Prior to coaching at Delbarton he had been an outstanding distance runner at Millburn High School and Georgetown University, and held the New Jersey high school records for the mile and two mile runs. He was also the marathon champion for the first Pan American games. The month before he died, one of his most outstanding runners, Barry Enright, won the New Jersey state cross country championship; and shortly before his death that cross country team won its first Morris County championship; and one day after Coach Passarelli's death the team won its fifth consecutive state title.

As Coach Passarelli's successor in 1979, Wayne Gardiner would continue the winning ways of Delbarton cross country, winter track and spring track and field from then until his retirement as head coach of the entire program at Delbarton in the late 1990s. In 1980, for example, Mr. Gardiner's teams won the New Jersey state, New Jersey prep, Morris County, and New Jersey Catholic Conference titles and remained unbeaten in their dual meet competition. Some important runners in the early 1980s included Tom Hanifin, Lou Ross, Kevin Walsh, Jim Rosenhaus, Kevin O'Brien and Ed Donoghue. The 1980-1981 indoor and spring seasons continued apace. The team won the New Jersey state prep championship, the New Jersey Catholic track championship, and Lou Ross was voted first team all state, John Wlader first team all county and Tom Hanifin, second team all county. Again, the anonymous writer in the 1981 *Archway* stated:

> *"When you ask someone why he runs track for Delbarton, the answer you receive depends on who you ask. Some might say for the satisfaction that comes from the sport, others for the challenge of participating, and one or two might even say that it is fun. But no matter whom you ask, the answer will always contain the phase "for the pride." For years Delbarton has turned out runners who have reinforced that spirit. Part of that pride comes from the mere fact that "Delbarton" is emblazoned across the chest of each jersey."*

The Delbarton cross country and track teams continued through the 1980s to be the winningest team at the School under the coaching of Wayne Gardiner. The runners, however, were not sure

> **"Part of that pride comes from the mere fact that "Delbarton" is emblazoned across the chest of each jersey."**
> – 1981 Archway

that their peers and parents understood that. The headline in the 1985 yearbook, for example, stated: "We won again – but nobody noticed." In a school where football and soccer were king during the fall, and increasingly, lacrosse in the spring, the cross country, track and field athletes often felt they did not receive the attention that they deserved. For example, in 1984, like 1978 before it, the School enjoyed its most successful sports seasons with outstanding teams in soccer and football. As for cross country, however, by 1984 the Green Wave team had not lost in regular competition for more than ten years. They enjoyed more than 100 consecutive victories in dual meets, and that record would continue through the 1980s. The most talented cross country and track runners then would continue to lead the team into the late 1980s. They included: Chris Shilakes, Todd Wells,

Pete Stewart, Bob Kulik, Andy Klein, Wally Carell, Paul Collins, David Gusmer, John Curley, and Matt Gilfillan.

Cross country and track and field excellence continued through 1989, when the team won its fifteenth consecutive state prep title and established the longest cross country undefeated streak in New Jersey history. Under the leadership of Keith Scott, Kevin Horty, Rob Failla, Jeff Forbes and Craig Spence, the team brought home a number of team titles, including the NJ Catholic track championship and the team's third consecutive Morris County championship.

And so, the winning ways of Father Peter Meaney and Coach Tony Passarelli continued under the tutelage of Wayne Gardiner as the School approached the last decade of the century. In that same year, 1989-1990, athletics at Delbarton reached something of a peak. The basketball team won the Morris County championship, the cross country team, as indicated, won the Morris County championship, football won the Northern Hills Conference championship, the hockey team won the Mennen Cup championship, soccer won the parochial A state championship, and swimming again won the Morris County championship.

HOCKEY

Father Donal Fox, O.S.B., founded Delbarton hockey in 1975 and Delbarton lacrosse a year later. As director of admission during Father Gerard Lair's administration, he had a sense of the future popularity of these two sports throughout the country in the 1980s and 1990s. In addition, he was encouraged by the prodding of some of the Delbarton students who needed administration support in establishing the sports.

Hockey was a club sport during the 1975-76 and 1976-77 winter seasons. In both years, the team skated at Danny Michael's ice palace in Florham Park. A Delbarton parent, Mr. Harvey Mell, served as the first coach, and Tom McKeown, a faculty member, and a graduate, John Holder, served as coaches in the second year. The School made hockey a varsity sport for the 1978-79 season with English teacher Dan Luker coaching. The team was not yet invited to join the Morris County hockey league, but many of the games they played were scheduled with teams in that league. Fortunately, the team did well enough to be invited to participate in the Morris County league the next year. Mr. Bruce Peckham coached the team between 1979 and 1981 and acquired ice time at 5:00 a.m. at the Essex Hunt Club in Far Hills, which began a tradition that continued until Delbarton left the Morris County hockey league. Playing at Mennen Arena, the hockey team was now able to draw a considerable number of Delbarton students to their games. As an anonymous editor of the 1981 *Archway* wrote:

> *"Fan support was a major contributing factor in this year's squad's attitude. Our souls were stirred by a rousing chant "Morristown eats bugs!" Most of the time we never let our fans down, especially with our specialty of the third period comebacks and puck handling that even surprised our coaches. We hope we gave our fans the excitement and thrills of well played sportsmanlike (usually) and just all around good hockey."*

In that year the team had 13 wins, 7 losses and 2 ties. More importantly, the storied and often electrifying rivalries began with Morristown Beard, Morristown High School and Chatham Borough. These rivalries often challenged the School administration, particularly in the 1980s, to improve the sportsmanship of the fans which it did by assuring a strong faculty presence at the games. In the 1980s, hockey in Morris County flourished. The regular crowds of more than 2,000 attending the Morristown and Delbarton games at Mennen Arena illustrate that.

In 1981 Bruce Peckham returned to graduate school, leaving a major gap in varsity coaching. At that time, three of the varsity players, Bill Clapp, Charlie Lazor, and Rob Bentley visited Headmaster Father Giles Hayes to ask him to hire Mr. John Magadini, an experienced college and All American hockey player formerly at RPI, but at that time a coach of youth hockey at the Essex Hunt Club. Mr. Magadini accepted Father Giles' invitation to meet with him to discuss the position, a meeting in which he indicated that if he was offered the job and took it, the headmaster should know that he was not going to be all that easy on his athletes. Recognizing, however, how those three young men who promoted Mr. Magadini's case both played for him and respected him as much as they did, Father Giles then hired Mr. Magadini. There began a five-year series of exciting hockey at Delbarton under "Mags," which brought the School its first two Mennen Cup victories and nail-biting competition in the state playoffs. Typically, Delbarton hockey games at Mennen Arena, both on weekends and school nights, attracted more than half of the Delbarton student body, and sometimes virtually the entire student body. Pep rallies often preceded major hockey games, especially those with Morristown High School, Morristown Beard, and Chatham, rallies to which Mr. Magadini frequently came to stimulate the interest and excitement of the students.

> "We hope we gave our fans the excitement and thrills of well played sportsmanlike (usually) and just all around good hockey."
> – 1981 Archway

Delbarton won its first Mennen Cup in 1984 behind the strong defense of Mark Miller and goaltenders Mike Silva and Marc Mestanas. Most exciting, however, was the play of Delbarton's strongest offensive player in both soccer and hockey of those days, Chris Gumm. In a memorable game against Chatham, sophomore Chris Gumm scored a hat trick and two assists on the way to a decisive 6-3 victory.

The School's first Mennen Cup came in late February, 1984, in a grueling double elimination tournament of the Morris County Hockey League. In the final game, archrival Morristown High School scored early, but the large and loud group of Delbarton fans never stopped cheering. As the editor writes in the 1984 *Archway,* the second period remained scoreless, but the third period started off with Ed Davis scoring immediately. The fans went wild, according to the *Archway* report, and the team knew that the School wanted this one too badly to let it get away. Because of the 1-1 tie, the game went into two sudden death overtimes. Finally, junior Tim Mahoney made it all worth while by scoring in the second half of the second overtime. After two previous appearances in the Mennen Cup finals, Delbarton finally claimed the championship.

Delbarton's first Mennen Cup victory team, February, 1984.

Veterans Bill Timpson, Marc Mestanas, Tim Mahoney, Joe Fodero, Peter Matthews, Chip Sawicki and Mike Manley graduated after the 1984-85 season, suggesting that the following year would be particularly challenging. In the end, in 1986, Coach Magadini's skaters won their second Mennen Cup and won 20 games, lost 1 and tied 1.

Superstars Pat Ramsey and Jeff Gorman captained the 1985-86 team, and Mark Balzarotti, who later won the Morris County Hockey League's most valuable player award, served as goaltender, earning 9 shutouts and allowing in only 24 shots in 22 games. Fan support reached the highest level yet during that season. The Delbarton tradition of student spectators standing through the entire game began during the 1986 double elimination tournament, when the student leadership insisted that since the team had to play on the ice all the time without sitting, the Delbarton spectators should also stand. Again, the author of the hockey article in the 1986 yearbook described some of the humor and the agony of playing hockey, and speaks to the coaching style of Mags:

> *"The alarm clock rings, it is 4:30am I can't believe it. Maybe it will be raining and*
> *our practice at the Essex Hunt Club will be gassed. There is no rain. The*
> *thermometer reads in the single digits. Pack another turtleneck. Hardly awake I*
> *grab the keys, pack and step into the cold. My body is shivering as I throw the*
> *equipment into the car and anxiously await the heat to kick in. There is nothing on*
> *the road. The soporific silence of the small warming room of the Essex Hunt is*
> *broken only by a quiet "hello" by a teammate. Then "ALL RIGHT, MEN!!"*
> *Oh no, Mags is here. Suddenly the room becomes animated as the team*
> *fights to get dressed before they are declared late and condemned to the*
> *punishment of extra sprints.*

Into the bitter cold and onto the ice. Time for a few quick stretches and then
hard skating around the periphery. The soggy equipment is no bother
now as I break into a sweat. Mags is right behind me, urging me to go faster.
The wind in my face stings briefly as beads of sweat freeze on my cheeks
and nose. The air is so hard and cold that my lungs hurt. Finally a rest,
but only a minute as the new drill begins.

The sun will be rising soon. This means the end of practice is nearing and so are
sprints. It gets worse before it gets better. Another beautiful sunrise in the valley
today. Mags is smiling. "All right everybody down here!" He yells! Oh no, sprints!!
It will be hell. "Okay, everyone inside, no sprints. We've got Mt. Olive tomorrow!"
the team lets out adrenalin-pumped hollers of joy.

The spirit carries on to the Mennen Cup finals against Mt. Olive. Posters and
banners are seen throughout the locker room and throughout the School in hopes
of boosting team morale. The door swings open, the crowd roars as the Green
Wave hits the ice. The trials and efforts of a long season culminate in a final battle
against the Marauders. The horn sounds to end the third period and the game is
forced into overtime. In the second overtime the Green Wave digs deep.

Sharp passes from the Gorman line connect with a winning goal scored by
Chris Gumm. To the team, getting up at 4:30am doesn't seem bad at all.
To the Delbarton fans that packed Mennen arena, their
team is number one. "

Many of the stars of that "best ever" Delbarton hockey team graduated in 1986, including Jim Chambers, Joe Corcoran, Jeff Gorman, Pat Ramsey, Clen Ryan, Bill Crutchlow, Chris Gumm, Woody Nash, Mark Balzarotti, Ned Cooper and Rob Reilly. Incorrectly, some thought that the 1986-87 team and those to follow would be much weaker. However, Delbarton continued to win the Mennen Cup through most of the remaining years in the 1980s and into the 1990s. John Magadini's assistant coach, Jim Brady, took over the program after John completed his fifth year in 1987. The 1987-88 team lost only 1 game within the conference, won the league, and again, the Mennen Cup. The records indicate that the team was the most productive offensively of all Delbarton's Hockey teams to date. They averaged seven goals a game and scored in double figures nine times. Brian Lonergan, Chris von Zuben, Peter Ramsey and Mike Pendy were standouts on offense, while Andy Craig and Derek Maguire along with Pat Hennessey, Martin Schwartz, James Olsen and Mark Rionda, contributed to the scoring and outstanding defense.

Delbarton hockey won its fourth and fifth consecutive Mennen Cup in 1988-1989 and 1989-1990. The team dominated the Morris County hockey league in 1989 with the season record of 15 − 0 − 1

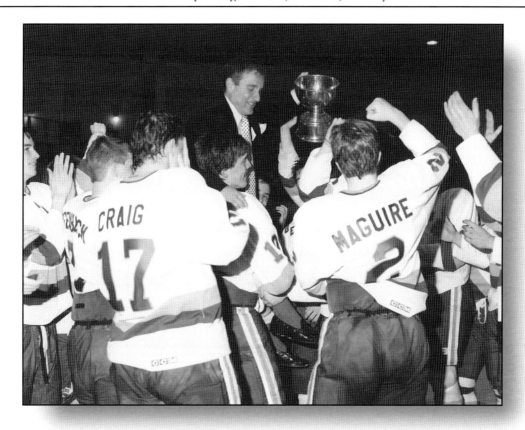

Peter Lazor and the Delbarton hockey team hoist Coach John Magadini on their shoulders after winning the 1987 Mennen Cup. In the background the packed Delbarton crowd yelled in appreciation: "Mags is god; Mags is god!"

and a Mennen Cup playoff of 3 wins, 26 goals for and only 2 goals against. They were ranked one of the premier teams in the state with a particularly strong defense and an offense which scored six or seven more goals then their opponents. Coach Jim Brady at that time in the late 1980s began to schedule more challenging competition outside of the state, in Massachusetts, Rhode Island and Connecticut, games the team often lost, but the competition itself made the team better. As the anonymous author of the 1989 yearbook wrote:

> *"Another recurring problem that the team experienced was a lack of team support, especially during the middle of the year. Strangely, the number of fans present at games was inversely proportional to the number of games won by the team. This relationship between the team and its supporters continued until the playoffs when, buoyed by promises of a celebration, large numbers of diehards showed up."*

This comment written in 1989 prophesied the characteristic of Delbarton hockey through the 1990s and beyond. The more successful the team became, the fewer students and parents showed up for the games. But the author of this article in the 1989 *Archway* had some other criticisms which suggest that the hockey boosters and the School administration itself may have not been as enthusiastic about hockey as the writer would have wished. He wrote:

"Finally, there were financial difficulties concerning accessories to overcome. After hearing tales of rolls of tape and "Wave" stickers stacked up to the ceiling in a remote room, players approached the athletic administration in hopes of acquiring entrance to this treasure trove, however, the "short arms, deep pockets" of the administration prevailed and the team had to resort to the shoestring and magic marker to fulfill their requirements."

Hockey parent boosters, as well as all team boosters through the 1990s and later could not be accused of that criticism. While the School budgeted more than $25,000 a year for the hockey team, the boosters, particularly because of very successful skate-a-thons run by Mrs. Agnes Lonergan and Mrs. Leslie Maguire over the years, supplemented the budget by another $25,000 or more.

Regardless, the team of 1989, one of the best in Delbarton's history, continued to dominate New Jersey hockey. Scott Ames held down most of the goaltending, while Greg Meyer, Tim Reilly, Mike Pendy, Brian Lonergan, Derek Maguire, Martin Schwartz, James Olsen, Jason Waite, Mike Phillips, Andrew and Chris Marshall, Pete Ramsey, Jon Mortenson, Pat Nelson and Michael Crutchlow continued to pour their hearts out for the School. While there was no one superstar, Derek Maguire, Brian Lonergan, Mike Pendy and Pete Ramsey were recognized among the best hockey players in the state.

Coaches "Buzz" Brown, Alec Walsh, Jim Brady (center) and Denny Wright, with Father Giles and captains of the 1988 Mennen Cup Champions: Paul Wagenbach, Brian Lonergan, and Chris Von Zuben with his brother Max.

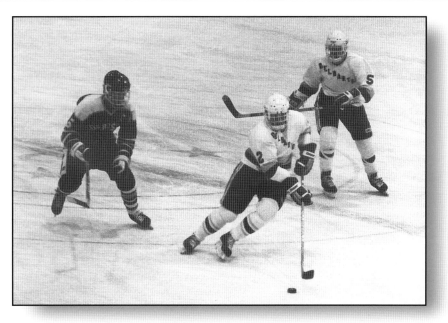

Derek Maguire about to score on a breakaway, 1989

Delbarton shared the New Jersey state championship in 1989. As the anonymous author in the 1989 *Archway* wrote:

> *"While no New Jersey team could stop the Green Wave, a virus did. A plague of measles struck Delbarton a few days before the team was supposed to play St. Joseph's of Montvale causing the state board of health to quarantine Delbarton from all athletic completion. Thus Delbarton never got to show its mettle against St. Joe's. The decision to declare Delbarton and St. Joe's co-championship brought some consolation. But, even after a fantastic season the team was left with the feeling of what might have been."*

No one was ever sure of how so many on the Delbarton team, first Jason Waite, the goaltender, then so many others, came down with the measles. The prevailing rumor suggested that a week or two before the final hockey game, Delbarton played Seton Hall in basketball in Delbarton's new gym. Some later learned that a number of students at Seton Hall were suffering from the measles when that game was held, but did not know they had the virus. When they came into the gym, it is thought, they unknowingly passed on the virus to a number of Delbarton faculty and students by handshakes. Just a few days before the scheduled state championship game, one after another of the Delbarton hockey players, a number of faculty, and many of the students came down with the virus. Mrs. Rabasca, by law, had to notify the State Department of Health about this sudden outbreak, which made the Department cancel the game. What an ironic end to one of the best hockey seasons in Delbarton's history!

Delbarton hockey began the 1989-90 season with a record 18-0 and continued their unbeaten streak to 39 games. Any photograph of this team, however, reveals on the left shoulder of each

Derek Maguire '90, Delbarton's most heralded
hockey athlete of the 1970s and 1980s. After
Delbarton, Maguire starred at Harvard and then
in the Montreal Canadian professional
hockey organization.

player the number 19. Tragedy occurred in early December when Derek Maguire's younger brother Terry died as the result of an injury in a hockey game where he so much enjoyed being on the ice with his older brother Derek. In spite of the tragedy, Derek, who, with his teammates, devoted the remainder of the season to the memory of Terry, led his team to the fifth consecutive Mennen Cup title. Assisted by Mike Crutchlow and sophomores Jim Bruce and Kevin Mahoney, as well as by the offensive line Jon Mortenson, Peter Ramsey, and Pat Nelson, by the penalty killing of the twins Chris and Andy Marshall and the outstanding play in goal of Jason Waite, along with the help of Matt Durney, Trey Whipple, Chris Louden, Keith Hennessey and Greg Pendy, Derek led the team to even greater distinction than earlier Delbarton hockey squads in the state and beyond.

The Maguire family, including Derek and Terry's parents, Ed and Leslie, anchored the hockey program with their undying support in the late 1980s and into the 1990s. Leslie ran the skate-a-thon for many years, and Ed was an ever present supporter, not only of his sons but of all the players.

Derek Maguire, the distinguished #2 in Delbarton's hockey program, played at Harvard University where he became an All American, and later a drafted member of the Montreal Canadians NHL organization. He followed Mike Pendy into professional hockey when Mike played professional hockey in Sweden following his sterling career at Bowdoin College. Anchoring

Delbarton's most distinguished hockey trio was George Parros, who played first at Princeton and then with Los Angeles in the NHL.

Brian Day, seasoned as a junior varsity and assistant coach under Jim Brady, succeeded Coach Brady in the early 1990s, a responsibility he held until Bruce Shatel became the head coach years later. Under both of these coaches Delbarton continued its sterling tradition of hockey, including two more State championships, and produced more than a dozen players who were recognized as choices for New Jersey All State hockey.

WRESTLING

Wrestling began at Delbarton as an intramural sport in the late 1950s and saw its first interscholastic competition as a varsity sport during the 1960-61 season. Mr. Don Grevara coached a strong contingent of two dozen athletes that year. Perhaps because it is such a demanding sport, and also because in the winter season it competes for athletes with five other teams at moderate-sized Delbarton, rarely after 1961 did the team have as many as two dozen wrestlers until more recent years. Mr. Ron Matakitis took over the coaching duties in the mid-1960s until he was succeeded by Coach Terry Hurley in 1980. Chris Wedholm succeeded Terry Hurley in 1987, until coach Ted O'Donnell became the varsity coach in the early 1990s.

The fledgling wrestling teams in the 1960s suffered a number of losses but always had competitive wrestlers in a few of the weight classes. In the early 1960s, for example, John Beasley, Ed Joffe and John Murdock did well, and in the late 1960s heavyweight Kevin Carlin always electrified the crowd. The strongest wrestling in the early years of the program occurred in the 1970s when coach Matakitis

Tom Anderson about to escape from a Morristown Prep opponent, 1965

had excellent wrestlers in Mike Beauchamp, Dan Gardner, Tom Reynolds, Glenn McCarthy, Mike Delaney, Ken Sachs, Kevin Kearney, Tom Joyce, Jeff McGovern, Greg Contreras, Jim Petrucci, John Kraeutler, John Hanlon, and Paul Beauchamp, Michael's brother. The team enjoyed a strong 12-2 record in 1977 and 13-2 record in 1978. The third of the Beauchamp boys, Jeff, as well as his brother Paul, John Hanlon, Dan Dalena, Matt McAleer and Ron Nagle led the team into the 1980s. With repeat state champion Jim Petrucci on the 1982 team along with Matt McAleer (1982 NJSIAA District Champion), Andy Anselmi, Glenn D'Angerio, Chris Speck, John Facciani and Ken Wedholm, all champions at one time or another, the team stayed strong in the 1980s. Chris Speck won the 1986 NJSIAA Regional Championship in 1986, and the District Championships in 1985 and 1986, and John Facciani won the Regional in 1989, and the District Championships in 1988 and 1989. John Hanlon's point total of 75 was the record for any Delbarton wrestler until John Facciani broke it in 1989. In the mid to late 1980s, the team continued to send strong teams to the mat, getting championship performances from Rob Bezzone, Jon Ponosuk, Rich Carella, Jamie Schwarz, and others. This winning tradition continued into the 1990s with NJSIAA District Championships being awarded to Avelino Verceles (1990), Mike Guerriero (1991), Jon Rose (1991) and Mark Facciani (1992). Jon Rose was also the Morris County Tournament Champion in 1991. In addition, John Hanlon at Boston College, Chris Speck at Duke University and John Facciani at Williams College all enjoyed strong college careers.

SWIMMING

The history of Delbarton swimming exemplifies the School motto *"succisa virescit"*, "cut down, it will grow up strong again." The School began to schedule swimming meets in 1946 with Father Adrian McLaughlin as the coach. The meets were held in the old Morristown YMCA on Washington Street. Through the 1950s and 1960s, rarely more than twelve athletes swam for the School. While some of them may have been outstanding in fall or spring sports, the School had few county champions and few, if any, state and nationally ranked swimmers in these early days. That all changed from the late 1970s through the 1990s when the team was under the leadership of Mr. John Romagna and Mr. Kent Manno. Outstanding swimmers and School record holders in the 1970s included Ken Stevenson, who held the School records for the 200 freestyle, the 50 freestyle, the 100 freestyle, and the 500 freestyle. In the early 1980s, the team began winning consecutive county championships from 1982 into the 1990s. They also competed occasionally against some of the perennial swimming powerhouses in the state, including Blair, Lawrenceville, and St. Joseph's of Metuchen. The distinguished team of 1983 set long standing records for the 200 medley relay and the 400 freestyle relay, and one member of the team, Brian Stagg, set the School record for the 200 IM. Victor Rios, Rob O'Mara, Chris McCumber, Chris Listo, Neil Coughlin, Ahktar Khan, Paul Dunnder, and Tim Barry anchored that team. In addition, the team at the end of the 1980s, after capturing its 7th consecutive Morris County title, became the only team in the county's history to win that many swimming titles. Outstanding swimmers and record holders of that team of the late 1980s were Kevin Burke, Alex Huck, Matt Whelan, Jamie Fitzpatrick, Kevin Joyce, Ed Sera, and Jim Fay.

Jeff Stanley (far right) and 1984 squash team.

SQUASH

Jeff Stanley, Sr., an attorney from Somerville, New Jersey, visited Father Giles Hayes, Headmaster of Delbarton, in the winter of 1982. Boldly, he asked Father Giles to establish a squash program at Delbarton and admit his son, a young Jeff Stanley, to anchor the future of the Delbarton squash team. At that time, Father Giles knew very little about squash, which was not a recognized sport in the State athletic organization. The research he immediately did, however, indicated that it was an important sport for physical conditioning, and students who could play squash well would be actively recruited by some of the most competitive Division I AA and Division III colleges in America. Father Giles quickly got back to Jeff Stanley, Sr. with a resounding, "Yes." Mr. Stanley's son tested for Delbarton and passed. After the admission of young Jeff Stanley, Father Giles found two members on the faculty who played squash and could coach the team, Mr. Olen Kalkus, and to assist him, Mr. Mark Koenig. Consequently, the Delbarton squash program was launched during the 1983-84 season. In the first year, Jeff Stanley, arguably the best junior squash player in the United States and perhaps in the world, won most of the tournaments he entered, and a few of his sophomore classmates performed well. In the second year of the program, 1984-85, Jeff continued to achieve while at the USSRA Nationals in Princeton and at other tournaments. Additional members of the team made the New England tour in January, but bowed to the Philips Andover and the Belmont Hill team, traditional squash powers. In late January, 1985, Rick Stanley, Dave Henry, and Peter McGratty scored within the top six at the New Jersey high schools tournament in Atlantic City. In the meantime, as the *Archway* indicates, Jeff Stanley was busy winning the Jacobs Trophy in New York City. February, 1985, saw Delbarton win all its dual matches. At the Chatham Squash and Racquet Club, the home location for Delbarton's

*Jeff Stanley, '85, later Princeton University squash
All-American.*

squash matches for more than twenty years, as well as the Plainfield Country Club, the team defeated Ridley College of Canada, 7 to 2 and 6 to 3, and continued undefeated by shutting out Princeton Day School twice. From then through the present, more than twenty students each year have joined the squash team, and dozens have followed Jeff to play squash in college. Jeff went on to Princeton University, where he led the squash team to the NCAA championships and continued his national and international winning ways.

Typically, in the 1980s and 1990s, the squash team played the Hunter Lot Tournament, the Princeton University JV, Portsmouth Abbey School, Tabor Academy, Phillips Academy, Belmont Hill, Noble and Greenough, Moses Brown, Mercersburg Academy, Shadyside Academy, the Episcopal School, Princeton Day, and a number of New Jersey schools which began organized squash programs. Annually Delbarton's squash athletes achieve among the top three in the State of New Jersey and receive top ten rankings for their age group in the United States. John Butter coached in 1986-87 and Craig Paris took over the program in 1987 and has been head coach to the present.

Jeff Stanley created a remarkable legacy for Delbarton athletics. As an athlete, he would be numbered among the greatest at Delbarton from the 1940s through the mid-1980s, a group that includes Vince Jazwinski for football, Bob Collins, Dennis Williamson and Bobby Kelly for basketball, Tom Sanfacon for football and track, and John Conner for track. Now married, the father of two children, and living in Summit while working in finance in New York, Jeff found himself a few years ago walking to the Magic Fountain with his young girls on a hot summer day to buy them ice cream. Immediately in front of him were two male teenagers, dressed in green Delbarton jackets with the words Delbarton Squash blazoned on the back of the jackets. While too humble to address the boys wearing those jackets, Jeff felt deeply about the legacy he established at the School and may have shed a few tears of joy that athletes of the next generation would gain so much from the sport he loved and introduced to so many young men at Delbarton.

BASEBALL

Few records for the baseball team exist, in part because baseball is played in the spring season which gets little coverage in the *Archway* or the *Courier,* a main source of information about the teams. Father Adrian McLaughlin and Father Phillip Hoover coached the elementary school and middle school teams in the 1940s, to be followed by Sam Arbes in 1949. In that first year of Ivy League play, the Delbarton team had an 11-2 record and won the Ivy League title. Father Felix Pepin took over the team in 1951 and coached it until his successor, Harry Stillwell, became the head coach in 1954. Coach Stillwell created an enviable record in the more than 17 years of his coaching into the 1970s. Father Karl Roesch began as head coach in the 1975 season and coached the varsity through 1987. Father Karl coached a particularly strong team in the late 1970s which advanced into the counties and amassed a record from 1976 through 1979 of 54 victories and 32 defeats. His team won the Morris County Tournament for the second championship in this strong baseball county in 1987. Ken Heaton was Delbarton's head coach in 1988 and 1989, followed by Ed Kim. Coach Ed Kim and Coach Brian Fleury very frequently won the Northern Hills Conference Championships in the 1990s and the School won two Parochial A State Championships

1985 varsity baseball team which went to the finals of the Morris County tournament, but lost because of a home run hit by the Morristown High School catcher, Brian Fleury, athletic director and head varsity baseball coach at Delbarton since 1996.

1985 Morris County championship varsity tennis team coached by Steve Diamond.

in 1996 and 2002. As Head Coach, Ed Kim's teams won 105 games and lost 56. Overall, Delbarton enjoyed a strong won-loss record between 1975 and 2005 of 500 wins, 285 losses, and five ties.

In the spring of 1970, Delbarton took its place among the better baseball teams in Morris County with the likes of Morristown High School and Parsippany High School, when Coach Stillwell's team beat Parsippany in the Morris County Tournament. As Harry said to Dan Castalano of the *Daily Record* on June 10, 1970, "I wanted this game more than any other. When you beat a Jack Mott-coached ball club you know you've earned it." The principal players of that distinguished Delbarton team included Ducky Grennan, Bob Cipolaro, Bill Williams, Pete Mehring, Gerry Waselik, Gary Milanesi and Terry Regan, who hit a line drive to right which scored Waselik and Milanesi to win the game.

TENNIS

Few sports at Delbarton have competed more successfully against other teams in the state than varsity tennis. From 1976 through the present, Delbarton tennis has won 23 county championships, and 11 state Parochial championships. Many Ivy League championships were won by the tennis team in the 1940s, '50s, and early '60s, but the records of that era are not available.

Father Kenneth Mayer occasionally coached the pick-up tennis team from 1948 until 1957 and enjoyed the help of Father Theodore Howarth in 1950. In that year, Bob Callahan won the Ivy League singles championship. He was joined on the victorious team by Adrian Doyle, Larry Battersbee, Ed

Connors, Jim O'Hara, Chuck Rye, Juan Noriega, John McMenaman and John LaVecchia. In 1955, the School won behind Bob Jenco, Patrick Henry, James Corroon, Bob Collins and Dave McBride.

The team became more organized in 1958 under the coaching of Father David Conway and won the Ivy League in 1959 and 1960. Competition became tougher with the demise of the Ivy League in 1961, so from 1962 through 1966, Mr. Ed Borneman and Mr. Michael Domas coached the team. The stalwarts then were Peter McBride, John Mountford, Norman Scott, John Furrey, Ted Furrey, Jack Janes, Hal Parmalee, Bernard Demoreuille, Charles Adams, Fred Balmer, Tim Larkin and Mark O'Brien. From 1967 to the present accurate information exists, in large part because Father Benet Caffrey took responsibility as coach for the tennis team from then until 1976. The team enjoyed winning records of 9-4 in 1969 and 12-1 in 1970, when Rick Kentz won the NJISAA first singles championship, assisted by his teammates Paul Kreiger, Peter Pizzi, Bill Conley, Joe Tracy, Mike Donohoe, Troby Laidlaw, Rich Dannemiller, Steve Plain, Chris Fittin, and Jim Hurley. Hurley, Plain and Webber led the team in the early 1970s with Tom Timpone, Andrew Kentz, Ed Hennessey, Dave Kennedy, Craig Low, and Dan Badenhausen. With them and Bob Scott in first singles, Delbarton won the Morris County Tournament for the first time in 1976. In the following three years, Joe Krakora coached the Delbarton teams to three consecutive Morris County championships, followed by Chris Stagg who led the School to two more State championships. Consequently, between 1977 and 1981, Delbarton tennis won more than 70 matches and lost fewer than 17. Players then who distinguished themselves with post-season recognition include Drew Robinson, Bob Scott, Ed Scott, Steve Gruen, Bill Burke, Chris Higgins, Donal Mastrangelo, Chris Benz, Rob LeBuhn, Drew Maldonaldo, Ed McDonnell, and Craig Paris. Steve Diamond's teams won more than 100 victories between 1982 and 1986, while sustaining fewer than 25 defeats. In 1984 alone the team secured its ninth consecutive Morris County Championship. Led by senior Eric Johnson, sophomore J.P. Flynn, and senior John Ojeda, the team posted a final record of 23-4. The first doubles team (juniors Jon Lubow and John Benz), and the second doubles team (juniors Pete Matthews and Jeff Stanley) won the competitive Northern Hills Conference for the second consecutive season. Coach Diamond was named *Star-Ledger* Coach of the Year after winning three consecutive parochial state championships in 1985, 1986 and 1987 as well as consecutive county championships from 1982 through 1990. One might say that the Golden Age of Tennis occurred at Delbarton when coach Steve Diamond coached J.P. Flynn, John Krawczyk, Brian Flynn, Tom North, Peter Ventimiglia, Jonathan Craig and Todd Rose through those years of the late 1980s and early 1990s.

Not to be outdone, John Thompson began coaching at Delbarton in 1992 and proceeded to win nine state championships, eight conference championships, and nine county championships from the time he took over until the present. Again, no Delbarton team has had a more successful record in the state of New Jersey than Delbarton tennis has in the last thirty years. Celebrating that, Coach Thompson and the School organized the Delbarton Invitational Tennis Tournament named after one of its important captains of the early 1990s who died in the terrorist attack of September 11, 2001, Bryan Bennett.

Father Kenneth Mayer, coach, fifth from left, with Delbarton's 1953 golf team, including championship college and amateur golfers, John Ruvane and Jim Noble, 2nd and 3rd from the left.

GOLF

Delbarton began an interscholastic golf program in 1950. For the first twenty years of the program, Father Kenneth Mayer and his brother Father Arthur Mayer coached the team, and were able to use the courses at Somerset Hills, Spring Brook and Morris County Country Clubs. In the early 1960s, Father Arthur's teams were particularly successful, especially when he coached Frank McGuire, Michael Hayes, A.J. Delaire and Kevin Maher. Although the number of golfers on the team through the early 1980s rarely exceeded one dozen, they experienced much success. Several achievements marked the success of the 1984 team. A defeat over Millburn softened the only loss of the 1983 team, and winning over Mendham was another satisfying victory. The team took third place in the State Preps at Peddie and second place in the Conference Tournament.

Well remembered among Delbarton's best golfers in the 1950s and early 1960s are John Ruvane, Jim Noble, Terry Gallagher, and Rob O'Mara. John Ruvane not only won most of his scholastic matches but also went on to be an outstanding collegiate golfer at Princeton University and amateur golfer.

From the mid-1970s through the early 1980s, Father Manus Duffy and Father Leo Beger coached golf. Mr. Jack Regan coached through the early 1990s. Under Coach Regan, young Matt Thompson, became the state regional champion and probably the School's most dominant golfer of that time. Under Coach Dan Whelan and his assistant Sean Flanagan, two teams in the 1990s and after the year 2000 won the state championship.

LACROSSE

Delbarton lacrosse is easy to write about, in part because the coaches over the years have kept excellent records, and also because it has become one of the most prominent sports at the School. Lacrosse began officially at Delbarton with young Matt Levine, a goaltender and graduate from Williams College who, at the age of twenty-two, came to Delbarton to teach history and establish a lacrosse team. Prior to that, Father Donal Fox, encouraged by Harry Rice and a few other young students, began to pressure the School to begin the sport. Father Donal knew little about it, but Harry, a resident of Summit where lacrosse was popular, knew a fair amount. They met on a regular basis by the flag pole in front of Trinity Hall and impressed the School leadership by their enthusiasm for the sport. When the opportunity came to hire a college lacrosse star for Delbarton's history department, Father Gerard Lair, the headmaster then, accepted it. Matt Levine began the program at the junior varsity level, but introduced varsity competition in 1976-77. With the help of captains Frank Lynch, Gary Ostermueller, Blake Phillips and Rob Quinn, the fledgling team earned an enviable record of 12 wins and 17 defeats in their earliest seasons.

Coach Mike Page replaced Matt Levine in 1977. Coach Page was an offensive record holder at the University of Pennsylvania who then, in his two years as head coach at Delbarton, earned a

Coach Jamie Jacobs and Delbarton's short-lived gymnastics team, 1976 and 1977.

record of 16 wins and 9 defeats. His principal captains and athletes were Jim Morrison, Phil Verhalen, Harry Rice, Marty Agacinski, Steve Faber, and Dan Pace. Coach Page gave the School two years and was followed by coach Loch Kelley, whose teams had 20 wins and 10 losses in two years. From 1982 through 1986, Ray Discolo succeeded Loch Kelley, earning 53 wins and 30 defeats. During the first ten years of the program the team won the state Prep B championship and the Garden State League Championship in 1978, and became league finalists and semi-finalists in 1979 and 1981. The team made the semi-finals of the NJ Coaches tournament and the state quarter finals in 1983 and 1984. Ray Discolo's captains included Bill Clapp, Mike Farina, Peter Shoemaker, Don Healy, John Shoemaker, John Dolan, Mike Silva, Mike Lonergan, Tim Mahoney, Kevin Sheridan, Pat Villoresi, and Paul Ferraro. Also in those first ten years many of the lacrosse players went on to play Division I lacrosse in college, including Dave Lewis, Mike Lynch, Rich Wickel and Dan Pace at Notre Dame, Peter Shoemaker, Don Healy, John Shoemaker and Tim Mahoney at the University of Pennsylvania, where John Shoemaker followed Mike Page as a record holder.

Delbarton lacrosse changed dramatically with the appointment of Chuck Ruebling to the head coaching position in 1987. While coach Ruebling had an enviable record in his first six years of coaching, 73 wins and 39 defeats, his record in his last six years, from 2001-2006, is 130 wins and 13 defeats. His teams reached the Morris County tournament semi-finalist or finalist level in 1988,

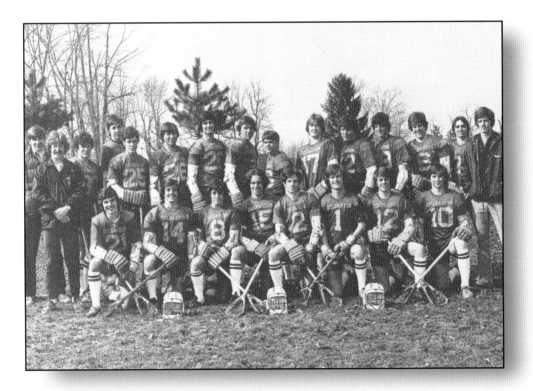

The 1978 Garden State Lacrosse League champions. Delbarton's first lacrosse championship team, coached by Michael Page, second row left, and including Charles Ruebling, #10, Delbarton's current coach; Harry Rice, fifth from left in the first row, and other founding student athletes of the lacrosse program.

1989, 1990, 1991, 1993, 1996, 2000, and 2002. They won the Morris County tournament championship in 1992, 1994, 1997, 1998, 1999, 2001, 2004 and 2006. They earned the state finalist or semi-finalist rankings in 1989, 1990, 1991, 1994, 1995, 1996, 1997, 1998, and 2001, and coach Ruebling's teams won the New Jersey State championship in 1994, 1999, 2000, 2002, 2003, 2004, 2005 and 2006. During those twenty years they were state division champions eight times. Also, during coach Ruebling's tenure, the number of high school All-Americans on his teams grew to over twenty. In addition, at least five of his graduates each year through the 1980s and as many as five to eight of his graduating athletes each year through the 1990s and into the year 2000 and beyond have played college lacrosse. During the first twenty years of the program, from 1975 through 1995, the following have been among the top three in career statistics: most career points – Kevin McLane, 204, Bob Sheridan, 128, Kevin Mahoney, 112; most career goals – Kevin McLane, 103, Bob Sheridan, 77, Max von Zuben, 60; most career assists – Kevin McLane, 101, Kevin Mahoney, 61, Brad Medd, 52; most career saves as a goaltender – John Servidea, 639, Tom McCabe, 426, and Dan Whelan, 279. All-American honors since then and through 1995 have included Brad Medd, Dan Wychulis, Dave Cashen, Kevin McLane, Justin Clavadetscher, Ryan Crane, John Servidea.

SCHOOL SPIRIT

School spirit has always been the hallmark of Delbarton's student body. An anonymous editor in the 1986 *Archway* wrote:

> *"Tankers in every hand...shirts on every back...buttons on every parent! It was impossible to escape the out-of-control enthusiasm of this year's fans. ...Delbarton was marked by an intensity and spirit undoubtly far superior to other schools. Is it not logical that we should have such School spirit? The soccer team won another championship, swimming won the counties, cross country was ranked seventh in the state, and the hockey team won the cup back. Delbarton has a lot to cheer about - - it's important to remember that we, the fans themselves, are very much a part of these victories. Ask any hockey player and he will tell you what a difference it makes, having 800 wild and screaming fans urging you on. It is this sort of enthusiasm that makes every victory a victory for everyone."*

The author here identified the source of Delbarton School spirit in the tight sense of brotherhood among the students, an energy driven by student leaders, the deanery system, and the sense of tradition passed down from class to class.

Coach Regan began that tradition by holding pep rallies at the beginning of the football season when he introduced each individual football player to the student body, and through the pep rallies he held at the beginning of the winter and spring seasons during which he talked about spectator sportsmanship and the importance of attending the games to support one's schoolmates. Typically,

Coach Bill Regan addressing the Delbarton student body at a pep rally in the footbal field stands, September, 1958.

he would bring the entire student body down to the stands at the football field for a rally or he would stand on the fire escape on the north side of the old gym and give his pep talks looking down on the student body assembled there.

Pep rallies became more complex in the last quarter of the century. In the late 1970s they were held during the midday free period in the new rotating schedule, but gradually the activities of the rallies required the use of an entire class period. Usually individuals in the Council of Seniors were assigned to create the activities, which often included student rock bands and a variety of comical skits, sometimes involving faculty actors along with the students.

Cheerleaders in each generation of Delbarton's history often promoted School spirit. In the 1950s, for example, often three or four seniors who were not playing one of the sports in season would don their green and white letter sweaters and ham it up as cheerleaders of the student spectators. In the 1970s a number of girls from girl's schools, usually sisters and friends of Delbarton athletes, and many from St. Elizabeth's Academy, would be dressed as cheerleaders for many of the games, particularly football and basketball. This practice continued periodically until the School leadership banned female cheerleaders in the late 1980s.

One of the more significant and appropriate Delbarton cheers came about quite by accident. Father Giles Hayes became Headmaster in the spring of 1980. There followed for him many months of hard work creating a new administration and building a faculty, a period when the orientation of new students seemed to be a "back-burner" responsibility. Suddenly, in late August, 1980, orientation had begun. At mid-morning on the first day of orientation, Father Giles was called upon to speak to the more than 100 new seventh and ninth grade students. Although his head and heart were filled with the values of the School, and after thirty years of being an integral part of the Delbarton culture, he walked before the new students that day without a prepared speech. Knowing that he had to get down to basics both to teach the new boys about the School and to make it possible for him to say something intelligent without preparation, he asked the boys to sit on the gym floor close to each other, seventh graders in the middle, surrounded by the ninth graders. When they were all assembled and quiet, he asked softly: "What School do you go to?" They answered softly, "Delbarton." Then he asked also softly, "How did you say that?" And they responded with a variety of answers: "Softly," "Quietly," "In unison," and a few said: "Together." Father Giles approved the last response, and then asked again, and more loudly this time: "WHAT SCHOOL DO YOU GO TO?" To which the boys responded loudly: "DELBARTON!" And then Father Giles asked: "HOW DID YOU SAY THAT?" And the boys shouted: "TOGETHER!" They then repeated the question and answer over and over again, "WHAT SCHOOL DO YOU GO TO?", "DELBARTON!", "HOW DID YOU SAY THAT?", "TOGETHER!" And so it was that Delbarton's memorable war cry was born. Down through the years, assembly after assembly, pre-game pep talk after pre-game pep talk, that cheer has been shouted by thousands of Delbarton students and athletes, affirming the brotherhood at Delbarton, and anchoring the spirit of the students and faculty.

School spirit in the 1970s

Spirit week began at Delbarton in 1982. This was a week set aside in early February for humorous and sometimes manic activities to give the students' spirit a boost during the depths of winter. Classes were held as usual, but special contests, activities and different dress-up or dress-down days energized the student body. In the late 1980s and into the 1990s individual classes and deaneries competed with each other in these activities. The fabled trike race, jousting, and wall-climbing were among the favorite competitive games. The student leadership held pep rallies during spirit week, especially prior to a Delbarton – Mendham basketball game or a Delbarton – Morristown or Seton Hall hockey game. Schola concerts and presentations by instrumental ensembles also spiced up spirit week.

Father Giles approved the last response, and then asked again, and more loudly this time: "WHAT SCHOOL DO YOU GO TO?" To which the boys responded loudly: "DELBARTON!" And then Father Giles asked: "HOW DID YOU SAY THAT?" And the boys shouted: "TOGETHER!"

Finally, School leadership in the 1980s and 1990s zealously promoted development of School spirit. Both the teachings of Kohlberg and St. Benedict emphasized that moral reasoning improves best in environments where the individuals are happy and proud of their institution. Indeed, the alliance between the School's administration and the junior and senior leadership during the 1980s and 1990s flourished especially when the students demonstrated pride in their School. This pride, enthusiasm and fellowship have continued to be the hallmark of the Delbarton students down to the present day.

Sisters and friends of Delbarton athletes filling in as cheerleaders, circa 1970s.

THE AFTERWORD

"Let nothing be preferred to the love of Christ," St. Benedict taught us more than 1,500 years ago. And Christ is one. All of us who have been baptized and who have taken vows have put on Christ and have become one in Him. All monks and nuns who are celebrating the sesquicentennial of Benedictines in New Jersey proclaim our unity in doing the Church's work of praise in celebrating the Eucharist and the Liturgy of the Hours, as well as in bringing the Kingdom of God to all human beings, the poor, the strangers and outcasts, the youth and the disenfranchised, and the faithful throughout this region. This has been our work for more than 150 years.

Most especially, loving Christ and putting on Christ has been the common work of the two ancient Abbeys of New Jersey, St. Mary's Abbey in Morristown and Newark Abbey in Newark. We are and have been one, more than we are different. We are one in Christ, in the sacramental life, in our history, and in our mission, though we have been different in our location and in those to whom we have been sent, urban and suburban children of God. When independent of each other, both communities of monks flourished. Both rooted themselves, often with the help of each other, in the values of the Rule of St. Benedict, both developed secondary schools which became the leaders of their kind in the United States, and both, finally, worked together to advance the values of Benedictine education worldwide.

More than that, all of this has only just begun. The past is prologue, and knowledge of the past frees us to follow the work of the Holy Spirit into the future. The common mission of both communities, the *ora et labora,* to praise and worship Almighty God on the one hand and on the other to make God's kingdom present to the urban and suburban communities of northern New Jersey, has these Benedictines poised for mighty work for God in our nation and world. The active and contemplative balance of Zilliox and Wimmer, the constant self-donation of both communities for each other and for the poor, the common commitment to human dignity and social justice, the love of Christ, and the sense of enthusiasm for doing God's work among human beings will make the New Jersey Benedictines in the next 150 years even more vibrant and successful in their work. "Unto the next generation" God's work will be continued by the monks and nuns of our land. Thanks be to God.

Sources

PUBLISHED:

Giles Hayes, <u>St. Mary's Abbey, Balleis to Zilliox: 1838-1886</u>, (Scriptorium, 1961)

Giles Hayes, <u>Wimmer-Bayley Correspondence</u>, (American Benedictine Review; Spring, 1963)

Giles Hayes, Unto Another Generation: <u>A History of St. Mary's Abbey/Delbarton, 1836-1966</u>, (Unpublished manuscript in SMA Archives, 1975)

Jeremy Steinemann, <u>A History of Delbarton School</u> (Internet, 2001)

<u>Delbarton Courier</u> and <u>Archway,</u> 1948-1995

These and assorted parish and abbey annuals were used to the extent that the information within them could be corroborated in the current research.

RECORDS:

Minutes of the Corporation of the Order of St. Benedict of New Jersey (1875-2000)

Minutes of the Chapter of St. Mary's Abbey (1885-2000)

Felix Fellner, Excerpts and Correspondence for the History of St. Vincent Archabbey Pertaining to the History of St. Mary's Abbey (1854-1887)

CORRESPONDENCE:

Wimmer-Bayley	Pfraengle-Bradley
Wimmer-Pilz	Zilliox-Pescetelli
Wimmer-Pfraengle	Zilliox-Reuss

MEMOIRS:

Vincent Amberg (tape recorded)

Patrick O'Brien (notes)

Augustine Wirth (tape recorded)

INTERVIEWS:

Over a second cup of coffee, from dozens of St. Mary's Abbey monks, checked against the official records and not found wanting.

In order to facilitate reading, footnotes for this essay have been omitted. When appropriate, sources and dates have been cited within the text.

PHOTOGRAPHS:

Newark Abbey and St. Mary's Abbey/Delbarton Archives

St. Benedict's Prep Website, OldNewark.com website

New Jersey: *A Mirror on America* by John T. Cunningham, Afton Publishing Co., Florham Park, NJ 07932, 1978

New Jersey: Life, Industries & Resources of a Great State, Published by New Jersey State Chamber of Commerce, Newark, NJ, 1928.

CHART:

Where Cities Meet: The Urbanization of New Jersey, by John E. Bebout, Ronald J. Girele, D. Van Nostrand Co., Inc., Princeton, NJ, 1964.

APPENDIX I

Essay on the life of Abbot Martin J. Burne, O.S.B., by Brother Eamon Drew, O.S.B., submitted as a graduate assignment at Immaculate Conception Seminary of Seton Hall University, 2005.

When one considers the landscape of Christianity in twentieth century America, certain topics quickly surface: the United States' involvement in multiple wars, civil rights, Pre-Vatican II Latin rituals, Post Vatican II renewals, ecumenism, education, mission and ministry. This and most lists could never be exhaustive. Be that as it may, rare is a person found involved so much in so many as the Right Reverend Martin J. Burne, O.S.B., salt of the earth who drew out the best in those with whom he interacted, a beacon of light to soldiers on the Pacific and urban peacemakers alike, a city with footholds atop High Street, Newark and the hills of Morristown. Recently, Abbot Thomas Confroy of St. Mary's Abbey reminisced about summer day trips as a young boy to those Morristown acres of Delbarton's campus whe the family visited his older brother, Fr. Mark. Thomas and his brother Jim would inevitably end their explorations at the swimming hole. Oftentimes they would mount the shoulders of two clerics and playfully splash and push one another. "Martin was always my horse!" he said.[1] If this Benedictine community has seen further over the past century, it is due in part to standing on the shoulders of Martin Burne, a workhorse whose burden he would most often deem light. "Sanctity of life is not attained overnight," he shared in a 19 June, 1991 Morristown *Daily Record* interview. This paper, then, examines, a lifetime, Martin's lifetime, for the sake of profiling a man fully American, fully Christian, fully integrated.

Martin J. Burne was born on 18 December 1914 in Irvington, New Jersey to benevolent parents. Irish Catholic immigrant Paul Dennis Burne and second generation German Protestant Anna Louise Kopf Burne, a convert to Catholicism just prior to her wedding witnessed the birth of four sons; the first two were stillborn, then Paul arrived, and two and a half years later, Martin. A cousin, Norma, joined the Burne clan when both of her parents died. She seamlessly enmeshed and the three considered themselves siblings amid a Clinton Hills neighborhood that provided a happy mixture of Jewish, Protestant and Catholic children, at the outset concerned more with the ballplayers they idolized than the God they worshiped.

They were all educated by the Chestnut Hill Sisters of St. Joseph at Clinton Hill's Blessed Sacrament Parochial School; Paul and Martin then followed their father's path to the Benedictine monks at St. Benedict's Preparatory School on High Street in Newark, the latter graduating in 1932. Extracurricular music instruction included piano lessons with Sr. Federica, S.S.J. and organ lessons with Mr. Edward Habig.

Upon graduation, Martin and three young classmates went west to commence their monastic careers with a novitiate year at St. Vincent's Archabbey, Latrobe, PA. There they were introduced to Benedictinism, a cenobitic existence stressing shared living, prayer, especially communal prayer, *lectio divina,* the goodness and necessity of work, the value of obedience, of stability, of self-denial and, or course, of a virtuous life in harmony with the Gospel. His introduction then to the *Breviarium Monasticum* proved vitally important throughout his vowed life; opening the Breviary does not mean instant communication with God, Martin believed, but faithfulness to its daily recitation proved to be a staple "in season and out of season" difficult to improve upon.[2] For all of his future travels, the rubrics of a Benedictine prayer life kept him close in heart to God and confreres alike.

The clerics returned from Latrobe to Newark, professing simple vows on 2 July 1935 and relocating to the community's theologate on the Delbarton campus a few days later. Coursework fell under the direction of Fr. Bede Babo (Dogma), Fr. Vincent Amberg (moral theology and canon law), Fr. Michael Ducey (liturgy), Fr. Ninian McDonnell (homiletics), and Fr. Hugh Duffy (Sacred Scripture). Returning to Latrobe, Martin graduated from St. Vincent's College in 1937 with a Bachelor of Arts in Philosophy with minors in music and English. Soon thereafter, he sought permission from Abbot Ernest Helmstetter to pursue a Master's degree from the Teacher's College at Columbia in music. After warning him that a confrere had preceded him to Columbia and wound up getting married (!), Ernest granted permission and Martin began his studies under the tutelage of Professor Peter Dykema; additionally, voice lessons were received at The Julliard School. He often observed burgeoning Navy Reserve ensigns training during his summers at Columbia: an image that would remain with him and affect later decisions. He professed solemn vows on 11 July 1938 and was ordained simplex at St. John's Cathedral on 18 May 1940 by Bishop Thomas McLaughlin, first Bishop of Paterson. Priests ordained simplex were as yet unable to preach or hear confessions but full presbyteral faculties followed one year later. In that same year, 1941, he attained his Master of Arts in Music Education, with his major instrument being the piano.

Martin remained in the classroom; with his degrees in hand he rounded the podium and began a teaching career at both his Newark alma mater and Morristown's newly founded Delbarton School. He was also put on the rota of convent missions and weekend parish work. "The work was joyful: one's priestly character came brilliantly to light, and one mostly felt that what he was doing was appreciated by those one served."[3] The scope of such service was to broaden quickly.

As the neophyte teacher was enjoying a most pleasant first year experience, the Japanese were repositioning troops in modern day southern Vietnam. The United States, favoring the pacifist movement enjoyed since the nineteen thirties preferred nonparticipation. It still shied away from military involvement yet was far from neutral. It froze Japanese assets and cut off oil supplies. The Japanese responded on 7 December 1941, bombing the Hawaiian Islands. The radio's "top of the news" was about Pearl Harbor and previous debates between isolationists and interventionists fell silent. "The churches shared the national consensus on war. Whether Protestant, Catholic, or Jewish, they showed no reluctance to support the war" which the United States entered days later.[4] Martin opined, "None of us present could have realized the changes that would be effected in our lives."[5] Martin approached Abbot Patrick O'Brien and broached the topic of volunteering for military chaplaincy with his own perspective much aligned with St. Augustine: "Peace is the desired end in war."[6] Pope Pius XII had already appointed then Bishop Francis Spellman as Military Vicar for the United States focusing great attention over Catholic chaplains and men of the Armed Forces. Yet, Patrick hesitated to send his young priest off. "Oh," he said, "you are much too young, and besides, you have been away from your parents so many years that you owe it to them to see them now and then." He added, "Besides, I shall not give permission to anyone to serve unless his parents are willing that he should do so."[7] When the topic first arose, his adamantly opposed mother reflected the consensus opinion put forth by Senator Robert Taft: "no American mother is ready to have her son die 'for some place with an unpronounceable name in Indo-China.'"[8] But after a few months she eventually relented: "Oh, who am I to keep you from the men who need you?"[9] Abbot Patrick made inquiries, Martin closed out the academic year, and by the fall of 1942 a new chapter opened.

The Military Ordinariate, which had increased its numbers from less than 200 in the nineteen twenties to nearly 9,000 during World War II, accepted Martin's application according to the guidelines of AR 605-30: he was a male United States citizen between the ages of 23 and 34 (26), he was regularly ordained, duly accredited by and in good standing with the Catholic Church according to academic requirements, and actively functioning as a priest.[10] Memories of Columbia's ensigns likely influenced his decision to enlist with the Navy corps chaplains. Tests and physicals were administered in New York where he was found to be underweight according to Navy parameters. But when the doctor ordered him to get dressed and weighed him again, the clothing tipped the scales and Martin was enlisted into the Navy Chaplain corps with the rank of Lieutenant JG (junior grade). He endured eight weeks of training at Norfolk, Virginia before shipping off to San Diego where he was stationed in the BOQ (Bachelor Officers Quarters). Whereas previously chaplains were often little more than "handymen," regulation revision AR 60-5 now stated:

Chaplains will be employed on no duties other than those required of them by law, or pertaining to their profession as clergymen, except when an exigency of the service...shall make it necessary.[11]

The senior chaplain of his M Company was Fr. (Capt.) William Maguire, a priest from the diocese of Newark, who helped make home away from home a bit more familiar. Orders soon came from the Commanding General, Third Marine Division that Martin would be on duty with the United States Marines. He transferred from San Diego to San Francisco and then to Pearl Harbor before boarding a plane for Nouméa. A boat then transported him to Guadalcanal where he hooked in with the 19th Marines who had arrived from New Zealand some months earlier.

Another contemporary transport boat, the SS *Dorchester,* had been sunk to the Atlantic floor between Newfoundland and Greenland on 3 February 1943, victim of a German torpedo. Chaplains half a world away were moved, not by fear of a recurrence in the Pacific arena, but by the heroism of the four chaplains aboard who helped men off the ship, offered their gloves and life preservers and went down into the icy waters holding hands and singing hymns in a saintly calm. Among them were Newark native John P. Washington, a Catholic priest previously assigned to St. Stephen's Church, Arlington, and Protestant Clark Poling who had earlier written to his father: "I know I have your prayers, but please don't pray simply that God will keep me safe. War is danger-ous business. Pray that God will make me adequate!"[12] Mirroring his Atlantic counterparts, reports and letters from veterans attest to both the bloody business through which and the faith and bravery with which Martin acted time and again.

In June, 1943, his division maneuvered further up the "slot" through the Solomon Islands, bound for Bougainville. Duties there were described as mostly pleasant and living accommoda-tions were simple but adequate. In the *Canons of Hippolytus,* number XIV states: a Christian soldier "should fulfill his obligation without deceit and in fear of God."[13] Within days Martin secured and erected a tent where he reserved the Blessed Sacrament and offered daily Mass. He heard confessions regularly and visited other priests available to hear his. Reports came that some would be forging further up the canal; Martin was disheartened to learn he was not among them. The majority of these volunteer chaplains "sought combat duty – not because they thought they would enjoy war, but because they felt they could make a more effective contribution in minister-ing to men under such conditions."[14] Martin boarded the next available ship and soon reassembled with his unit.

Repositioned in Bougainville, Martin set up another tent chapel and with the help of a Marine organist and a number of male voices, developed a rich liturgy, employing among other things, a Mass he wrote for the troops. The Newark *Evening News* cited the chaplain's work in its 24 January 1944 edition. He had administered four sacraments to Private John Paul Raby, Jr. of Port Providence, RI: baptism, penance, Holy Eucharist and confirmation in the span of an hour with special dispensation granted by Bougainville's bishop. "Nothing was too much!" he recalled, "My enthusiasm knew no bounds."[15] At the same time the local newspaper was reporting Martin's doings, stateside news was reaching him. Mail call one day brought equally sad and joyous news. Father Eugene Polhemus, his fellow confrere and classmate who was similarly serving with the army, died in Louisiana shortly after digging a foxhole. Meanwhile, a nephew had been born and graced with the name Martin. With little time for home front reflection, he boarded the *Windsor* which steered from Bougainville to the Mariana Islands, reaching Guam in July.

Martin was overcome, once topside, by the number of nearby ships, all of which seemed to be firing at Guam. He and others debarked, climbing down the ship into Higgins boats which transported them to an extended reef where they changed over to amphibious vehicles capable of handling both water and coral. They ventured ashore, landing near Agaña, Guam's capitol. Too close to the hostilities they were told to make their way down the beach. Serpentining along, they paused behind a disabled tank to catch their breath. Japanese shells rained close by and Martin's companion, Dr. Shepherd cried out: "Dr. Goetsch has been hit!" Martin drew close and anointed him. He died from his shrapnel wounds moments later. They saw to identification and then continued down the beach. Martin did not recall whether or not they had buried Dr. Goetsch which speaks to one of a few things. First, the frenzy of the firefight may have fogged his memory. Martin's own memoirs recount:

> *Burials became one of our principle occupations during those early days...We buried the men reverently, carefully marking the places of burial and the identification of those interred. Scarcely a few days later, the doctors asked us to exhume those we had buried, and graves registration now came with trucks to transfer our dead to more suitable resting places."* [16]

Second, whereas it seems like a horrific moment someone could hardly forget, it is likely that the chaplains found themselves in such situations more often then they would like to recall and at different times different events may have ensued. Third, war death is an experience unlike those with which civilized society is more familiar: a slow succumbing to disease, wake, funeral, eulogy, repast with friends and relatives. "War death results from a hostile act precipitated by human failure...The soldier who witnesses war death is doomed to random recall of the event...The final, enduring image of war death is horror." [17] But the final image may not necessarily equate with death, often wounded soldiers are "dusted off" the battlefield with no follow-up reports, no closure. The image of Dr. Goetsch, of death, may have etched so harshly and recurred so frequently in Martin's mind that memory of ensuing events were forever blocked. Martin and another chaplain, Ed Cunningham finally reached "safety" and dug a foxhole under tree coverage where they planned to spend the night. However, a sergeant informed them of another nearby hole occupied by six men that had been hit. Martin and Ed anointed the wounded, prayed over the dead, and attached their dog tags.

Once situated inland from the beaches of Guam's shore, Martin began ministering to the island's residents, nearly one hundred percent of whom were Catholic. The temptation he fought most often in the tropics was the "manana" syndrome. Irregular schedules seemed to be protocol and many people excelled at putting non-essential tasks off until tomorrow, but idleness is a friend of the devil; Martin kept busy. It was not out of the ordinary to be called upon to conduct services for the burial of fallen infants, victims of the unhealthy conditions present prior to the Marines' landing. He also heard adult confessions regularly. The sacramental prayers were still in Latin at that time, a great consolation as they provided some familiarity to the penitents. Although the Mass also was in Latin, Martin even dared to deliver homilies in the local dialect of Chammora! St. Basil once wrote in *Letter* 106, "It is possible even in the military profession to maintain perfect love for God and that a Christian ought to be characterized not by the clothes he wears but by the disposition of his soul."[18] Martin feared not foes before him, but welcomed fellow members of the Body of Christ and co-heirs and co-architects of the Kingdom of God.

While in Guam, he wrote to Abbot Patrick in what has characteristically and good-heartedly come to be known as a Martinized style, that is, an account unsoiled enough to make the dry cleaners of the same name proud. For example, he described his trip as "pleasant" and expanded on his landing there on D-day no further than coming through "without a scratch." In the same note, he revealed his continued concern with his home community, Benedictinism and the world's troubles beyond his Pacific parameters, expressing agreement and gratitude to St. Mary's Abbey for voting to support Monte Cassino in its rebuilding efforts after the unfortunate errant British bombing incident.[19] More immediately, South Carolina Navy chaplain Fr. Al Kamler approached Martin with a concern. Both of their tours were rapidly coming to a close, yet their divisions were preparing for an important mission further north. Both men feared for the safety of their green replacements and subsequently sought extensions to their tours. The guilt of leaving behind buddies and unknown replacements in harm's way is a pain with which veterans constantly grapple. Their requests reached as far as Washington but were denied, and rather than landing on Iwo Jima, Martin made his way to Yorktown, Virginia and the nearby Naval Mine Warfare School in Norfolk.

From Yorktown, Martin was asked to visit a nearby camp where German prisoners of war were housed. He met Fr. Neugebauer, a priest drafted into the German army and twice wounded. Given the option to spend his imprisonment in either officers' quarters where he could not function as a priest or with grunt soldiers in far poorer conditions but where he could function, he chose the latter. He petitioned Martin for occasional deliveries of Mass wine and bread. Those visits nourished a friendship between men separated by national loyalties but bound in priestly mission.

It was in Virginia that Martin discovered Ronald Knox's recent translation of the New Testament from Vulgate to vernacular and was mesmerized by the English translation, purchasing it on the spot. He soon purchased the second volume as well and thence began the practice of reading Sacred Scripture straight from Genesis through Revelation on a continuum for the duration of his life.

In the weeks prior to Martin's discharge from the Navy "in dominant public interest," Fr. Adrian McLaughlin's and Martin's mothers were both in Beth Israel Hospital, Newark having been hit by a city bus as they were crossing 12th Street and Clinton Avenue on their way to a Benedictine Mother's League function. Martin requested a leave which was granted when the subsequent call came from Fr. Lambert Dunne that Martin's mother's injuries had proven fatal. He entered his father's home and arms and both cried before arranging the funeral. "The vagaries of life!" Martin recalled, "Looking forward to returning to the abbey in less than two months and now mother's funeral!"[20] World War II came to a close aboard the battleship Missouri. There in Tokyo Bay, General Douglas MacArthur declared:

> We have had our last chance. If we do not now devise some greater and more equitable system Armageddon will be at our door. The problem basically is theological and involves a spiritual recrudescence and improvement of human character that will synchronize with our almost matchless advance in science, art, literature and all material and cultural developments of the past two thousand years. It must be of the spirit if we are to save the flesh.[21]

Martin was detached with the rank of Commander in the Naval Reserve in 1946, armed for spiritual warfare, and perhaps a prep school's senior religion classes.

Back in the classroom, teaching religion, music, Latin, and German, Martin soon became involved in extracurricular activities including the New Jersey All-State Orchestra and Chorus. He was a member of the N.J. Music Educators Association during the mid-nineteen fifties at which time he earned a Doctorate of Philosophy in Music Education from New York University (1956). He garnered knowledge, wisdom and spiritual depth only to in turn bestow it upon his students. "He had a sense of gravitas," recalled Mr. Paul Thorton, St. Benedict's Prep alumnus and current development director. "Some priests tried to be pals with students. Father Martin respected young men. He always knew he was their teacher."[22] He also taught Sacred Scripture to postulants and novices at the Convent of the Mercy Sisters at Mount Saint Mary's in Plainfield as well as at Caldwell College and homiletics at Immaculate Conception Seminary, Darlington. All the while he ministered as a weekend assistant at St. Rose of Lima Parish in Short Hills where he and the pastor, John Ryan shared a great love of John Henry Newman. He also lived for a year at Sacred Heart in Elizabeth working in the parish and ministering as chaplain at Elizabeth General Hospital (Elizabeth's two other hospitals, operated by the Alexian Brother's and St. Elizabeth's had their own chaplains). For several years Martin weekly visited the Little Sisters of the Poor in Newark in the capacity of teacher and confessor beginning in 1965. At that time he was also the chaplain of the Newman Club at the Madison campus of Fairleigh Dickenson University.

Terms in the offices of both subprior and prior, respectively the third and second in the chain of command within monastic houses, at Newark were trying periods for Martin. Beyond the cloister, his father, Paul Burne died 10 July 1962 while vacationing in Belmar; Martin spent days at his hospital bedside anointing him in his final hours. His first experiences as superior of some capacity within the community revealed discrepancies between monastic ideals he held and the day-to-day realities of cenobitic life. A series of letters exist between Martin, Abbot Patrick, Rt. Rev. Archabbot Denis Strittmatter, then President of the American Cassinese Congregation, and

Abbot Cuthbert Goeb, St. Mary's most recent visitator, regarding Martin's anguished feelings of "right Church, wrong pew." His sense of ordered life did not seem to jibe well with his confreres at that time, and he quietly sought dispensation from his monastic vows. Although his eyes set on a diocese or a religious community more strictly adherent to the *Holy Rule* of St. Benedict, he instead observed obedience and remained in place as was the want and advice of those with whom he consulted.

In 1963, the centennial year of the signing of the Emancipation Proclamation, Martin made a pilgrimage to the steps of the Lincoln Memorial to be in attendance when Dr. Martin Luther King, Jr. delivered his "I Have a Dream" speech. "Nonviolent resistance is also an internal matter," Dr. King had preached previously in 1958. "It not only avoids external violence or external physical violence but also internal violence of spirit. And so at the center of our movement stood the philosophy of love."[23] Abbot Melvin Valvano, Newark Abbey, recognized and verbalized Martin's outward flow of internal love; he wrote:

> *He saw his countrymen inured to [slavery and racism] and for the most part*
> *exhibiting a cunning 'innocence' that the Civil Rights movement was struggling to*
> *unmask, crack open and overcome and this – mysteriously and remarkably – by*
> *non-violent action! Martin became a disciple of Dr. King and sought wherever*
> *and however to join him in this often bloody battle for freedom for all people.*[24]

Martin realized that Dr. King's message resonated strongly and applicably in the rapidly evolving City of Newark. King wrote in a posthumously published essay, "A Testament of Hope," "The Newark riots could certainly have been prevented by a more aggressive political involvement on the part of that city's Negroes."[25] At the 1968 St. Benedict's Preparatory School Centennial Dinner, recently elected Abbot Martin Burne joined voices with his slain namesake in addressing those in attendance. Citing Scripture, Vatican II's *The Declaration on Christian Education, The Church Today,* and President Johnson's *Report for Action,* he challenged the alumni, the monks and the City at large.

> *I propose to the business community of Newark...the challenge of a lifetime. I*
> *challenge any man to ask me what I am doing, or what I – and my brothers in*
> *Saint Benedict – are willing to do. I challenge a society that talks a great deal*
> *about helping the underprivileged to let Saint Benedict's do just that. Let not the*
> *leaders of industry and business...deplore the racial disturbances to which our City*
> *has been heir. Let each of us show what he can – and will – do.*[26]

The perceived "unwise and untimely" activities of the peace movement attested to by King from his Birmingham jail cell served as catalysts for Martin. While noting certain exceptions to the rule, King expressed great disappointment in the white church and majority of Catholic leaders.[27] Taking up his own gauntlet, Martin introduced a resolution at a chapter meeting on 3 March, 1970 seeking approval of "A Better Chance" (ABC) Program through which four disadvantaged students a year would receive scholarships to Delbarton School. A lack of funds ultimately squelched the program then, but similar awards are granted today. The larger world observed a fresh sense of social concern within the post-Vatican II Church, emphasizing the need to be involved "with the downtrodden, the ill, the poor, and the neglected. That emphasis was well placed, Martin believed, but for proper balance, all action must flow from prayer; "however much time the Savior of mankind gave to his ministry, to the needs of others, never does one conceive Jesus as anything other than a man of prayer."[28] Regardless of his office or state of health, Martin's desire for national and world peace remained firm; evidenced as late as the summer prior to his passing when he wrote a letter to President George W. Bush disappointed by media reports of impending war. "We, [the United States], are not widely known as aggressors..." he noted, "I write you ask that you desist from the anti-Iraq attitude that you seem to exhibit, and pray that you will not be the agent of war, with its really terrible suffering for countless law-abiding citizens and children."[29] Acknowledging the value of life and horrors of war, Mrs. Desiree Thompson, Special Assistant to the President and Director of Presidential Correspondence, replied to Martin's letter on the Feast of St. Patrick, who legend says rid Ireland of its snakes. Thompson, in similar fashion, said the President was fully determined to rid Iraq of their dictator Saddam Hussein and his regime by disarming them of weapons of mass destruction the United Nations' weapons inspectors have since reported to be non-existent.

Martin returned to Delbarton at Abbot Patrick's request to function as novice master beginning in the summer of 1963, and additionally vocation director a year later. The relocation and reassignment provided opportunity for Martin to petition the prior, Fr. Michael Collins, regarding a *resourcement* of the monastic horarium. Permission was granted and the inclusion of daily chanting within Vespers started up, a tradition passed down to the present. Confreres have lovingly joked over the years that in a Lawrence Welkian tone, they learned to "Swing and sway with Martin J." All four novices in Martin's charge pronounced vows on the feast of St. Benedict, 11 July 1966, two of whom, Frs. Edwin Leahy and Philip Waters remain prominent figures today of the Newark community in their roles as St. Benedict's Prep headmaster and St. Mary's Parish pastor, respectively.

During the same time frame, Abbot Baldwin Dworschak, Abbot President from St. John's Abbey, Collegeville, MN presided over the visitations of the Morristown and Newark communities. He announced that Abbot Patrick, who had previously petitioned the Holy See for permission to resign if his ill health continued, additionally requested the election of a coadjutor abbot, someone to carry on the administration of the abbey while Patrick continued to decline in health and who would smoothly transition into his own abbacy upon Patrick's death. Permission was granted. On the second ballot of 28 November 1966, Fr. Laurence Grassman announced the results: "Father Martin Burne received the required two-thirds vote (62) of the 93 ballots cast...With faculties recently received from the Holy See, Abbot Baldwin then confirmed the election."[30] The Newark

News described him on this occasion as "A saintly man, well liked by priests and lay people alike."[31] His friend and confrere, Abbot Lambert Dunne, then serving with the Abbot Primate at Sant' Anselmo, Rome sent his congratulations: "To say that I am thrilled with the election is to put it very mildly, and I am given to understand there is universal approval. *Ad multos annos.*"[32] The booklet printed for Martin's Solemn Blessing as Coadjutor Abbot states:

> *In this age of Vatican II renewal, Abbot Martin faces formidable challenges which*
> *he must accept both for his monks and for the Church. In this process of monastic*
> *growth and development, adaptation and implementation, Saint Benedict reminds*
> *him...: "The Abbot ought always remember what he is and what he is called, and to*
> *know that to whom much has been entrusted, from him much will be required"*
> *(Holy Rule, Ch. 2).*[33]

Within the Mass, Martin reflected: "I pray that I will be able to make our monastery one that is relevant to the world...I hope to be the kind of abbot that Benedict wants me to be, a man among men."[34] He echoed the theme in his first school Mass homily, challenging each student in much the same way as in his centennial address mentioned above, to "play the man."

The community that had lived under an ill and often absentee abbot since 1937 and that now was just beginning to digest the Second Vatican Council hoped for change. Months prior to Martin's election, St. Mary's had undergone its triennial visitation. The report drafted therein by Abbot President Baldwin reflected the spirit of Vatican II: "The Council has given us an incentive for renewal and reform which cannot be denied, if we hope to survive and flourish in the next generation. What cannot be avoided is self-study, self-criticism, a clear exposition of our problems, and a genuine *aggiornamento.*"[35] Martin encouraged frequent meetings to generate more community-wide ideas and initiated a renewal committee of twenty members under the guidance of Prior Michael Collins; however, the changes he addressed first dealt with men whose health conditions were hampering their leadership roles both in parishes and the prep schools. The committee eventually listed three areas for concentration: an awareness of prayer in all of its ramifications, and in some daily visible manifestation; a conviction regarding *lectio divina* in its full sense as formative of a community; and work, rather than being seen as the almost exclusive concern of the community, must be given a more honest appraisal.[36] The new abbot quickly heeded advice from confreres as their letters attest. In one instance, former Headmaster of Delbarton School and Director of Development, Fr. Stephen Findlay answered one of Martin's queries on 4 December 1966 regarding school affairs both in Newark and Morristown, strongly supporting an increased presence and role for duly qualified laymen, under the influence of Vatican II in actively supporting the Benedictine way of life, and the schools were proper receptacles in which to channel their talents, training and experience. An influx of lay faculty and staff continued thence. He also oversaw the construction of a new dormitory, Schmeil-O'Brien, dedicated to both a benefactor and his predecessor, and a monastic cemetery on the Delbarton campus.

Beyond Morristown and Newark, Martin visited the community's men in Brazil who were studying Portuguese and planning a South American Benedictine foundation, however the monks in the Garden State were not overly supportive of planting a mission beyond its borders. A chapter meeting devoted largely to the question of foreign missions bore witness to the renewal committee running into enough problems of its own; therefore it was "inadvisable to saddle another committee with these problems."[37] Martin urged continued pondering and prayer over the question so that in the future, the community could find some sense of unison and move forward accordingly. Eventually it was decided that Fathers Edmund Nugent, Sebastian Joseph and Columba Rafferty would continue their missionary work but not seek replacements upon their retirement or property for a foundation.

Martin began his longtime membership with the Morristown Clergy Council in 1968. That same year, St. Mary's Abbey celebrated the dedication of the abbey organ on 8 December. The guest organist Mr. Dennis G. Michno of Trinity Church on Broadway and Wall Street in Manhattan played the instrument designed by Mr. Eric Fiss, who constructed it over a three month span. Its final cost, $8,800.00, was funded primarily through the financial gifts received at Martin's abbatial blessing.

Martin's musical degrees came to the fore again when he spearheaded a Congregation-wide Consilium for the revision of liturgical music within the monastic offices. Copious correspondences between liturgical committees throughout the Congregation channeled through Martin as revision and renewal helped reshape the monastic horarium of Benedictine houses throughout the United States. Areas of concern ranged from pitch range to retention of Gregorian hymns alongside a sprinkling of folk music, to proper instruments to be played, and so on. The massive effort and wide involvement from many fronts helped form settings and structures still in place today.

Martin led with gallant strides but felt the increasing stress of serving two communities as one abbot. Pressure compounded with the City of Newark's growing pains illustrated most tellingly in the 1967 riots. Concerning those particularly disturbing events he addressed the community:

All of our men resident there should be commended for the steadfastness with which they accepted their very difficult and trying position. No one panicked, and everyone tried to follow the suggestions given by those trying to restore order to the City. Father Maurus asked that the community contribute money for food, along with several parishes in and around the city, and this we did....More than ever, the City needs acts of confidence....I plan to write a letter to Governor Hughes. I shall assure him of our continued interest in the City in such a way that he will feel free to call upon us should our help be needed in ways of which we are capable.[38]

Martin's Statement to the Chapter on 29 June 1968 focused on the struggles of leadership in a house divided. Not inclined to 'love the one and despise the other,' he simply felt that the two roles demanded something beyond the capacity of the ordinary mortal. The malaised Newark community felt itself orphaned, in part because Martin believed one cannot stand at two helms simultaneously. He found their unrest understandable but unacceptable and therefore sought action in the matter. He proposed to either phase out operations in Newark altogether or to seek an abbot for an independent house in Newark. Discussions regarding the withdrawal of the Newark Priory revealed a substantial number of men still believed in its mission. An initial straw vote trisected support between the status quo, Newark's independent status, and a phasing out of the Newark operation. That shaped the resolution before the chapter: the separation of the Morristown and Newark communities. The resulting vote overwhelmingly favored separation. On 21 November 1968, the High Street Benedictines again attained independent status, taking the name Newark Abbey under the patronage of the Immaculate Conception.

The separation did not distance Martin from the stress he felt prior. If his election as coadjutor was unusual, equally so was his early resignation from a post generally held until death. For all the grandeur with which he was ushered into his abbacy, the July edition of the Newark *Advocate* tellingly stating "Abbot Burne, 56, will be plain Father Burne in his new role." His resignation took effect 1 July 1971. Martin could scarcely be described as plain, yet being counted once again as an equal, a confrere hastening alongside his fellow monks, was a desire burning in him at least since his naval days when he often wrote to Abbot Patrick concerning his attempts to be more charitable to others. In the interim years, he had fine tuned that virtue which is perhaps the reason he accepted his next position despite internal anger over his even being nominated.

Martin had been elected by the General Chapter of the American Cassinese Congregation to the Council of the Abbot President, Abbot Baldwin a few years earlier. It was this very council on which he sat to which he submitted his resignation naming stress as his primary reason. Within three months of his fellow council members' sympathy and approval for resignation they looked to him to head the Congregation. He acceded. In the same year he accepted Bishop Lawrence Casey's request to sit on the Paterson Pastoral Council. All the while he continued to teach a partial load of senior religion classes at Delbarton.

As Abbot President, Martin traveled to many abbeys for the purpose of visitations. "The president of the Congregation need not serve as a visitor, but early on I resolved that either I or a Council member would be part of each visitation team. Such firsthand information would help the Council and me when we met to consider the stability and solidity of our various houses."[39] These experiences strengthened his resolve in the Benedictine charism of balance between ora et *labora,* prayer and hard work. Each community had its own particular issues with which to deal but no one expected quick fixes or visitators to provide cure-alls. Conversely, one visitation taught Martin, the visitor, an important lesson in patience. Predecessors had suggested certain changes which had not been effected. By the time Martin arrived, he "felt like a new broom that ought to sweep clean" and strongly urged a change in the house's leadership.[40] The changes were set in place, and the results were disheartening. In hindsight, Martin realized that the previous administration had been working rather well and that the insights of those living within that particular monastery, in that instance, were keener than those of the outside visitators. He was never again as quick with verbalized opinions.

His re-election equated to a twelve year commitment, all totaled as Abbot President; he informed the Council that he would not be a candidate for a third term. In those twelve years he oversaw numerous visitations, twenty-nine abbatial scrutinies and elections throughout the United States, Puerto Rico, Bahamas, Canada and Mexico, and organized Congregation-wide meetings regarding liturgy, music, formation, finances and the like. During that span, Abbot Joseph Gerry of St. Mary's daughter house, St. Anselm's Abbey, Manchester, New Hampshire petitioned Abbot Brian Clarke in 1981 for Martin's services at their Woodside Priory in Portola Valley, California. "I realize," he wrote, "that I am asking for more than a man, I am asking for Abbot Martin."[41] The timing was amiss for that mission, but shortly after resigning a similar request came forth. When he stepped down in 1983, Bishop Frank Rodimer's took advantage of the opportunity to write Martin regarding the formation of a new position: the Diocese of Peterson's Director of Liturgy, a responsibility he felt Martin was "uniquely suited to assume."[42] He wrote: "I know that your personal interest, your experience, your extensive knowledge of liturgy and music, and your life as a Benedictine all contribute to making you well equipped to take on the position of Director of Sacred Liturgy."[43] Martin accepted, serving in that role until another S.O.S. sounded.

The year was 1985. Holy Cross Abbey in Canon City, Colorado was in trouble. Martin stepped in as Administrator, arriving 7 March. The community prayer life there seemed strong and their apostolates in parishes, jails, hospitals and their prep school were in order, although student enrolment was low and drugs were present in the school. The problem was financial. Martin sought Congregation-wide support; petitions proved fruitful. He called home Father Kenneth Hein, who had been working at St. Anselm's College to serve as headmaster and to work in the finance department, but the paucity of pupils registered (less than 40) for the following academic year proved fatal. The state of the Abbey was bleak when Martin addressed a letter to the abbots and priors of the congregation on 25 October 1985. The school had been closed, weekend parish work was not in demand, the property was being divided for the purpose of sale and/or rent, and horses and house antiques were being auctioned off. Nevertheless, the letter contained notes of gratitude for financial assistance from other houses (a particular "shot in the arm" was the more than generous amount given by St. Mary's Abbey, attested to in a letter dated 23 January 1986 to Abbot Brian Clarke), and hope in that the community boasted several young monks working through philosophy and theology studies. By the summer of 1987 he was able to report to the abbots and priors of the congregation that the Holy Cross Chapter had voted to overturn its initial decision to sell the property and relocate. Through continued soul-searching, serious dialogue and much hard work, it seemed they could steer themselves out of dire straits and these men in black could operate in the black once again. With the financial picture more firmly settled, Martin returned to Morristown in the summer of 1985.

Positions in the Delbarton religion department did not open until the second trimester of that academic year and therefore the abbot emeritus occupied himself with retreat work. He occupied a place on the Delbarton faculty until 1995. Additionally, he continued offering weekend assistance in local parishes, as well as lecturing and teaching Scripture classes to the abbey's formation classes. He compiled a number of his lectures and reflections into a book of meditations, *A Furiously Sweeping Woman,* published in 1991; notes for a second book remain unpublished at present. In one chapter Martin focused upon Moses: "Had his vision been less, had his trust in God been less, he might easily have given up. But he sees what others do not see: it is God who leads one into the unknown future; and the best human efforts, apart from trust in God, cannot guess all that lies ahead."[44] Through his pouring over Scripture in *lectio continua,* Martin had come to embrace, exemplify and exalt the Good News. What he found in Moses became internalized and imaged through his words and works. "When he published his book," current Abbot President Timothy Kelly offered on the occasion of Martin's passing, "he told me that many people have one book in them. But the best book was his presence, his life, his witness to what it means to shine the light of Christ on others and then discover in them the same Christ who was in him."[45] St. Benedict cautions monks, in accord with Scripture, against criticizing the speck in someone else's eye while missing the log in one's own; Martin conversely excelled at noticing and bringing to light others' talents, interests and assets.

With the onset of the frailties of human life, Martin traveled less frequently but it would be inaccurate to say he slowed down. His work in the abbey archives and his letter correspondences remained at full strength. Most impressive to most, however, was Martin's undying faithfulness to prayer, both private and communal. The strength and wisdom to see to completion his life's accomplishments could be made possible only with God as his source. Fittingly, then, God forever remained his summit to Whom he returned. Naysayers regret his short lived term as abbot and suggest it points to a lacking in a monk who professed stability alongside obedience and *conversatio morum,* however, stability speaks to more than geographic location. Martin was unfailingly the first in his choir stall for each of the abbey's four daily offices. He adopted the psalmist's mantra rising at midnight to offer praise with a private Mass daily. In the end, he was able to sing with the angels a Newman classic dear to his heart, "Lead Kindly Light" as he reached his heavenly reward 25 July 2003.

Footnotes:

1 Abbot Thomas Confroy, St. Mary's Abbey, interview by author, 4 June 2005, Morristown, NJ.

2 Martin Burne, "Autobiographical writings, 2001-2003,"p. 6, St. Mary's Abbey Archives.

3 Ibid., 12.

4 Robert Gushwa, *The Best and Worst of Times: The United States Army Chaplaincy 1920 – 1945,* volume 4. (Washington, DC: Office of the Chief of Chaplains Department of the Army, 1977), 95.

5 Burne, "Autobiographical writings, 2001-2003," p. 14.

6 Louis Swift, *The Early Fathers on War and Military Service,* (Wilmington, DE: Michael, Glazier, Inc., 1983), 114.

7 Burne, "Autobiographical writings, 2001-2003," pp. 14-15.

8 Gushwa, 93.

9 Martin Burne, "Autobiographical writings, 2001-2003," p. 16.

10 See Gushwa, 98-99.

11 Ibid., 21.

12 Ibid., 127.

13 Swift, 93.

14 Gushwa, 148.

15 Martin Burne, "Autobiographical writings, 2001-2003," p. 11.

16 Ibid., page not numbered.

17 Paul Drew, *Jenny 4,* (Spring Lake Heights, NJ: Charleson and Associates, 2004), 30-31.

18 Swift, 94.

19 Martin Burne, Guam, to Abbot Patrick O'Brien, 9 August 1944, St. Mary's Abbey Archives.

20 Ibid., "Autobiographical writings, 2001-2003," pp. 32-33.

21 Rodger Venzke, *Confidence in Battle, Inspiration in Peace: The United States Chaplaincy 1945-1975,* volume 5. (Washington, DC: Office of the Chief of Chaplains Department of the Army, 1977), 1

22 Braun, "An Abbot of Grace and Strength Saved St. Benedict's," First of five in a series titles

"Lives Well Lived," Newark Star Ledger, 22 December 2003, pp. 1, 20.

23 Martin Luther King, Jr., "The Power of Nonviolence," I Have a Dram: Writings and Speeches that Changed the World, (New York: Harper Collins Publishers, 1986), 31.

24 Abbot Melvin Valvano, Testimonial on the occasion of Martin Burne's death, 25 July 2003, Newark Abbey.

25 James Washington, ed., *"A Testament of Hope," A Testament of Hope: The Essential Writings and Speeches of Martin Luther King, Jr.,* (New York: Harper Collins Publishers, 1986), 319.

26 Martin Burne, "Address at the St. Benedict's Preparatory School Centennial Dinner," June 1968, St. Mary's Abbey Archives.

27 See Washington, "Letter from Birmingham City Jail," 298; and *Playboy* Interview," 345.

28 Martin Burne, "Autobiographical writings, 2001-2003," p. 100.

29 Ibid., Morristown, to President George Bush, 13 July 2002, St. Mary's Abbey Archives.

30 Ibid., "Autobiographical writings, 2001-2003," p. 41; cf. Minutes of Chapter Meeting for 28 November 1966.

31 *News* (Newark), page unknown, 29 November 1966

32 Abbot Lambert Dunne, Rome, to Coadjutor Abbot Martin Burne, 12 December 1966, St. Mary's Abbey Archives.

33 Program for the Liturgy Celebrating Martin Burne's Abbatial Blessing, 2 February 1967, 3.

34 *The Beacon* (Paterson), 9 February 1967, 6, St. Mary's Abbey Archives.

35 Abbot Baldwin Dworschak, "Recessus of Visitation held at St. Mary's Abby, Morristown, New Jersey, 4-9 February 1966," St. Mary's Abbey Archives.

36 Committee on Renewal, "Recommendations to Abbot Martin Burne," 13 February 1968, St. Mary's Archives.

37 Fr. Simon Gallagher, "Chapter meeting notes for 21 April 1969," St. Mary's Abbey Archives.

38 Martin Burne, Morristown, to Confreres, 23 July 1967, St. Mary's Abbey Archives.

39 Ibid., "A Different Kind of Presidency," *Delbarton Today,* Winter 1990, 9.

40 Ibid., "Autobiographical writings, 2001-2003," p. 49.

41 Abbot Joseph Gerry, Manchester, NH, to Abbot Brian Clarke, 27 January 1981, St. Mary's Abbey Archives.

42 Bishop Frank Rodimer, Paterson, to Abbot Brian Clarke, Eve of the Ascension, 1983, St. Mary's Abbey Archives.

43 Ibid., to Abbot Martin Burne, 21 June 1983, St. Mary's Abbey Archives.

44 Burne, *A Furiously Sweeping Woman: God's Loving Pursuit of Each Person,* (Denville, NJ: Dimension Books, 1991), 57.

45 Abbot Timothy Kelly, Collegeville, MN, Tribute to Martin Burne, 29 July 2003, St. Mary's Abbey Archives.

WORKS CITED

Beacon, The (Paterson), 9 February 1967, St. Mary's Abbey Archives.

Braun, Bob. "An Abbot of Grace and Strength Saved St. Benedict's." First of five in a series titles "Lives Well Lived." Newark *Star Ledger,* 22 December 2003.

Burne, Martin. "A Different Kind of Presidency." *Delbarton Today,* Winter 1990, 9.

_____. "Address at the St. Benedict's Preparatory School Centennial Dinner." June 1968, St. Mary's Abbey Archives.

_____. *A Furiously Sweeping Woman: God's Loving Pursuit of Each Person.* Denville, NJ: Dimension Books, 1991.

_____. "Autobiographical writings, 2001-2003." St. Mary's Abbey Archives.

_____. Guam, to Abbot Patrick O'Brien, 9 August 1944. St. Mary's Abbey Archives.

_____. Morristown, to Confreres, 23 July 1967, St. Mary's Abbey Archives

_____. Morristown, to President George Bush, 13 July 2002, St. Mary's Abbey Archives.

Committee on Renewal. "Recommendations to Abbot Martin Burne." 13 February 1968, St. Mary's Archives.

Confroy, Thomas, Abbot of St. Mary's Abbey. Interview by author, 4 June 2005, Morristown, NJ.

Drew, Paul. *Jenny 4.* Spring Lake Heights, NJ: Charleson and Associates, 2004.

Dunne, Lambert, Rome, to Coadjutor Abbot Martin Burne, 12 December 1966, St. Mary's Abbey Archives.

Dworschak, Baldwin. "Recessus of Visitation held at St. Mary's Abbey, Morristown, New Jersey, 4-9 February 1966." St. Mary's Abbey Archives.

Gallagher, Simon. "Chapter meeting notes for 21 April 1969," St. Mary's Abbey Archives.

Gerry, Joseph, Manchester, NH, to Abbot Brian Clarke, 27 January 1981, St. Mary's Abbey Archives.

Gushwa, Robert. *The Best and Worst of Times: The United States Army Chaplaincy 1920 – 1945*. volume 4. Washington, DC: Office of the Chief of Chaplains Department of the Army, 1977.

Kelly, Timothy, Collegeville, MN, Tribute to Martin Burne, 29 July 2003, St. Mary's Abbey Archives.

King, Jr., Martin Luther. *I have a Dream: Writings and Speeches that Changed the World*. Edited by James Washington. New York: Harper Collins Publishers, 1992.

News (Newark), 29 November 1966.

Program for the Liturgy Celebrating Martin Burne's Abbatial Blessing, 2 February 1967.

Rodimer, Frank, Paterson, to Abbot Brian Clarke, Eve of the Ascension, 1983, St. Mary's Abbey Archives.

_____. Paterson, to Abbot Martin Burne, 21 June 1983, St. Mary's Abbey Archives.

Swift, Louis. *The Early Fathers on War and Military Service*. Wilmington, DE: Michael Glazier, Inc., 1983.

Valvano, Melvin. Testimonial on the occasion of Martin Burne's death, 25 July 2003, Newark Abbey.

Venzke, Rodger. *Confidence in Battle, Inspiration in Peace: The United States Chaplaincy 1945-1975*. volume 5. Washington, DC: Office of the Chief of Chaplains Department of the Army, 1977.

Washington, James, ed. A Testament of Hope: *The Essential Writings and Speeches of Martin Luther King, Jr*. New York: Harper Collins Publishers, 1986.

THE ABBOTS OF ST. MARY'S ABBEY

Rt. Rev. James Zilliox, O.S.B.	(1884-1886)+
Rt. Rev. Hilary Pfraengle, O.S.B.	(1886-1909)+
Rt. Rev. Ernest Helmstetter, O.S.B.	(1910-1937)+
Rt. Rev. Patrick M. O'Brien, O.S.B.	(1937-1967)+
Rt. Rev. Martin J. Burne, O.S.B.	(1966-1971)+
Rt. Rev. Leonard G. Cassell, O.S.B.	(1971-1975)
Rt. Rev. Brian H. Clarke, O.S.B.	(1975-1995)
Rt. Rev. Gerard Parker Lair, O.S.B.	(1995-1998)
Rt. Rev. Thomas J. Confroy, O.S.B.	(1998-2006)
Rt. Rev. Giles P. Hayes, O.S.B.	(2006-)

THE HEADMASTERS OF DELBARTON SCHOOL

Rev. Augustine Wirth, O.S.B.	(1939-1942)
Rev. Stephen Findlay, O.S.B.	(1942-1967)
Rev. Francis O'Connell, O.S.B.	(1967-1972)
Rev. James O'Donnell, O.S.B.	(1972-1975)
Rev. Gerard Lair, O.S.B.	(1975-1980)
Rev. Giles Hayes, O.S.B.	(1980-1985)
Rev. Bruno Ugliano, O.S.B.	(1985-1990)
Rev. Beatus Lucey, O.S.B.	(1990-1995)
Rev. Giles Hayes, O.S.B.	(1995-1999)
Rev. Luke Travers, O.S.B.	(1999-2007)

DELBARTON MOTHERS' GUILD PRESIDENTS

Mrs. Maria Cannon	1946-50	Mrs. Nancy Higgins	1979-80
Mrs. Helena Hasney	1950-52	Mrs. Elizabeth Gilfillan	1980-81
Mrs. Gertrude Gallagher	1952-54	Mrs. Ann Longo	1981-82
Mrs. Mary Veronica Noble	1954-55	Mrs. Marie Stanton	1982-83
Mrs. Henrietta Baran	1955-56	Mrs. Grace Fiocco	1983-84
Mrs. Mary Corroon	1956-57	Mrs. Else Benz	1984-85
Mrs. Helen Gallagher	1957-58	Mrs. Joyce Henry	1985-86
Mrs. Sandra Fittin	1958-59	Mrs. Gloria Sweeney	1986-87
Mrs. Wendy Martin	1959-60	Mrs. Roberta Ferguson	1987-88
Mrs. Catherine Moran	1960-61	Mrs. Lottie Hladick	1988-89
Mrs. Joan Scott	1961-62	Mrs. Valerie Conroy	1989-90
Mrs. Peggy Stearns	1962-63	Mrs. Paula Baker	1990-91
Mrs. Marion Whitney	1963-64	Mrs. Marjorie Collins	1991-92
Mrs. Patricia Werring	1964-65	Mrs. Mary O'Mara	1992-93
Mrs. Rosalie Arlinghaus	1965-66	Mrs. Rosemary Dangler	1993-94
Mrs. Joan Garten	1966-67	Mrs. Trudie Rainone	1994-95
Mrs. Jeanette Lansdell	1967-68	Mrs. Louise Spirig	1995-96
Mrs. Hilda Maloney	1968-69	Mrs. Kimberly Krieger	1996-97
Mrs. Patricia Kelley	1969-70	Mrs. Cheryl Redpath	1997-98
Mrs. Emily Terzis	1970-71	Mrs. Carolee Kallmann	1998-99
Mrs. Marge Nugent	1971-72	Mrs. Cathleen Vermylen	1999-00
Mrs. Jane Nichols	1972-73	Mrs. Nancy Cox	2000-01
Mrs. Eileen McCoy	1973-74	Mrs. Virginia Walsh	2001-02
Mrs. Jayne Ferrante	1974-75	Mrs. Sharon Cocoziello	2002-03
Mrs. Faith Broderick	1975-76	Mrs. Patricia Petri	2003-04
Mrs. Marie Contreras	1976-77	Mrs. Jane Kilcullen	2004-05
Mrs. Patricia Lynch	1977-78	Mrs. Judy Lee	2005-06
Mrs. Barbara Leddy	1978-79	Mrs. Jessica Fiddes	2006-07

DELBARTON FATHERS & FRIENDS PRESIDENTS

Mr. William G. Foster	1947-49		Mr. John G. Gilfillan III	1979-80
Mr. Charles A. Snyder	1949-50		Mr. Frank A. Delaney III	1980-81
Mr. John J. Cross	1950-52		Mr. Gerald A. Cerza	1981-82
Mr. Frank V. McBride	1952-54		Mr. George J. Kadri	1982-83
Mr. Harry F. Tappen	1954-55		Mr. John G. Engler II	1983-84
Mr. Edwin R. Feste	1955-56		Mr. Robert W. Sheridan	1984-85
Mr. Walter E. Maloney	1956-57		Mr. Francis V. Goodwin	1985-86
Mr. James P. Fittin, Jr.	1957-58		Mr. Thomas G. Ferguson	1986-87
Mr. Robert J. Dunn	1958-59		Mr. Samuel F. Champi	1987-88
Mr. Edward C. Stearns, Sr.	1959-60		Mr. Eugene R. Sylva	1988-89
Mr. Gerard H. Keller	1960-61		Mr. James J. Meenan	1989-90
Mr. Arthur Venneri	1961-62		Mr. George F. Thompson	1990-91
Mr. J. Nevins McBride	1962-63		Mr. Jack Plaxe	1991-92
Mr. Frank E. Connery Sr.	1963-64		Mr. Kenneth Bertaccini	1992-93
Mr. Max A. Minnig	1964-65		Mr. Henry A. Collins	1993-94
Mr. Elmo E. Crump	1965-66		Mr. Anthony V. Bastardi	1994-95
Mr. Robert H. Lansdell, Jr.	1966-67		Mr. Daniel T. Scott	1995-96
Mr. Carmen C. Ottilio	1967-68		Mr. Joseph P. Nacchio	1996-97
Mr. Louis P. Thebault	1968-69		Mr. John A. Maione	1997-98
Mr. James F. Villere, Sr.	1969-70		Mr. Michael J. O'Donnell	1998-99
Mr. Robert A. Matthews	1970-71		Mr. Dennis M. DiVenuta	1999-00
Mr. Raymond M. Cantwell	1971-72		Mr. Robert G. Chandis	2000-01
Mr. Donald A. McMahon	1972-73		Mr. Russell L. Hewit	2001-02
Mr. Austin E. Kearney, Sr.	1973-74		Mr. Michael X. McBride	2002-03
Mr. Thomas J. McCoy, Jr.	1974-75		Mr. Thomas Pecora	2003-04
Mr. Leonard Pace	1975-76		Mr. Gerald C. Crotty	2004-05
Mr. Herbert R. Jordan	1976-77		Mr. Robert Waldele	2005-06
Mr. Thomas M. Leddy	1977-78		Mr. Larry Schillings	2006-
Mr. Joseph J. Longo	1978-79			

Delbarton Alumni Association Presidents

1948-51	Francis J. Haynes '48		1975-76	Richard L. Wade '61
1951-53	John B. LaVecchia '50		1976-77	John A. Catillo '55
1953-55	Edward F. Broderick '50		1977-79	Carmine J. Galdieri II '57
1955-56	Joseph P. Laico '52		1979-80	Edward J. Dwyer '64
1956-57	Joseph R. Hillock '51		1980-81	Lee S. Trumbull '58
1957-59	James A. Ferrante '52		1981-82	Franz E. Vintschger '57
1959-61	John B. LaVecchia '50		1982-84	Perry L. Beneduce '74
1961-63	Ronald P. Mealey '50		1984-86	Frederick J. Honold, Jr. '70
1963-65	Walter J. Flaherty '51		1986-89	Joseph R. McDonough '68
1965-67	John F. Sanfacon '57		1989-92	Kevin T. Kenny '78
1967-68	James A. Ferrante '52		1992-95	Anthony M. Nugent '74
1968-69	Edward F. Broderick '50		1995-97	Thomas J. Luby '72
1969-70	Edward J. Butera '56		1997-99	John E. Luke, Jr. '78
1970-71	James M. Corroon '57		1999-01	Lee D. Esposito '74
1971-72	William O. Storch '53		2001-03	William J. Waldron III '65
1972-73	Robert C. O'Mara '60		2003-05	David A. Lewis '78
1973-74	James M. Maloney '56		2005-	Kurt W. Krauss '81
1974-75	Frank D. Visceglia '60			

DELBARTON PARENTS OF GRADUATES ASSOCIATION PRESIDENTS

1985-1987	Mr. & Mrs. John and Mary Hanifin
1987-1989	Mrs. Colleen O'Loughlin
1989-1991	Mr. & Mrs. Robert and Grace Fiocco
1991-1993	Mr. & Mrs. John and Betty Gilfillan
1993-1995	Mr. & Mrs. James and Lorraine Farrell
1995-1997	Mr. & Mrs. Reginald and Marie Stanton
1997-1999	Mr. & Mrs. John and Rita Engler
1999-2000	Mr. & Mrs. William and Roey Dangler
2000-2002	Mr. & Mrs. Frank and Loretta Zupa
2002-2004	Mrs. Joyce Henry
2004-2006	Mr. & Mrs. Bill and Jean Gowski
2006-2007	Mr. & Mrs. Peter and Pat Giammarino

Delbarton Valedictorians

William G. Foster	1948	Robert E. Somol, Jr.	1978
Edward F. King	1949	Steven C. Gruen	1979
James J. Cannon, Jr.	1950	Alberto J. Luzarraga	1980
Richard E. Wolke	1951	Martin J. Marchaterre	1981
Marco R. Grassi	1952	Thomas C. White	1982
Frank V. McBride, Jr.	1953	Gerard H. McCarren	1983
Martin E. Weber	1954	William J. Benson	1984
James D. Noble	1955	Douglas J. Beck	1985
Terence J. Gallagher	1956	James M. Armstrong	1986
Harry J. Pinto, Jr.	1957	Louis J. Magnotti	1987
John F. DiLorenzo, Jr.	1958	Gregory E. Mrva	1988
Stephen J. Pribula	1959	Eric Schnell	1989
John E. Feldman	1960	Todd S. Kim	1990
Douglass A. Roby	1961	Michael D. Preston	1991
George J. Meister	1962	Todd A. Rose	1992
David M. McCarthy	1963	Peter A. Gibbons	1993
Kevin J. O'Neill	1964	Edward Shen	1994
Jasper A. Cragwall, Jr.	1965	Joseph A. Ferraro	1995
Edward S. Binkowski	1966	Albert Pan	1996
Raymond W. Kosley, Jr.	1967	David J. Jamieson	1997
Mark J. Flannery	1968	Christopher Janson	1998
Michael J. Cheng	1969	Brian J. Rissmiller	1999
David A. Cole	1970	L. Charles Shioleno	2000
Gerald T. Reilly	1971	Kartik Venkatram	2001
James G. Glicker	1972	John P. Romankiewicz	2002
Michael Plantamura	1973	John-Thaddeus Keeley	2003
James E. Hurley	1974	Christopher T. Soriano	2004
Sean M. Hanifin	1975	Stephen D. Zoller	2005
James R. Baumgardner	1976	Alexander M. Stephan	2006
George G. Holder	1977		

DELBARTON STUDENT COUNCIL PRESIDENTS

Francis J. Haynes	1948		Kevin T. Kenny	1978
John V. Spinale	1949		Stephen B. Faber	1979
John B. LaVecchia	1950		Donal F. Mastrangelo	1980
Joseph R. Hillock	1951		John P. Hanlon	1981
Robert A. Lilly	1952		Joseph P. Chernik	1982
Paul J. Jernigan	1953		Andrew E. Anselmi	1983
Nicholas A. Keating	1954		Glenn D'Angerio	1984
James D. Noble	1955		Pietro Petino	1985
Peter J. Hayes	1956		Richard O. Leggett, Jr.	1986
Lawrence A. McLernon	1957		Jeffrey R. Krilla	1987
John F. Sena	1958		Brendan J. Brown	1988
Frederick X. Fittin	1959		Stephen C. Henry	1989
Henry J. Hayes	1960		John B. Murphy	1990
Michael J. Hayes	1961		Lawrence P. Whipple, III	1991
Anthony E. Merrey	1962		Mark D. Facciani	1992
W. Peter McBride	1963		John M. Sullivan	1993
Michael J. Guerriero	1964		Michael Henry	1994
John H. Werring III	1965		Timothy J. Fitzsimmons	1995
Daniel J. Mitchell III	1966		Jed Y. Lewis	1996
L. Philip Thebault	1967		Michael C. Saunders	1997
James P. Geiss	1968		Evan Andrew Hammitt	1998
James F. Nugent	1969		Douglas R. Skinner	1999
William N. Peck	1970		Owen M. Bowness	2000
John A. Burke	1971		Matthew J. Hanlon	2001
Jerome J. McDonald	1972		Grant M. Hewit	2002
Michael C. McFadden III	1973		W. Timothy Vecchione, Jr.	2003
Andrew W. Kentz	1974		Riley R. End	2004
Peter F. Harty	1975		Clinton W. Morrison	2005
Paul M. Yearwood	1976		Stephen A. Popper	2006
Steven G. Yevak	1977			

HALL OF HONOR MEMBERS

1984	Jules G. Spada '48		1996	Kary W. Antholis '80
				Rev. Adrian McLaughlin, O.S.B.
1985	Frank D. Visceglia '60			
			1997	Daniel T. Scott '62
1986	Lee S. Trumbull '58			James E. Nugent '69
				W. Michael Murphy, Jr. '67
1987	Rev. Manus Duffy, O.S.B. '60			
	Joseph K. Pagano '63		1998	Kevin T. Kenny '78
	W. Norman Scott '64			Robert E. Mulcahy III
				Boyd A. Sands '55
1988	Edward F. Broderick '50			
	D. Peter Keller '65		1999	Elizabeth T. & John G. Gilfillan III
				Anthony M. Nugent '74
1989	Edward J. Dwyer '64			Peter L. O'Neill '59
	John F. Sanfacon '57			
	Louis P. Thebault		2000	E. Pat Brady '70
				David F. McBride '65
1990	F. Daniel Foley '50			Rev. Peter J. Meaney, O.S.B.
	Carmine J. Galdieri '57			
	Robert C. O'Mara '60		2001	C. Sean Closkey '85
				Donald L. Criqui
1991	James M. Corroon '57			Robert L. Sheridan '81
	Frank A. Delaney			
	Rev. Giles P. Hayes, O.S.B. '56		2002	Lawrence H. McLernon '57
				J. Craig Paris '82
1992	Rev. Stephen W. Findlay, O.S.B.			
	William F. Sittmann '67		2003	John F. Conner '53
	Joseph R. McDonough '68			Hilda Maloney
				Bill Smith '63
1993	Robert B. Collins '56			
	William O. Regan		2004	Abbot Brian H. Clarke, O.S.B.
				Eugene "Doc" Doherty '54
1994	Brian T. Fitzgibbon '74			J. Brian Thebault '69
	Rev. Kenneth H. Mayer, O.S.B.			
	William J. McFadden '59		2005	Abbot Thomas J. Confroy, O.S.B.
				William J. Waldron III '65
1995	Edward J. Butera '56			Ronald P. Mealey '50
	Harvey C. Jones, Jr. '70			
	Skip Livera '63			

Delbarton Lay Board of Trustees 2006